SEEING MATTERS

In *Seeing Matters*, Sarah Awad offers a psychological exploration of how images shape our actions, perceptions, and identities. She examines how we use images to symbolically and materially influence the world, others, and ourselves, while also revealing how the images around us shape our thoughts, emotions, and memories. Awad investigates the social and political dynamics of visual culture, questioning who is seen, how they are portrayed, and why these representations matter. By using clear language and real-world examples, she makes complex theories accessible to readers, offering diverse methodological approaches for analysing a wide range of image genres – such as graffiti, digital memes, photojournalism, and caricatures. This comprehensive analysis addresses the politics of visual representation, making the book an essential guide for researchers across disciplines, while providing valuable insights into how images impact society and our everyday lives.

SARAH H. AWAD is Associate Professor of Sociocultural Psychology at Aalborg University, Denmark. She received her PhD in Cultural Psychology from Aalborg University and her MSc in Social and Cultural Psychology from the London School of Economics and Political Science. She studies processes by which individuals make sense of change through visual and narrative tools and the influence of visual culture on identity, collective memory, and politics within a society. She has coordinated different art facilitation programmes and public service visual campaigns in cooperation with the United Nations Development Programme and the British Council. Her most recent co-authored books include *Remembering as a Cultural Process* (2019), *Street Art of Resistance* (2017), and *The Psychology of Imagination* (2017).

THE PROGRESSIVE PSYCHOLOGY BOOK SERIES

This book is part of the Cambridge University Press book series, Progressive Psychology, edited by Fathali M. Moghaddam. As the science of human behavior, psychology is uniquely positioned and equipped to try to help us make more progress toward peaceful, fair, and constructive human relationships. However, the enormous resources of psychology have not been adequately or effectively harnessed for this task. The goal of this book series is to engage psychological science in the service of achieving more democratic societies, toward providing equal opportunities for all. The volumes in the series contribute in new and unique ways to highlight how psychological science can contribute to making justice a more central theme in health care, education, the legal system, and business, combatting the psychological consequences of poverty, ending discrimination and prejudice, better understanding the failure of revolutions and limits on political plasticity, and moving societies to more openness. Of course, these topics have been discussed before in scattered and *ad hoc* ways by psychologists, but now they are addressed as part of a systematic and cohesive series on Progressive Psychology.

SEEING MATTERS
A Psychology of the Image and Its Politics

SARAH AWAD
Aalborg University

Shaftesbury Road, Cambridge CB2 8EA, United Kingdom

One Liberty Plaza, 20th Floor, New York, NY 10006, USA

477 Williamstown Road, Port Melbourne, VIC 3207, Australia

314–321, 3rd Floor, Plot 3, Splendor Forum, Jasola District Centre, New Delhi – 110025, India

103 Penang Road, #05-06/07, Visioncrest Commercial, Singapore 238467

Cambridge University Press is part of Cambridge University Press & Assessment, a department of the University of Cambridge.

We share the University's mission to contribute to society through the pursuit of education, learning and research at the highest international levels of excellence.

www.cambridge.org
Information on this title: www.cambridge.org/9781009272070
DOI: 10.1017/9781009272100

© Sarah Awad 2026

This publication is in copyright. Subject to statutory exception and to the provisions of relevant collective licensing agreements, no reproduction of any part may take place without the written permission of Cambridge University Press & Assessment.

When citing this work, please include a reference to the DOI 10.1017/9781009272100

First published 2026

Cover image: Sculpture by sculptor Henrik Voldmester. Photograph by Ivan Lind Christensen (Used after permission)

A catalogue record for this publication is available from the British Library

A Cataloging-in-Publication data record for this book is available from the Library of Congress

ISBN 978-1-009-27207-0 Hardback
ISBN 978-1-009-27211-7 Paperback

Cambridge University Press & Assessment has no responsibility for the persistence or accuracy of URLs for external or third-party internet websites referred to in this publication and does not guarantee that any content on such websites is, or will remain, accurate or appropriate.

For EU product safety concerns, contact us at Calle de José Abascal, 56, 1°, 28003 Madrid, Spain, or email eugpsr@cambridge.org

SEEING MATTERS
A Psychology of the Image and Its Politics

SARAH AWAD

Aalborg University

Shaftesbury Road, Cambridge CB2 8EA, United Kingdom

One Liberty Plaza, 20th Floor, New York, NY 10006, USA

477 Williamstown Road, Port Melbourne, VIC 3207, Australia

314–321, 3rd Floor, Plot 3, Splendor Forum, Jasola District Centre, New Delhi – 110025, India

103 Penang Road, #05-06/07, Visioncrest Commercial, Singapore 238467

Cambridge University Press is part of Cambridge University Press & Assessment, a department of the University of Cambridge.

We share the University's mission to contribute to society through the pursuit of education, learning and research at the highest international levels of excellence.

www.cambridge.org
Information on this title: www.cambridge.org/9781009272070

DOI: 10.1017/9781009272100

© Sarah Awad 2026

This publication is in copyright. Subject to statutory exception and to the provisions of relevant collective licensing agreements, no reproduction of any part may take place without the written permission of Cambridge University Press & Assessment.

When citing this work, please include a reference to the DOI 10.1017/9781009272100

First published 2026

Cover image: Sculpture by sculptor Henrik Voldmester. Photograph by Ivan Lind Christensen (Used after permission)

A catalogue record for this publication is available from the British Library

A Cataloging-in-Publication data record for this book is available from the Library of Congress

ISBN 978-1-009-27207-0 Hardback
ISBN 978-1-009-27211-7 Paperback

Cambridge University Press & Assessment has no responsibility for the persistence or accuracy of URLs for external or third-party internet websites referred to in this publication and does not guarantee that any content on such websites is, or will remain, accurate or appropriate.

For EU product safety concerns, contact us at Calle de José Abascal, 56, 1°, 28003 Madrid, Spain, or email eugpsr@cambridge.org

To Adam

Contents

List of Figures	*page* viii
Acknowledgements	x
Introduction	1

PART I THE IMAGE AND WHAT WE DO WITH IT

1	Why a Psychology of the Image?	9
2	Theoretical Conception of the Image	29
3	What We Do with the Image	49

PART II THE SOCIAL LIFE OF IMAGES: AN ANALYTICAL FRAMEWORK

4	The Birth of the Image	79
5	The Body of the Image	100
6	The Environment of the Image	123
7	The Viewing of the Image	147
8	The Development of the Image	166
9	The Death and Afterlife of the Image	191
10	Concluding Thoughts: The Mattering of the Image	212

Appendix	235
References	239
Index	259

Figures

1.1	The blue bra incident, Cairo, December 2011	page 9
1.2	Banal and insignificant everyday images from Saudi Arabia and Denmark	26
2.1	A typical image representing the mind, its processes, and its sufferings as puzzles or gears inside the brain	29
2.2	Image taken in a small town in Ghana, highlighting the lack of access to clean and safe water	40
3.1	The mushroom cloud over the Japanese port of Nagasaki, 9 August 1945	49
3.2	An image of an anti-nuclear weapons campaign poster	61
II	The social life of images' analytical framework	75
4.1	Image of the Ancient Egyptian queen Nefertiti wearing a gas mask	79
4.2	An illustrative collage of different caricature images	95
4.3	Andeel's caricature, 2013	97
5.1	Lifejackets piled up on a beach in Lesbos, 2015	100
5.2	An illustrative collage of different poster images	119
6.1	Berlin-based artist Prizmu's stencil art piece of 'Fuck Wars'	123
6.2	Street posters in Aalborg, Denmark, 2015–2023	133
6.3	Photographs of *fuck* graffiti from different countries	144
6.4	Image of a wall in Cairo covered in different layers of graffiti	145
7.1	An image of a Muslim woman wearing a headscarf	147
8.1	Alan Kurdi and Omran Daqneesh, illustrated by Khalid Albaih	166
8.2	The Palestinian flag and its transformation into a watermelon symbol	174

8.3	An illustrative collage of different transformations of Alan Kurdi's photograph from different online platforms	184
9.1	An image of absence, to represent the many absent images we cannot use for illustrative purposes due to copyright regulations	191
9.2	Protest poster against censorship and prolonged Covid-19 regulations in China, 2022	208
10.1	Photographed from a ceramic shop in Belgrade, Serbia, May 2024	212

Acknowledgements

In preparing this book, and in the years of discussion that led to it, I would like to thank the many students and colleagues who accepted to think along with me, providing me with relevant literature and ideas for the book content, structure, and title. I am particularly grateful to Ivan Lind Christensen, Louisa Celine Klatt, Bo Allesøe Christensen, Brady Wagoner, and Robert Innis for reviewing parts of the book manuscript. I am also very thankful to Fathali M. Moghaddam, the inspiring scholar and series editor, for his continuous support and trust in this project.

Introduction

We use images to immortalize precious moments, keep static what is passing, and pick from the countless life scenes, the scenes that represents us and how we see the world. In an image we can construct how the world looks to us, or how we imagine it ought to be. We find certain images that capture how we feel towards a person or a global event. We seek images that bring abstract and distant ideas into a concrete material meaningful form or make that which we thought we knew strange again. When talking to people about images that move them, they refer to images that captured what they could not express in words, images that captured the essence of a person or a phenomenon, images that represent how things used to be, or images of rupturing moments that changed life as they knew it.

This book is about the psychology of how we use images for social and political action and how images in our environment influence us. Whether it is an image of a bereaved loved one, a political event, or a significant moment, there is a choice made by a person, a group, or an authority, of what image – among all possible images – that will be the one best capturing how we feel – or ought to feel – about that which is represented in the image. Images that we choose, and those that surround us beyond our choice, shape not only who and what we remember and think about but more importantly how we remember and feel about them. They become sources of our common-sense knowledge and a continuous source for the reproduction – and, potentially, transformation of – our culture. This calls for a psychological approach to images that interrelates the individual, social, cultural, and political dynamics involved in how we relate to images.

The significance of images to human life is not new. Prehistoric cave paintings stand as a witness to how humans, beside fulfilling their basic needs of food and shelter, were also driven by the idea of representing their world through pictures. The 27,000-year-old Cosquer cave, for example, in Marseille is home to hundreds of paintings of animals, hand stencils, and sexual symbols. What purpose did those images serve for those painting them? Painting could have been a ritual in a religious or a social practice. It could have provided a way to represent and give meaning to their experience. It could have been a way of communicating with present and imagined others. There could also have been a motive – similar to many graffiti painters today – to mark: 'we were here'.

These are all intriguing questions, and the same sense of wonder is behind the focus of this book, namely what purposes do images serve in contemporary society. Many aspects have changed when looking at our relationship with images today, while some core aspects remain the same. There have been major technological developments that facilitate our access to images as tools to express ourselves and share everyday experiences. If you have a smartphone and access to the internet, you can take photos, create images using software programs and artificial intelligence, share and edit other people's images, and even report and censor them. This change in accessibility presents us with different possibilities and challenges.

For the sceptic, this change has made us over-occupied with self-representation. As image producers, we take *selfies*, document where we go and what we eat, and at times prioritize taking photos of experiences rather than actually experiencing them. We take images of others and represent them in ways that might polarize, dehumanize, or defame. As viewers, we are immersed in an abundance of images, learning to swipe through them to know what is happening in the world and in people's lives, to shop, and to find dating partners. As image subjects, we are continuously looked upon and surveyed. In one hour today, more images are produced and shared than those created in all of the nineteenth century (Sturken & Cartwright, 2018). Did this abundance take away something from what images mean? There is a common idea about the power of the image and how it is worth a thousand words, but what happens when we have a thousand images of every moment? Throughout the book, I tackle how this abundance has influenced the power of the image, its credibility, and ideas about its originality and authorship as images spread and transform every second and are harder to trace to one artist, photographer, or even human in the case of artificial intelligence.

For the hopeful, this change has a democratizing potential. With growing access to representation and documentation follows a promise to de-centralize the control over what is seen and who is seen. We can see more images of world happenings from the perspective of eyewitnesses rather than the images news agencies decide to publish. We can document injustices and state violence, and have the tools to look back at authorities and hold them accountable. We can also, like the cave painter, represent ourselves and our world the way we see it, and counter misrepresentations. However hopeful this perspective is, not everyone has the same tools or platforms for visibility. Governments, news agencies, and corporations and their algorithms, still have a privileged access in moderating who is seen and how they are seen. Hence it is important to look for who among this new accessibility and abundance is still made absent from public visibility.

I examine the critical and the hopeful perspectives through a theoretical and methodological framework with a focus on one key fascinating aspect about images: their transformative social lives. When followed, they can show us why, when, and how images can matter as powerful cultural tools. An image's social life starts when it is created by a person in a certain social context that drives their motivation and informs what is in the image and where it is placed. The image, once out there in the public space, takes on a social life of its own with certain affordances. It is seen by many viewers who each interprets it according to their own position. Some viewers would be so intrigued by the image that they would share it, move it from one context to another, or change how it looks and produce a new version of it with their own meaning. Some viewers would feel so violated with the image that they would decide that its life must be cut short, that neither they nor anyone else should see what the image represents any longer. They would then try to censor it by attempting to physically or virtually stop its life, and – if radical enough – go after those who created it.

Images vary in their lives. Some have short lives with little public attention. Some go viral and live on in many different forms to become famous visual symbols we identify with. Their lives are dependent on what we do with them and what they mean to us. Each of us is an image producer, viewer, and censor, shifting positions based on what we see and what we feel about it. The lives of images reveal the individual psychological level of how we think, feel, and remember through images as cultural artefacts that carry multiple and changing meanings. The transformation in the images' social lives also show the interactional level of how images are tools for social action that we use on ourselves, others, and the bigger society. And, finally, seeing the meaning transformation, contestation, and development of an image's social life shows the broader societal and political context that facilitates or inhibits a visual dialogue. In other words, images' social lives happen at the intersection of the individual and the sociocultural, and the private and the public.

Throughout this book, I present an invitation to revisit the language and approach we use to analyse images to be able to understand their psychological influence in today's visual culture and how people make meaning of them in everyday life. Images today are accessible and abundant like never before, and they need to be studied through accessible methods and accessible language. They are not only hidden valleys of the unconscious that can be revealed by the psychoanalyst, they are not only exclusive art objects that can be understood by the art expert, and they are not only bound by a signs system that can be decoded by the semiotician. Some of the most popular and viral images today are quite far away from what many would conceive as art. This requires an approach that pays attention to the ordinary, the banal, the redundant, the unnoticeable, and the ugly images that circulate and mobilize people. What is attractive about President Trump hugging the American flag, or Pepe the Frog wearing a Klu Klux Klan hood, or a Grumpy Cat meme image?

The meaning of the image is not confined within the image or in the mind of its producer but is acquired throughout the image's circulation as different people do different things with it. The meaning changes throughout the image's social life as it becomes part of different social practices of production, reproduction, and viewership, and as it is situated in different environments. The social lives of images show what we do with images and, more importantly, show what images do to us; how they make us look, look away, relate to, or repel from what we see. The metaphor of images having a social life does not mean that images are vital beings that act on us, rather it means that we do things with images that affords them with certain potential affordances to act back on us.

I argue throughout the book that there is an inherent psychological and political aspect in studying images in public space. In any given space, there are politics of representations: who has the privileged access to image production and circulation, who is represented in those images, and how they are represented. Those processes inform our understandings of group identities, collective memory, social positioning, and power. Those topics are essential for a progressive psychological science that investigates how inequalities are reproduced in everyday visual culture, how social movements shape emotions and mobilize action through images, and how the visual could be used to promote inclusion and recognition of different communities. I aim with this approach to bring in the image as an object and method of study to inform a psychology that is oriented towards social change and concerned with power and how it is exercised, acknowledging how our lives are social and communal, with thoughts, feelings, and actions as not just individual but also collective in nature.

In the first part of the book, I start Chapter 1 by identifying what I mean by public images in visual culture and why they are relevant psychologically. I will then present in Chapter 2 the theoretical framework, where images are conceptualized as cultural artefacts that are both signs open for meaning making and tools open for social action. They are also dialogical and political artefacts that take part in knowledge production and circulation. Then, in Chapter 3, I integrate sociocultural psychology with other disciplines within psychology such as cognitive, social, and neuro psychology, and outside psychology such as sociology, visual studies, and philosophy, to tackle the power of images to influence our seeing, thinking, feeling, and remembering.

In the second part of the book, I present the analytical framework by following the social life of images. I start in Chapter 4 with the birth of the image and ways of understanding the intentions and motivations of image producers. I then look in Chapter 5 at the body of the image itself and present ways of interpreting what is contained in an image. After that, I address in Chapter 6 the immediate material environment and placement of the image and the extended environment that includes the sociocultural, historical and political context in which the image circulates. Then I move in Chapter 7 to look at the viewers of the image and the different ways people appropriate images informed by their social positions. In Chapter 8, I turn to the development of images, and how they are transformed as they travel and circulate. Then in Chapter 9 I tackle the destruction of images, which leads to a discussion of the death – and potential rebirth – of images. In each of the chapters in Part II, I draw on a case example from a specific context with a specific image genre that varies from protest posters, caricatures, graffiti, political campaigns, and photojournalism to social media memes. Rather than presenting one method for doing visual research, I draw on my own and other researchers' empirical work to present a range of methodological possibilities that are suited for different image genres, different focus areas based on which aspect of the social life one focuses on, and what datasets one has access to.

In Chapter 10, the final chapter, I end with a discussion about when do images still matter despite their abundance and why images have an ambivalent relationship with reality. Can we distinguish between images that reflect reality, manipulate reality, or help us imagine an alternative reality? Can we talk of a 'good' image, a powerful one that lives on, and invites dialogue? Can we talk of a 'just' image? We want images that do us justice, whether it is for our personal memories or grieving, or for our collective identity and society. In our effort to be seen and recognized, we do not just seek an image, we seek a 'just image' – as Roland Barthes (1981) puts it. We seek an image that would do us justice and an image that would survive among the abundance of images surrounding us.

PART I

The Image and What We Do with It

In Part I, I present a theoretical conceptualization of images and argue for their psychological relevance. I explore the nature of their social lives in visual culture, what it means to investigate their social lives, yet not consider images as 'alive' per se, and why it is challenging to write about images.

Using a sociocultural psychological perspective, images are theorized as cultural artefacts that we use to mediate our own higher psychological functioning, as well as our relationship with others and with the environment around us. This theorization puts the focus on what we do with images in a specific sociocultural context, rather than on the image as an independent object. We can use images as signs to construct and exchange meaning, thus influencing our mind and the minds of others. We can also use images as cultural tools to materially act on the physical world.

Our engagement with images shapes their social lives and how they come to be part of the dialogic process of knowledge production in society. This is an inherently political process that shapes what is seen, what is knowable, and what is made invisible.

The significance of images in relation to our psychological, social, and political practices is brought forward through an analysis of how images influence our seeing, thinking, feeling, and remembering.

CHAPTER 1

Why a Psychology of the Image?

Figure 1.1 In December 2011, while the army forces were dispersing a protest in Tahrir Square in Cairo, they attacked an unarmed protestor, hitting her and dragging her on the ground, which stripped her of her top garment, revealing her blue bra.
Source: Photograph by Rana Jarbou

The image shown in Figure 1.1 became a known symbol for the *blue bra* incident after many protestors and news reporters captured it on camera and shared it on digital media and news channels. State media and religious media used the image as a proof of the vulnerable and shameful position women put themselves through when they join protests. Activist graffiti artists reproduced the *blue bra* image to represent the heroic position of women activists despite the violence they are exposed to. The image travelled and transformed among activist networks and became a protest symbol, the meaning of which elaborated from being a symbol of women protestors and the abuses they face, to a symbol of the Egyptian revolution more broadly, to a protest symbol that is used in other struggles in other geographical contexts. The image in Figure 1.1 with the statement 'against the regime' was painted on a wall in Jisr El-Cola, Beirut, during Lebanese protests in 2013. The image was captured by Rana Jarbou, a social documentarian and graffiti archivist, who gave me permission to reproduce the image in this book, bringing it to this new context, and to a new viewer, you.

The social life of the *blue bra* image captures many aspects of what this book is about. The image, first as a still photo from a video, and later as a graffiti stencil and an online image, is a sign with changing meanings, based on who is using it, where, and for what purpose within a contested societal dialogue about women, protest, and violence. The image was used as a tool for political action, whether by protestors to document the violence and mobilize for the continuation of the protests, or by state and religious media as a propaganda against the revolution and women who do not follow traditional roles.

Tracing the transformative life of this image shows how the representation of the woman in the photograph, dragged on the ground by soldiers, was reconstructed by the activists to represent how they see the incident; it is not one of humiliation as the media showed it, but it is one of heroism. For example, graffiti painter El Tenin produced a stencil image of the woman with a cape, as a superhero, not laying on the ground, but standing strong and determined. Also, artist Bahia Shehab reproduced the blue bra as a symbol of resistance as part of her 'A Thousand Times No' project and painted it on many walls and exhibitions around the world. The different reconstructions of the blue bra by activists were all attempts to represent the revolution in the way they would like it to be seen and remembered. In Chapter 2 and Chapter 3 I tackle how images as social and political artefacts influence our ways of seeing, thinking, feeling, and remembering.

The social life of the image started with the moment of its birth, when a photographer captured the incident in the specific context of the protest and the specific place of Tahrir Square. The photographer was not the only image producer; the image became famous because it attracted many other image producers who shared it on news channels and digital media, and who reconstructed it and used it as a material graffiti documentation in the city space. Every image producer had intentions and motivations that drove what they did with the image and what meanings they promoted by their reuse of it. By placing the image in this book, I am also reproducing it as an illustrative example and extending its social life to a new context. The birth of the image and its producers will be the topic of Chapter 4.

The different reproductions of this image transformed its body: what is portrayed in it and how it is portrayed. The interpretation of what is in an image, as presented in Chapter 5, starts from the specifics of the image, such as the colour of the bra, the posture, and the accompanying text. The interpretation then proceeds to the meanings from the immediate context of the image – such as, is it a photograph documenting the incident, is it a graphic remake showing protest meanings, who took it? The interpretation then draws on the meanings we can interpret from broader contextual knowledge. To see the image in Figure 1.1 as a powerful protest symbol, one needs to be familiar with the history of it – possibly how this image in an Egyptian context captures how the woman's body is often the terrain of cultural, moral, and political subjection (Hafez, 2014) or how the bra has been used as an object of protest in women's movements globally. With those associations one can react to the image's elaborate meaning, possibly feeling connected to it or being repelled by it based on our political views. The aim of the interpretation process is not to reach one meaning of the image but to interpret what kinds of meanings the image affords and how different viewers with different social positions can make sense of it.

The interpretation of the image is always embedded in its environment. The environment of the image, which is the topic of Chapter 6, involves the material medium of the image and its placement – for example, a graffiti stencil painted on a wall in urban space or a digital photograph on a social media platform – and the cultural, social, and historical context in which the image lives. The meanings of the later reproduction of the image in Lebanon relies on our knowledge of not only the political context of Egypt and Lebanon in 2011 and 2013 but also the connection and solidarity among the activists in the region and the awareness of the shared struggles they face.

Besides what interpretations an analyst can come up with from the aspects just mentioned, it matters to follow the reception of the image in public space, how it is being met by different viewers with different social positions, in different contexts, how the viewers make meaning of the image – this is the focus of Chapter 7. In a previous study (Awad, 2017), I presented the image in Figure 1.1, without text, to participants who were all frequent visitors to the Tahrir Square area. This was part of several interviews I conducted in 2016 that tackled the collective memory of the revolution. Among the twenty-five participants, the image triggered the memory of the incident for nineteen of them. What was interesting was not that they remembered but how they affectively reconstructed the incident from the image. Based on the participants' political position, the incident was either recalled with a solidaric 'we' and a re-emphasis of the honourable position of the women against a 'them', or with a passive recall of what happened to the women, without mentioning an actor doing the dragging and the violence to her. I was curious to know what associations the image would bring to someone who is not familiar with the context at all. I showed the blue bra image, again without text, as part of a survey, to my Danish undergraduate students with a few simple questions, among them: *Have you seen this image before? What meanings do you associate it with?* Out of 170 participants, 134 said they had not seen it before and only one participant associated it with Egyptian protests and violence. However, sixty-seven participants associated it with meanings in relation to feminism, the bra-burning movement, protest, liberation, and the Danish women's rights Red Stocking Movement.

This, in part, is why this image had a rich transformative life, I argue. It dialogued with a known familiar symbol that already has an older social life with feminism and, building on that old symbol, the image reproduced it with new meanings and emotions in relation to the violent incident. The image transported a private object, especially in a conservative society, to the public space, to stand as a witness to violence and as a symbol of solidarity. It circulated between the material urban space, news and online spaces, and books, and travelled from its local context and its meaning in relation to the specific incident to a neighbouring protest context with its elaborated meaning in relation to protest and resistance. The development of the image through circulation, travel, and transformation will be the topic of Chapter 8.

Not every viewer just looked, looked away, or reproduced the blue bra image. The image offended some to the extent that they decided to censor it. Some reported the original video and photograph as sensitive material that should be censored by news and digital media. Some also destroyed the image on the walls by spraying paint over it. The government systematically whitewashed any revolution graffiti including the blue bra from the streets, arresting some artists and confiscating books that documented images of the revolution. These are all attempts to end the social life of an image. Do these attempts kill images? Or do they trigger people to circulate them even more, giving them another life, maybe in another context? I will tackle the death and rebirth of images in Chapter 9.

The story of the blue bra is one of an image that became a travelling transformative protest symbol, with multiple layers of meanings all becoming part of the collective memory of the 2011 Egyptian revolution. It still has a rich social life despite censorship – or maybe because of censorship. Not every protest image or graffiti got the same social life. In Chapter 10, the final chapter, I discuss what makes a powerful image that lives on and attracts engagement.

Going back to the chapter's question, what is then psychological about images' social lives? The study of images from a psychological perspective is a study of how people act, think, remember, and feel in relation to and through images in their everyday environment. This is especially relevant to the fields of social and cultural psychology that focus on how we shape and are shaped by people around us, cultural signs and tools, and the built and social environment we inhabit.

If I were to sum up the psychology of the image that I present in this book into one question it would be: how do people act and are acted upon through the use of images? In other words, how do individuals and groups use images to symbolically and materially act on the world, others, and themselves, and how, in return, do images surrounding us in the environment shape our thoughts, emotions, and memories?

These inquiries are inherently psychological and political; they deal with the politics of seeing and being seen. Many of the examples I use in this book draw on the visual production of social movements and the production and transformation of protest symbols. I investigate when and under which conditions images could disrupt the status quo and mobilize action against perceived injustices, and when do images confirm the status quo by reproducing prejudices and discriminations. For this investigation, I draw on psychological processes such as identity construction, social positioning, and social cognition. These are processes that the psychological science has long been interested in, but research on them has mainly relied on spoken and written language. I propose that using a visual lens to investigate these processes could give us a new insight into how humans interact and shape their environment through the cultural artefacts of images.

A revisited psychological inquiry into images is needed to respond to the developments in today's visual culture and the technological advancement that has changed our access to images. In our everyday life we see images all the time in the street, on the news, and on digital media. Sometimes we notice them, reflect on what they mean, and engage with them. But more often than not we walk by them or 'scroll' through them with little attention. After all, we are used to being surrounded by environments that are overpopulated by images, where we know about other people, world events, new products by seeing images of them rather than reading about them. This development has not only changed our access to images as viewers, it has also given us access to be image producers and broadcasters. Through a mobile phone one could document an incident as it is witnessed, share an image or a video of it, and if enough people share it and talk about it, news media catch up, and it can become a topic for public attention and debate, possibly a mobilizing factor for protest and even revolution! A clear example of this is the video of the murder of George Floyd in Minnesota in 2020 and how Floyd's image and what it represented mobilized support and solidarity to the Black Lives Matter movement and its fight against police brutality and racially motivated violence. Another example is the image of Khaled Said, who was beaten to death by Egyptian police in 2010. An image of his disfigured corpse next to a portrait photo of him spread through social media, the latter showing a relatable face of a young Egyptian man, and the former showing the 'after violence' photo, giving a concrete image of brutality and injustice. The image with the slogan 'we are all Khaled Said' became one of the driving forces for solidarity with anti-regime protests, leading up to the Egyptian revolution of 2011.

It is easy then to argue that our relationship with images has developed; today we are continuously producing, circulating, viewing, and even censoring different images. This is different than when images were only the product of a professional artist or photographer, and we were allowed access to them as consumers of mass media or as spectators in an art museum. This does not mean that we all now have equal access to representation and visibility, or that we all can create images of our version of reality and be seen and recognized. The power dynamics of visual culture persist in different ways. We do not all have the same means to visual production or the same access to platforms of visibility. Having the access to self-representation on social media as a refugee is by no means equal to having the power and resources to produce images of a refugee 'crisis' in news media. Also, producing an image of injustice or dissent in a democratic society does not equate with the risk of doing the same in an authoritarian society where the government monopolizes visual culture and what is allowed to be seen in public space.

It remains, however, that there are new dynamics of visual culture and new accessibility to images as a mode for engagement in social and political dialogues. This opens up new questions for the field of psychology, especially for a progressive psychology that engages with social action and works in the service of achieving more just, open and equal societies.

1.1 What Is an Image?

The word image can refer to many different things from mental images to material images, to moving images. My focus is on graphic material images that circulate in different public spaces such as news media, digital media, and urban space. They take different forms such as photographs, paintings, graphic designs, caricatures, comics, memes, posters, and graffiti spray painting. They are also created for different purposes such as commercial advertisement, political campaigning, propaganda, news reporting, entertainment, and protest.

There are different reasons why it is difficult to delineate what an image is and how it is distinct from other communicative means. First, even though I focus on images rather than language, these two forms of communication are often interrelated. Second, the examples I mention are all public external images in our visual culture, rather than internal mental images, yet again the internal-external distinction is interdependent. Third, they vary in their purposes between political, entertainment, and advertisement, but as I will argue there is always a political factor in public images even for what could be considered apolitical images. Fourth, the public images do not include private images such as family photographs and personal digital images, yet images in their social lives can often travel in between the public and private spaces, which is often the case in scandal images, and as I will argue, the private-public distinction could also be a problematic one. I will tackle each of those four distinctions, as any attempt at defining images through them should come with the awareness that these categories are not binary ones that we can separate fully and investigate independently.

As you read this text, there are images shaping the space you are sitting in, and as you read those words, you might recall a mental image of a relevant image you have seen recently. If I was presenting the book at a conference, your perception of my spoken language is not only verbal but also combines it with visual cues such as my facial expressions and posture. Also, you might be visualising the words you read or hear, and verbalizing the images you see. To take an example, can you see an image of an apple without thinking of the word apple? And can you write the word apple without thinking of a mental image of an apple? It gets more complicated if we move from the example of an apple, to questioning what images come to your mind when you hear the words freedom, democracy, terrorism, or immigration. What are the different images that came to your mind and where did they come from? Meanings of images are always related to – and dependent on – language (Barthes, 1978). Visual and verbal communication together realize the same fundamental social feature: that of meaning (Kress & Leeuwen, 2021). Images cannot carry meaning on their own – their meaning is always intertextual, relying on other images and texts; they accumulate meanings and play off their meanings against one another (Hall, 1997a).

Despite how interrelated those two modes of communication are, we can still look at how we perceive them differently. Research in neuropsychology and visual perception indicates that the areas of the brain devoted to visual perception are significantly larger than areas devoted to other brain faculties (Mather, 2014). This line of research shows generally that we perceive and interpret images in a similar way to perceiving natural visual scenes, rather than how we perceive language. This perception requires flexibility in the use of visual cues, unlike language interpretation that relies on arbitrary learned associations (Mather, 2014). Research in visual communication also shows that the two modes 'communicate' to us differently: textual communication is based on argumentation and follows certain narrative structures, while visual communication is based on association, where certain patterns and memorized visual precursors are more or less spontaneously associated by the viewer (Müller, 2008). This means that the visual meaning creation is less standardized and more context dependent than meaning communicated by language, especially written language.

Those features of image perception are relevant to image analysis and interpretation. However, I argue that instead of focusing on distinguishing a clear line between the visual and the linguistic and how they work differently, a more meaningful approach would be to find how words and images meet, and together shape our meaning making. We look at the intersection where the entanglement of images and words together form our representation of the world and our memory (Mitchell, 1994; Zelizer, 2004).

Distinguishing how we perceive images from how we perceive language is complex, so is distinguishing internal and external images. One attempt at categorizing images across distinctions of visual-verbal and internal-external comes from visual culture scholar William J. T. Mitchell. He presents five areas of research in relation to image investigation: graphic images (such as pictures, designs, statues), optical images (such as mirrors and projections), perceptual images (such as perception of visual information), mental images (such as dreams, memories, ideas), and verbal images (such as metaphors and descriptions) (Mitchell, 1986). Using those distinctions, my starting point of investigation would be graphic images, while interrelating them with perceptual, mental, and verbal images. From a psychological perspective, one can also distinguish between two interdependent images: the external image that is culturally produced such as posters and photographs, and the internal image that is based on perception and cognition that could include mental imagery, imagination, and dreams (Forrester, 2000). I focus on the external images with an understanding of how they are internalized into internal images and how internal images are expressed in external image production. The psychology of the image is one that explains how the external meets the internal, and how – as psychologist Forrester (2000) puts it – 'the private finds expression in the public, as well as how the public underpins, reproduces and constrains, the private' (p. 4).

My interest in those external images is in their accessibility and exchange in everyday public life. This drives my attention away from fine art in the traditional sense that is bound within certain museums and cultural spaces – though the boundaries of high art, non-art, and mass media images are continuously changing and involve much travelling and transformation in between different media types. Also, since I have been researching protest and political campaigning images, inevitably much of my focus has been on images circulating in relation to specific political contexts. However, I argue that images with their function in representation and visibility are inherently political even when they are not explicitly tackling a political matter, an argument that I will elaborate on in Chapter 2. Even with explicitly political images, throughout their lives, they get appropriated for a variety of political and seemingly apolitical causes. Examples of making the political apolitical can be seen in the political visual symbols of Che Guevara's portrait, the rainbow flag, or the Palestinian keffiyeh, which are continuously commercialized and turned into fashion symbols. An example of appropriating an apolitical image to a variety of political causes could be the image of Pepe the Frog, a cartoon image of a fun apolitical frog originally drawn for a comic book that was then transformed into a hate digital meme by white supremacy groups online, to be later appropriated as a protest symbol in the 2019 Hong Kong protests. This is an interesting case to come back to in Chapter 9.

The political–apolitical distinction is closely tied to the public-private distinction. Feminist theories have long warned against the division of the public and the private as mirroring the political–apolitical division. Since

I study images' transformative lives as they travel between different spaces, including private and public spaces, I do not assume a clear distinction of public images versus private images. Rather, I assume that any image's social life involves both, but my lens of investigation is on the public part of its life. Even the most famous public images of presidents or of war, went through a private process of production, selection, decision-making, and possible modification, before they became the images we know today. Also, many forms of image censorship are about the attempt to bring what is public to be private again, not seen by the masses. Sometimes, what makes an image viral in the public space, and perceived as 'scandalous', is the mere fact that it came from the very private space; it shows what should not have been seen.

1.2 Are Images Alive?

The book's title and the conceptualization of images so far is clearly suggesting that images do have social lives. So, it is important early on to clarify what that implies in relation to the vitality of the image; are images alive, having agency, and an independent existence in social life? My short answer is no. The lens on the images' social life is a lens on human interaction with images and human agency in thinking and acting with and through images.

Theories of art provide different views on the independence of the image and where the focus of investigation should be (Haynes, 1995). One view looks at the image as having an independent existence and therefore should be a site of investigation in its own right. Another view looks at images as inseparable from the thoughts and biography of the person creating them, and therefore has a primary focus on the subject of the artist. A third view moves away from focusing on the image or its producer to focusing on the role of the viewer and the nature of the gaze. This third view is clear in the poststructuralist writings around the 1960s of Roland Barthes and Michel Foucault, and Jacques Lacan's psychoanalysis. Both Barthes and Foucault claimed the disappearance or the 'death' of the author, refusing to limit a work of art – whether a piece of literature or a painting – by its origin in its authors' intentions and biography, and instead looking at the processes of consumption and the multitude of possible meanings that could be produced by readers or viewers (Haynes, 1995); thus, understanding the texts/images as products of – and a node within – a network of discourses and meaning systems.

The visual culture scholar William J. T. Mitchell (2005) tackles the idea of the vitality of the image differently; he proposes that images have lives and attributes that make them into vital signs – not merely signs for living things but signs as living things. His analysis tackles the way images become alive and 'want' things, focusing on the idea of the images' desires. He asks questions such as what do the images want from us? Where are they leading us? What is it that they lack, that they are inviting us to fill in? What desires have we projected onto them, and what form do those desires take as they are projected back at us, making demands upon us, seducing us to feel and act in specific ways? He argues that the life of images is not private or individual but social, that is, images live in genealogical or genetic series, while reproducing themselves over time as they travel between cultures. This is clear in how images do not stay put, they continuously circulate in between different material medium forms (e.g. paint, paper, wall, electronic impulses). His conception of the social life of images is one that has a parallel existence to the social life of their human hosts.

Mitchell's exploration of the vitality of images, looking at them as having desires, demands, and drives, is productive and has inspired many of my ideas in this book; however, I would not adhere to the idea of images as independently alive. Rather than asking Mitchell's (2005) question of what images want, I would ask what humans do with images and what do those images, inscribed by human actions and desires, do to individuals and society at large.

I propose the social life of images as a lens that brings focus to the agency of social actors (e.g. producers, viewers, censors) as they construct and reconstruct an image and its meaning. The meaning is thus not limited to the composition of the image itself, the producer, or the viewers but in understanding those aspects in relation to each other within a certain material and social context. The image does not have agency or an independent parallel life in and of itself but rather its social life is interdependent on what individuals and groups do with it, emphasizing the dynamic process images go through in reaction to different social actors' production, perception, transformation, and destruction processes. By this lens, I investigate the image not as a constant static object but as an instance in a dialogue that travels, transforms, and constantly changes meaning and shape over space and time.

This lens also helps us understand what philosopher and cultural critic Susan Sontag (1977) referred to as the 'ecology of images'. Similar to ecologists' concern with the interrelationship between organisms and their environment, an ecology of images is concerned with the interrelationship between the image and its environment, including the social actors, social practices and structures, and other images and discourses surrounding the image. The ecology of images shows us how certain images resonate within certain contexts, histories, processes, and structures of meaning, and urges us to take images seriously as part of reality (Manghani, 2012).

Using this approach, I hope to give a broad interdisciplinary approach to understanding our complex relationship with images. I build on different disciplines such as psychology, sociology, anthropology, philosophy, and visual studies. I integrate ideas with the purpose of constructing a comprehensive way of investigating images, while maintaining a practical and accessible language for this investigation. The title of the analytical framework *the social life of images* borrows from philosopher and literary critic Mikhail Bakhtin's (1981) ideas on the social life of discourse that liberates the work of art from a sole author or a sole meaning, suggesting that a work of art presents an open and continuous dialogue. The title also borrows from Marxist and cultural critic Walter Benjamin's (1935) ideas on the reproduction and 'afterlife' of artwork, where he argues that even in perfect replication through mechanical reproduction, an image takes on a new presence in time and space and that new presence is reactivated with every new viewer. The title is also inspired from anthropologist and postcolonial theorist Arjun Appadurai's (1986) book *The Social Life of Things*, which highlights the value of following the forms, uses, and trajectories of material artefacts to understand their meanings, the culture, and the person-object relations. I will return to their ideas throughout the book.

1.3 Visual Culture

Analysing images involves an analysis of visual culture and its dynamics in relation to knowledge circulation and power. Those broader conceptions cannot be studied in abstraction. To capture their complexity, they need to be investigated as they are manifested in certain material artefacts (Appadurai, 1986; Beer, 2013). I follow what cultural geographer Gillian Rose (2016) presents as critical visual methodologies, which refers to approaches that interpret the visual accounting for cultural significance, social practices, and power relations in which the image is embedded. Through critical visual methodologies, I am concerned with how power relations are produced, articulated through, and challenged by ways of seeing and representation. This involves an investigation of: the site of production – where an image is made; the site of the image itself – its visual content; the site of circulation – where an image travels; and the site of viewing – where the image encounters its spectators (Rose, 2016).

Following this, the investigation becomes not 'just' of images or of visual culture but of culture and society at large. From a sociocultural psychological lens, culture exists in between the human minds and the environments they live in (Valsiner, 2014). Culture is a process by which humans use different shared resources in their environment as they think, develop, and act in relation to social others. These resources could be, for example, language, tools, symbols, or rituals. An analysis of culture and cultural resources and practices is thus concerned with the production and exchange of meanings (Hall, 1997b). Looking at culture through these processes suggests an understanding of culture as dynamic and in continuous change as it is co-constructed through the interaction between individuals, cultural symbols, and social structures (Much, 1995). This is different than conceptions of culture that equate it with nation states, suggesting cultures as more like stable containers with fixed boundaries.

Cultures in themselves do not have agency, humans do, and their agency in culture is enabled or constrained by different cultural resources and social structures with certain power distributions. As cultural theorist Stuart Hall (1997b) argues, it is participants of a culture who give meaning to things; things rarely – if ever – have any one single fixed meaning. It is humans' use of bricks that can make bricks into a house, and it is humans' thoughts and feelings that make a house a home. Meanings arise by the way we talk about things, the stories we tell, the images we produce, and the emotions and values we associate with those (Hall, 1997b). Cultures do develop to be powerful, however, as they accumulate human meanings and symbol creation, and become powerful influencers on how people think and act (Valsiner, 2014). This dynamic will be elaborated on throughout the book: individuals and groups with access to different resources co-construct culture, and cultures as powerful resources influence people's ways of seeing and thinking about the world.

Within the broader conception of culture, visual culture refers more specially to the aspects of everyday life that we experience visually. It is the scenery and landscape of the spaces we live in and the still and moving images we see around us. In other words, visual culture is the plethora of ways in which the visual is part of social life (Rose, 2016). It plays out through the variety of multimodal and multisensory cultural practices that inform the broader multisensory networks of meanings and experiences (Sturken & Cartwright, 2018). That practice does not only include images, but it incorporates the different practices we engage in when we see and the ways in which our environment is visually organized in relationship to power (Sturken & Cartwright, 2018).

An interest in visual culture, therefore, entails an analysis of 'visuality'; the practices of seeing the world, what we do when we look, gaze, and show, and when we refuse to look or show (Mitchell, 2005, p. 337). This analysis requires overcoming the familiarity surrounding the experience of seeing, looking at how vision is learned and cultivated, not just simply given by nature. This allows us to unfold the ethics and politics of seeing and being seen, as well as the visual construction of the social. This complex field of visual reciprocity is not merely a by-product of social reality but actively constitutive of it (Mitchell, 2005).

1.4 On Writing about Images

If studying images and visual culture entails studying practices of looking and how we learn to perceive the world in certain ways, then the analyst needs to also reflect on how they themselves look, what they have learned to pay attention to, and what they have learned to look away from. Our ways of seeing are historically, geographically, culturally, and socially specific, and we need to acknowledge this in analysing images ourselves (Rose, 2016). Positioning ourselves helps us become aware of where we see from and how this influences the knowledge we produce (Haraway, 1988) and makes us acknowledge the difficulty of engaging in this reflective task (I. Rogoff, 1998).

My academic interest in images started with a research paper during my postgraduate study. The research paper was about the street art of the 2011 Egyptian revolution. This was in 2013, two years after the protests started and the protest street art was grabbing local and international attention. It was a new form of political expression in a public space that was previously dominated – and its visual culture monopolized – by the government. Before the revolution, the image one would be certain to see everywhere – besides commercial advertisement images – was that of Mubarak (Egyptian president from 1981 until his ousting in 2011). Like the trees, buildings, and roads, Mubarak's image was part of the 'natural' urban environment. The image would be placed in public offices, schools, and on billboards. The continuous 'presence' of Mubarak and the way he was presented reaffirmed who was in power. Only one version of this image was populated: that of the one leader, forever young, always present, and always overlooking his people. There was no room for this portrayal to be contested, at least not in the public space.

I grew up in Egypt. Mubarak was the president for three years before I was born and continued to be the one and only leader until I was twenty-seven years old. I grew up with his controlled national media as the only source for representing 'reality' on TV, newspapers, and the urban space. It was not until my teenage years that we had access to satellite channels and, later, to the internet. Those transitions from national, to satellite, to online media mark my generation's experience with access to information and visual culture, not only in Egypt but globally. Those transitions also marked a new challenge for state-controlled media.

In 2010, a news image was taken of the Middle East peace talks meeting in Washington. The image showed the then US president Barack Obama walking in the lead on a red carpet, and slightly behind him Israel's prime minister Binyamin Netanyahu, the Palestinian president Mahmoud Abbas, Jordan's King Abdullah, and Mubarak further behind them. When the Egyptian state-run *Al-Ahram* newspaper reported the story, it used this image but after editing it to show Mubarak in the lead with the other leaders behind him. The original image was in violation of how Mubarak 'should be' seen in Egyptian media. However, those practices could not pass unnoticed. In 2010, Egyptian bloggers called attention to the altered photo, showing it side by side with the original one used in international media. The newspaper's editor-in chief responded by defending the altered image, saying it was an 'expressionist' photo illustrating the 'true' expression of the prominent position of Mubarak (Associated Press in Cairo, 2010). This will be a theme I will return to as I discuss authoritarian monopoly of visual culture and the control over who is represented and, more importantly, how they are represented.

There was a rupture with this control of the visual culture when the streets were proclaimed by the 2011 protestors and in those proclaimed areas street art started to flourish. It was powerful in how it proclaimed public spaces and presented a process of contagious group creativity (Awad & Wagoner, 2014), where one image after the other deconstructed the 'holy' portrayal of authority in the public space. It turned city walls into a platform for the protestors to represent themselves and reconstruct many social representations of the nation, freedom, and social justice.

This provided a clear case for analysis that shed light on group creativity in times of social change and on the use of art in protest movement. Based on my research paper, I later developed a PhD proposal on same topic for a PhD position in Denmark. However, as I started my PhD in 2015 many political and social changes were taking place in Egypt. The initial success of the revolution in toppling the old regime of Mubarak was followed by an elected Muslim Brotherhood presidency for one year, that was then ended by a military coup which resulted in El-Sisi becoming the current president.

This meant that all empirical material of protest street art has been white-washed and replaced by new government images – now the image of El-Sisi instead of Mubarak. This made me start my PhD with questions such as: Am I analysing a time that has passed and has no presence in the current counter-revolution measures in Egypt? And what is the value of researching political agency and creativity at one point in time without dealing with the crackdown that followed? The changes had a strong impact on those who had hope and belief in the cause of the revolution, myself included, and it left me questioning what constitutes meaningful research in a time of loss. I started interviewing activists and graffiti artists, most of whom felt more despair than hope. They were mourning the future dream that never came to be and the heavy price of this dream, not least the loss of many young lives in the protests. But their stories also provided a more complex narrative.

Their activism was not a singular act of resistance in a time of protest that disappeared when the protest was over. Their protest, public space occupation, and street art images were an outcome of long years of underground resistance, that took form in a moment of collective action, and started a new dialogue that lived on beyond its erasure from the urban space. Despite the empty streets and the replacement of revolution images with government ones, the visual production of the revolution travelled locally and internationally, acquiring new lives in news media, books, social media, online archives, and even body tattoos. The political meaning of the revolution images was also elaborated and taken up by other movements such as in the example of the blue bra image mentioned earlier. Among Egyptian activists today, the images form a significant part of the collective and affective memory of the revolution.

The political developments – though tragic – showed something fascinating about images: their emergence and circulation, their travel and transformation to mobilize new movements, and how they become so tempting for physical and symbolic destruction by new regimes. The images' social lives showed the fluidity and transformability of this form of communication and shaped my research to move on from looking at protest street art as a fixed object of aesthetic political expression, to looking at the dynamic social lives of the images. I started investigating not only protest street art images in urban spaces but also images that preceded them, reproduced them, and responded to them, including graffiti, posters, online images, and government billboards. Today, there is an even stronger presence of El-Sisi's image in the public space than in the time of Mubarak. In a recent trip to Egypt during 2023, my son counted how many times he was 'greeted' by El-Sisi's photo. By the second day he had already counted over thirty-three photos, he then lost interest.

Although this book mainly draws on my academic endeavour with images, my interest has not always been academic, I started working with images in my professional practice shortly after my bachelor's degree. Drawing on my training in graphic design and communication in my undergraduate study, I worked with developing public service campaigns advocating for child rights within the framework of a United Nations Development Programme in cooperation with the National Council for Childhood and Motherhood in Egypt. This work started me thinking about the process by which major social causes such as fighting domestic abuse, child labour, or female genital mutilation could be communicated visually in a way that influences attitude and behaviour change. More broadly it made me reflect on the field of visual communication for behavioural impact and its potential – but also constraint – in combating deeply held beliefs and practices.

Reflexivity in relation to one's position also involves overcoming the familiarity surrounding the experience of seeing and reflecting on one's socialization in different visual culture environments. There are many visuals that I normalized seeing when I lived in Egypt, the United States, Saudi Arabia, the United Kingdom, and Denmark but now reflect upon differently because of moving in between those contexts (see, e.g., Figure 1.2). I remember how alienating it was at times in Saudi Arabia to be surrounded by many women without being able to see their faces. Even human faces on product boxes, such as an image of a family in an inflatable pool, were covered by a black marker. I also remember how I was charmed and absorbed by the consumer culture in the United States when I first moved there as an exchange student. One cannot escape being bombarded by images of what advertisers claim one 'needs' and must 'rush' to get and the many ads calling for bigger dreams, bigger houses, and bigger cars. I was also surprised by the normalization and continuous banal use of the national flag in Denmark.

Now that I have been living outside of Egypt for over fifteen years, when I visit, I am always fascinated by what I see and even more by what is concealed from vision. Authoritarian societies that have a rigorously

Figure 1.2 Banal and insignificant everyday images, such as bathroom signs, can provide interesting reflections about normative ways of thinking in a culture, that are not considered until one sees them contradicted in a new sign. I took the photos in Saudi Arabia (a) and Denmark (b).
Source: Author's photographs.

policed visual culture regulating everyday practices of visuality could in fact be a good case example to understand the dynamics of visual culture. When seeing is prohibited and invisibility is mandated, it is then that we see the visual culture in its sharpest form (Mitchell, 2005). The politics of visuality in Egypt do not only revolve around the image of authority and how it is displayed but also the invisibility of the opposition, the poor, and the unholy. Going through Cairo one can see many walls concealing slum areas and other walls separating the growing number of gated communities from the rest of the society. One can also see lots of billboards advertising the exclusive safe luxurious life one can have if one is rich enough to buy a home on the 'right' side of the gated community walls. Invisibility is also mandated on all that contradicts with 'religious and family values'. This includes a variety of practices such as censoring any material that is considered blasphemy, attacking 'inappropriate' social media content and its producers, and censoring books or entertainment content that promote prohibited identifications or sexualities such as homosexuality.

This comes in clear contradiction with Danish visual culture, and there are several cultural clashes that made this clear. According to Islam, it is prohibited to visually depict God or the prophets in images or statues. It was thus a controversial moment when images of the prophet Muhammed were depicted in the Danish newspaper *Jyllands-Posten* in 2005. Here, the most holy and invisible in one culture was not only made visible and banal but also ridiculed. In a more recent incident, Rasmus Paludan, who leads a Danish far-right party and has been previously jailed for several offences including racism and defamation, has become famous for going to public areas especially in neighbourhoods with high immigrant population and burning the Islamic holy book, the Quran. He would then record his visual performance showing the material burning of the holy Islamic symbol and sharing the video online for provocation. Those incidents and the reactions to them open many questions regarding freedom of expression and censorship and the clash of visibility and invisibility in different cultures.

These examples drive my current research interest into practices of visuality in different cultures and how we see and represent the 'other'. I look, for example, at processes of 'othering' in far-right parties' visual campaigns in Denmark and how the visual is used in the dialogue about the refugee 'crises' in Europe. I also look at how, in more conservative cultures, such as Egypt, the 'West' and Western values are seen and represented. I approach those processes of othering as a reciprocal gaze where each group constructs an image of the 'other' that primarily serves the group's own social identity, its value significance, and distinction. I will draw on some examples from this line of research in Part II of the book.

In writing about and analysing images I try to adopt an accessible and practical approach. This comes from a frustration about how the accessibility of images is made inaccessible through obscure and exclusive language of some approaches in visual analysis, and how the analysis of images in an increasingly visual culture still draws on the minority group of images that are considered art. If I propose that images are accessible tools that are utilized in everyday meaning and social action, then we should be able to analyse images in an accessible language and be able to attend to what meanings people make out of images in everyday life. I follow Michael Billig's (2013) and George Orwell's (1946) advice in translating and appropriating jargon technical terms to utilize them for the purpose of the book. Their advice comes from a critique of how academic writing has become overpopulated by complex nouns and jargon that do not necessarily explain social phenomenon clearly and passive verbs where the actors are invisible. They propose that a writer should attempt to simplify and translate jargon-filled sentences in their writing. This exercise would reveal when we have an idea or a meaning to communicate and when we are just hiding behind complex words. When sentences are written in humble words, losing their shiny jargon nouns, they reveal even to the writer themselves whether they had something to say and ideas to contribute or were they just sentences empty of meaning. Using accessible language allows the possibility of a theoretical dialogue that is inviting to different voices, rather than one that uses special jargon that is created as if to let only the chosen ones understand (hooks, 2001).

My empirical work also drives my interest in this writing approach. Many of the image producers I have spoken with did not define themselves as artists in the traditional sense, or at least did not want to contest a protected field with rigid exclusive boundaries and preferred to identify as activists who are using images for social action. In writing about those participants, I will use stories of what they did with images and how they produced and contested meanings through intervening in the social lives of different images. The images that were especially powerful were those that resonated with a general local and global public that did not necessarily have easy access to or familiarity with fine art institutions. Images can sometimes provide an accessibility that transcends spoken and written language.

CHAPTER 2

Theoretical Conception of the Image

Figure 2.1 A typical image representing the mind, its processes, and its sufferings as puzzles or gears inside the brain.
Source: designed by Freepik, www.freepik.com

The image in Figure 2.1 and many similarly looking ones come up when one searches for the terms mind, thinking, creativity, or psychology on the Freepik website that offer free-licensed images. This is a typical image that one sees in psychology textbooks, therapy clinics, and in online articles that represents the mind, its processes, and its sufferings as puzzles or gears inside the brain, that with the right expert hand could be explored and fixed. Such images inform everyday common-sense knowledge about the mind and its workings, and promote certain ideas that thinking, remembering, mental illnesses, and the mind more broadly reside inside the brain of the individual, and to understand how a person thinks, comes up with ideas, or suffers, we need to look inside their brain and try to solve the 'puzzle' of how things work within.

Unlike the meanings communicated by the image in Figure 2.1, the human mind and its processes are always interdependent on the social others and the environment surrounding the person, and therefore cannot be understood in isolation from the social, cultural, and historical contexts. This approach has defined the field of sociocultural psychology and its inquiry into human development, well-being, and suffering. The field of sociocultural psychology is quite broad and hard to define as a distinct field of study with clear boundaries, but one key idea that informs the approach is that the mind is situated in the society rather than in the brain (Vygotsky, 1978). This approach incorporates different lines of work labelled as cultural psychology (Cole, 1996; Shweder, 1991; Valsiner, 2014), societal psychology (Himmelweit & Gaskell, 1990), and critical social and political psychology (W. S. Rogers, 2020) among many others. The breadth of the approach is also due to it being an interdisciplinary one, combining elements from psychology, anthropology, sociology, and history.

My interest in sociocultural psychology comes from an interest in the reciprocal relationship we as humans have with our social, cultural, built, and natural environment. This is how we, individually and in groups, influence the environments we live in and how those environments shape our thoughts and emotions. This has informed my theoretical conceptualization of images, which I will present in this chapter through four key ideas:

- Images are cultural artefacts, which are both signs for meaning making and tools for social action.
- The agency of individuals in this meaning making and social action is interdependent on an environment with certain enabling as well as constraining conditions.
- Engagement in image production and viewership entails a dialogic process of knowledge circulation.

- This knowledge circulation through images is inherently political, shaping what and who is visible and knowable and what is invisible.

2.1 Cultural Artefacts: Signs, Tools, and Symbols

Conceptualizing images as cultural artefacts means that they are always embedded in a specific sociocultural context and cannot be understood independent of that context and the social practices surrounding people's interaction with the image. Looking at images as cultural artefacts places them alongside other artefacts that humans have created to mediate their relationship with the environment; this includes tools that help us intervene in our space from sticks and stones to spaceships and robots, and signs that help us exchange meaning such as languages.

The focus on signs and tools as mediators of the human–environment relationship draws on the work of psychologist Lev Vygotsky (1896–1934). He introduced a sociocultural, developmental, and historical approach to the study of the human mind (Vygotsky, 1978). He analysed the mechanisms through which culture becomes part of each person's nature, explaining how changes in societies and material life influence changes in people's consciousness and behaviour. He argued that human mental life is not isolated inside the brain as the image in Figure 2.1 shows but is connected to the objects and artefacts in the environment around us such as language, material tools, and cultural rituals. He focused specifically on how humans use signs and tools to transform their environment and, in so doing, transform themselves. Both signs and tools mediate our higher psychological functions such as thinking, remembering, and representation of reality.

Cultural artefacts are created collectively in the society over time and are continuously changing as societies change and develop. They are not just material 'objects' out in the environment but also conceptual aspects of the material world that has been modified through goal-oriented human action (Cole, 1996). This view acknowledges the unity of the material and the symbolic in human cognition and that our cognition is a distributed process that happens across our brain, bodies, interactions, material spaces, technologies, and cultural artefacts (Hutchins, 1995).

Vygotsky stressed a distinction between signs and tools. Tools are means of labour by which we master our environment. Examples of tools are an axe, a carving knife, a brush, a print machine, or a camera. Here he builds on Karl Marx's idea of humans' use of the mechanical, physical, and chemical properties of objects to make them act as forces in regulating and transforming the environment for their use and interests. Signs, on the other hand, represent a psychological process of creating systems of meaning. The most fundamental example of signs is language, but signs could also be images, narratives, cultural symbols, and body language.

Both signs and tools are interrelated in their mediation of higher psychological functioning and in their regulation of human behaviour, but their mediation operates in different ways: tools operate as material mediators while signs operate as semiotic mediators. In other words, tools allow us to externally act on the physical world while signs mediate our relation to our own mind as well as the mind of others (Gillespie & Zittoun, 2010). This distinction is not rooted in the cultural artefact itself but rather in how it is used; for example, a shovel is a tool for digging a hole but if placed next to the door as a reminder of the task of digging, then it is used as a sign for reminding oneself or others of the task (Gillespie & Zittoun, 2010). If the image of the brain in Figure 2.1 is printed on the cover of a psychology textbook, it serves as a material tool on cardboard to cover and distinguish the book as a sales object, and at the same time it is a sign communicating a meaning about the content of the book and possibly a promise of how by reading the book you can solve the puzzle.

Another example is a barricade or separation wall set by an authority to block access to certain groups of people. The wall is a clear tool that modifies the physical environment and turns a street access into a dead end. For those who know who put it up and why, it is a clear sign of an authority's power in blocking access and giving a warning message to those intending to surpass it. Some activists could try to intervene with the material barrier and try to break it down. Others could choose to symbolically destroy the meaning of the wall by transforming it into a canvas for their counter-authority images and paintings that traverse the wall and show the scenery beyond it (see, e.g., the 'no walls' street art on the barricade walls in Egypt in 2011, and street artist Banksy's paintings on the West Bank barrier in Palestine in 2005). Here the wall is both a tool and a sign that has been transformed into a canvas for protest images.

Vygotsky's distinction of tools and signs has informed two lines of work within cultural psychology: the activity tradition and the semiotic mediation tradition (Valsiner, 2007). Activity tradition focuses on tools as material mediators and how they enable action in the world, thus it tackles the external dynamics rather than the intra-psychological dynamics, while the semiotic tradition tackles the intra-psychological side through looking at signs as mediators of thought (Gillespie & Zittoun, 2010).

2.1 Cultural Artefacts: Signs, Tools, and Symbols 33

I combine those two traditions to look at images as both semiotic and material mediators, while keeping in mind the conceptual distinction between them. With a focus on meaning, I look at how images carry meanings as signs, and how those meanings are realised in what people do with the image as a tool. For example, a political image on a billboard in the street is a material tool that modifies the environment and a sign that refers to a meaning the producer attempts to communicate to viewers. Looking at the image as a tool highlights the material objects that make its creation possible, such as printing and billboard construction, and how its material form invites or inhibits certain interactions with it, such as spray painting over it. Looking at it as a sign sets focus on the meanings communicated in the image and how those meanings are seen differently by different pedestrians passing by it.

Following the image's meanings and uses throughout its social life could also reveal its symbolic value. Signs in an image often constitute more than one meaning, but when a sign is able to accumulate and condense several elaborate meanings that allows it to be an independent visual, travelling with its accumulated meanings, and having an affective value in itself, then it becomes a visual symbol. I draw here on psychologist Frederic Bartlett's (Bartlett, 1924) definition of symbols as signs that potentially embody multiple meanings as they communicate a face value as well as an underlying sentiment that makes them affective. What distinguishes a symbol from a sign here is the underlying and affective meanings a symbol accumulates, that allows it to have its own new social life. This is different to the distinctions often used in the semiotic tradition building on Charles Sanders Peirce's (1998) categories of a sign as either iconic (where form or meanings are related through similarity), indexical (where form or meanings are related through physical or natural connection), or symbolic (where meaning is conventional). This is also different from semiotician and structural linguist de Saussure's distinction of signs as having an arbitrary relation to meanings, with symbols as having non-arbitrary motivated relationship to meaning (de Saussure, 2021). From a psychological perspective, I limit my focus to the meanings people make of signs in an image, and when do some of those signs become affective symbols. Symbols could be conventional and non-arbitrary as per Peirce and de Saussure, but that is not always the case, especially in digital media images. I will elaborate in Chapter 9, with examples from digital media memes, that symbols could develop from novel and random associations.

An example of an image turning into a protest symbol is that of the blue bra example of Chapter 1. The blue bra was a sign, alongside other signs, in the initial photograph with the women and the army forces. In the reproduction of the image into graffiti images and online images, the blue bra came to be the symbol that condensed the elaborate meanings of revolting against oppression. The symbol on its own became a travelling image, carrying the meanings and triggering certain memories. We can further follow how, just as a sign could develop into a symbol, that symbol's social life and transformation could lead to it losing its symbolic value and dying in a sense. For example, many protest symbols lose their symbolic, historical, and affective meanings when they are overused as tools for commercialization on t-shirts, mugs, and tattoos. They then become signs for new different meanings and identifications.

If images are signs carrying meanings – potentially of symbolic value – that are realized in their uses as tools, how then do those artefacts become part of our higher psychological functioning? Vygotsky uses the term *internalization* to refer to the process by which an external sign/tool (such as an image) is transformed and reconstructed internally in an intra-psychological process (such as remembering) (Vygotsky, 1978). Note here that we are not always consciously aware of our use of artefacts (for a distinction between reflective and non-reflective use of artefact resources see Gillespie & Zittoun, 2010). We are often non-reflectively seeing images every day that re-enforce certain memories and ways of remembering over others; when we become attentive to this and choose to appropriate certain images differently, then we are engaging in a reflective *externalization* of those artefacts. Vygotsky would thus argue that the distinguishing feature of human psychology lies in humans' development through the internalization and externalization of socially routed and historically developed activities. This idea has influenced the development of a broad cultural psychological line of research looking at the internalization and externalization processes in different contexts (Cole, 1988; B. Rogoff, 1990; Shweder, 1991; Valsiner, 1987; Wertsch, 1985).

Cultural psychologist Jaan Valsiner (2014) shows how both internalization and externalization are constructive processes that allow us to transform 'incoming' messages into a new form and reconstruct them into 'outputs' to the social world to be further internalized by others. An interpreted (internalized) image is a new sign even if physically it has not changed. As this internalized meaning is shared, it is externalized into a new meaning or a new way of seeing or feeling, that then becomes an input in the internalization processes of other persons. Meaning making through images is thus a constructive process happening in between people in the society through dialogue as will be elaborated later in this chapter.

The internalization and externalization processes highlight human agency in creatively appropriating artefacts to influence our minds, people around us, and our environment. However, as much as the reflective use of artefacts can produce individually unique selves and ways of seeing the world, it can also produce socially coordinated similar and dominant world views, and instead of an open dialogue, it can create a basis for consensual validation of potentially illusory or oppressive ideas. We are not always reflectively thinking about all the images we see; we often non-reflectively perceive and use many images with their taken-for-granted meanings. Then, there are times when we pause and question the meaning of an image and actively appropriate and reconstruct its meaning, possibly producing a counter-meaning or a counter-image to refute its meaning. This is what social critic and feminist scholar bell hooks (2001) refers to as an oppositional gaze, which I will refer back to as I discuss viewership in Chapter 7. In Section 2.2, I discuss the question of our agency within the environment: what is our power in representing ourselves and our ideas through images and what is the power of dominating images in the public space to influence the way we think and feel?

2.2 Agency and Social Action

Looking at human agency in relation to the environment deals with the broad and philosophical question of how much freedom of thought and action we have as humans in shaping our environment and creating our own realities and how much are our thoughts and actions determined and shaped by factors outside of our control. I argue that our agency is interdependent on the environment that surrounds us and the different enabling and constraining factors in this environment. This shapes my focus to be on how humans as intentional agents psychologically navigate their lives within the perceived and material constraints and affordances of their surroundings.

One aspect of agency that is relevant to visual culture is about how people make meaning of themselves, others, and the social world. To understand human action, we need to look at how human experiences are shaped by the mind within a cultural system of meaning (Bruner, 1990). Our actions are not direct responses to biological and environmental stimuli as some classical psychological models would presume; behind our actions are meanings, motives, and moral evaluations that need to be understood to explain human complexity (Brinkmann, 2006). To study humans as intentional agents presumes that humans are not causally reacting entities but acting persons who have intentions and can explain and justify their actions in complex ways that are not controlled or predetermined by causal laws (Brinkmann, 2012; Harré, 2004). This goes in line with the pragmatist approach of philosopher and psychologist John Dewey (1896), who opposed the mechanistic stimulus–response psychology of his time and the idea that the mind subjectively observes the objective world. He argued instead that perception, cognition, and action form a dynamic system of adjustment, where the mind is the means through which we reconstruct our relationship to the world. Our thoughts and feelings are intentional acts, subject to normative moral evaluations with the norms and practices of the societies we live in; those norms influence us, yet they are not deterministic, as our evaluations and subjective moral judgements develop and change over time (Brinkmann, 2006). Those intentional acts are historically embedded (Gergen, 1973) and cannot be studied as static causes and effects, as one would study an object in natural science, as humans do not act in identical, repeatable, or predictable ways.

Human agency and meaning making are interdependent on an environment with enabling as well as constraining conditions that are natural and material (e.g. human biology, nature), structural (e.g. social, political, and economic structures), and discursive (e.g. language, narratives). Here, it is neither argued that the environment has a causal deterministic effect on us nor that all reality is socially constructed by subjective positions. Those two ontological and epistemological approaches are not exclusive and can be combined together beyond the realism–constructionism divide through a pragmatic pluralist sociocultural psychological approach (Brinkmann, 2012; Cornish & Gillespie, 2009; Gillespie et al., 2024). The pragmatic pluralist approach to knowledge here sets focus on knowledge as a tool for action rather than a representation of reality, and thus accounts for multiple forms of knowledge and ways of seeing. Through this approach I take my primary unit of analysis in the social acts in which human agency interacts with the environment in a dynamic mutual influence process – hence the social life of images' analytical framework. My interest is in the everyday mundane interactions, practices, and actions through which people use images to construct and negotiate knowledge. This goes in line with Bakhtin's (1986) process philosophy – discussed in Section 2.3 – where he analysed language and art as dynamic, living, and contextual, criticising de Saussure's (1916) approach in claiming static structures and abstract rules that can explain language use. Through the social life of images framework, the focus is not in static structures or meanings, but on

2.2 Agency and Social Action

what different pragmatists have referred to as acts (J. Dewey, 1896), experiences (James, 1912), or social acts (Mead, 1912) through which meaning is constructed. This pragmatist focus moves away from the subject–object dualism, emphasizes processes over things, highlights change and development, and provides a framework for testing theory – via consequences – and generating theory – via abduction (Gillespie et al., 2024).

Images are not meaningful in isolation but become meaningful in terms of their psychological role within a broader context and the different knowledge they (re)produce or contest. However, this does not mean that all knowledge is equal or relatively 'correct'. I take a pluralist non-relativist approach that acknowledges that some constructions are morally or epistemologically superior (e.g. knowledge backed up by scientific and ethical standards) to others (such as oppressive non-dialogical knowledge that maintains inequalities). Knowledges produced by images should be always critically analysed, moving beyond a simplistic representation versus reality opposition.

From this perspective, images as material objects do not have agency that acts independently, nor is there a causal relationship of how images are variables with direct predetermined influence or effect on the human mind. Images are artefacts through which individuals can exercise agency, act on and modify their world, and negotiate meaning within certain environments. As a community we use photographs, paintings, and monuments to shape our collective identity and collective memory. Our ability to have a say in what memories are represented and how they are represented varies greatly based on where we live and our power position. Through images we can reconstruct certain significant historical events, and the meanings those events have on who we are and who is our 'in' group. Through those identifications we assign different social positions, such as the heroes, the victims, and the threatening 'other'. In every representation there are also absences: those events we conceal and those people we do not represent. As those images circulate in the public space, they live on as signs in the environment regulating what we – and generations to come – identify with and remember, as well as what we forget.

From a pluralist non-relativist approach, those different constructions, and the knowledge systems they rely on, are important to study in order to understand the contestation over collective identity and collective memory. Those constructions are not seen as all equally valid; they could vary in their reliance on historical evidence, and they could vary in how they rely on their in-group representation on stigmatizing and oppressing a minority 'other'. Studying the multitude of ways in which images can construct reality shows the enabling as well as the disempowering potential images can have on different groups. There is a material reality to images themselves as artefacts, and every image can reflect different material realities and can also construct different ways of knowing and seeing the world. Those different layers of realities need to be recognized to understand the power of images in social and political intervention and knowledge circulation. This is key to creating useful and ethical knowledge, where not every knowledge is true if it pragmatically 'works'. The question is, who does it work for and what is its consequences? Images have historically been used by those in power to objectify, survey, exoticize, and exploit different groups. An analysis of knowledge production cannot be separated from value and ethics.

2.3 Dialogic Knowledge Circulation

Knowledge is produced, exchanged, and transformed in everyday life through the internalization and externalization of images. This knowledge is dialogical; happening in dialogue between individuals within a co-created and dynamic culture. Dialogue here is not limited to the physical presence of two or more individuals in dialogue with each other. More fundamentally, dialogue refers to the coexistence of different voices in any process of knowledge construction. Those voices are in dialogue inside our mind and in our socially shared world, as we think, create artefacts, and interpret them.

The emphasis on dialogue follows the main argument presented earlier, that our minds are not isolated entities inside the brain filled with puzzles, ideas, and knowledge as Figure 2.1 suggests. Our minds are intrinsically social and our development as a social self relies on our ability to see ourselves through the perspectives of the other, whether a specific other (a person, group) or a generalized other (a society) (Mead, 1934). This means that even when we are in total physical isolation, we still think in dialogue with social others. This does not refer to a pathological condition of hearing voices nor does it refer to an over-obsession with what others think, denying an individual agency and independence. Rather the conception of the mind as dialogical emphasizes the deep link between the individual and the social and highlights how thinking and meaning construction is a social process and how dialogue is fundamental to all human thinking and action.

This conception of the mind provides an alternative to the individualistic perspective that has traditionally dominated the field of psychology,

2.3 Dialogic Knowledge Circulation

by bringing in the interaction of the mind with the 'other', which includes individuals, groups, institutions, and cultures within a historical perspective (Marková, 2016). The dialogical mind emphasizes how the capacity of humans to create, understand, and communicate meaning is always rooted in history and culture (Marková, 2003) and is mediated through signs and tools, in an intersubjective process that is happening in relation to others (Gillespie, 2009).

With this conception of mind comes an understanding of the socially shared everyday knowledge as a dynamic co-construction of different voices and perspectives in dialogue with one another in a socially shared space. Social representations theory offers one explanation to how commonly shared social knowledge is formed, maintained, diffused, and transformed within a society (Moscovici, 1984). Unlike many psychological theories of social knowledge that focus on stable universals, regularities, and tendencies for non-change in thinking and action, Moscovici does not presuppose stability but looks at the dynamic continuous change and dialogue in the circulation of knowledge. This poses knowledge creation as an affective and ambiguous process rather than a mere accumulation of data from the environment (Valsiner, 2014).

How, then, are images sites of dialogic knowledge construction and meaning exchange? Using Moscovici's (1984) terminology from social representations theory, images provide one way of making the unfamiliar familiar, and turning the abstract unknown into everyday common-sense knowledge. Images objectify abstract ideas into concrete tangible objects and anchor what is unfamiliar through familiar representations. Those two processes of objectification and anchoring are key cognitive processes through which we make sense of the world (Moscovici, 1984). I use the image in Figure 2.2 to elaborate on those two processes and connect them to the dialogic aspect of knowledge construction.

What images comes to mind when you think of Africa and its living conditions? If you do not have personal experience with living in or visiting the continent, your mental images might come from knowledge you have accumulated over the years from books, news, talking to people, and images you have seen in the media. There are common images often used in humanitarian aid campaigns trying to mobilize support and donations for different humanitarian crises in Africa, such as starvation. Photographic images used in charity public service ads have a significant influence on how people think and feel about charity. Radley and Kennedy examined people's conceptions of need when they see images of aid agencies such as UNICEF; their analysis shows that people constructed out of the images

Figure 2.2   This image was taken by Boamaeric1 in a small town in Ghana, to highlight the lack of access to clean and safe water.
Source: The image is shared for free use through Wikimedia Commons and is licensed under the Creative Commons CC BY-SA 4.0 licence.

extended narratives about the moral and economic aspects of charity, where they entered into an imaginary – culturally situated – relationship with the subject presented in the image (Radley & Kennedy, 1997).

There are common elements one sees in those charity images. There are children in dire condition, deserted villages with rough landscapes, and an outsider person or celebrity who is advocating for the cause and speaking on behalf of those suffering. There is a good reason why campaigners construct the images that way, and why they often 'work' for aid purposes. We have a cognitive and emotional limitation to act in response to numbers and abstract ideas (Scott et al., 2021). It is difficult to conceptualize global inequality and poverty as concepts or to sympathize with the quantitative information that more than 600 million people around the world live in extreme poverty. An image of a child in need can transform these sufferings into relatable social knowledge through objectifying the abstract concepts and humanizing the numbers into the image of one child, while familiarizing the crisis through the eyes of a goodwill ambassador. This framing positions the viewer as a witness to the crisis and therefore having the obligation to help. I elaborate further on positioning and argumentation through images in Chapter 3.

This knowledge presented in an ad is not static or finalized but rather presents one voice in a dialogue that viewers engage with as they view, empathize, or contest the image. One ironic response to this typical humanitarian image comes from the comedian Trevor Noah in his show *You Laugh But It's True*. Noah, who is South African, criticizes how those ad images reproduce ideas of victimhood and helplessness. He says those images of American campaign ads always show sad children with flies on their faces and wonders:

> [Y]es there are people starving in Africa but I do not understand why they need to make us look that bad ... because I grew up in a poor family in Africa, and no matter how poor we were, no matter how hungry we were, no matter what, we could still do this [waves his hand over his face as if shooing away a fly].

Noah's humorous and critical response to the image adds one perspective to the meaning of the image that makes it almost impossible to look at the image in the same way again with 'just' its original meaning. The meaning in every image constitutes several voices in dialogue: the perspective of the producer, the producers' imagined others' perspectives in the process of production, the perspectives of the viewers, and the perspectives the image respond to, negate, or borrow from. This could be summarized in the triadic interdependent relationship of Ego–Alter–Object, which forms the basic unit of social psychological analysis (Mead, 1934). The Ego refers to the individual, the Alter refers to the social other, and the Object refers to the artefact of knowledge. Social psychologist Ivana Marková (2003) argues that this triadic relationship shows how social knowledge is a reflexive and intersubjective process that relies on humans' social and interactional capacity to dialogically construct it.

The idea of images as taking part in complex dialogical dynamics could be further elaborated on using the work of philosopher and literary critic Mikhail Bakhtin. The idea of the dialogic nature of meaning is central to his work, not only on literature, but also on art, creative action, and ethics (Haynes, 1995). According to Bakhtin, meaning is not static or finalized in a piece of literature or an image; meaning is found in dialogue between the author (producer), the object (artefact), the viewer, and the social context. He asserts that there is neither a first meaning nor a last one; any artefact could be understood as it exists among other meanings, as a link in a chain: an utterance (Bakhtin, 1986).

Images are utterances in a continuous dialogue, and an utterance is inherently responsive. Any image producer is to some extent respondent: the producer is not the first speaker who is disturbing the eternal silence of the universe, the author presupposes the existence of a system of meaning that she is using, she also presupposes the existence of preceding utterances (of herself and others) with which her given utterance enters into a dialogue with. In this dialogue, her utterance could build on and reproduce previous utterances or could problematize them and refute them by reconstructing them. Every new production affirms, supplements, or refutes previous productions, and its meaning relies on those previous productions and presupposes knowledge of them to be understood. Thus, every act of speech or creative work such as an image is a co-production with varying degrees of 'otherness' and 'our-own-ness' (Bakhtin, 1986, p. 89). No matter how monological an utterance may seem, it cannot be anything but a response to what has been already said about a given topic. It becomes one's own only when we appropriate it and adapt it to our own intentions (Bakhtin, 1986).

Bakhtin mainly relied on literature analysis in his use of the term 'utterance'; however, the term could be applied to images (Wagoner et al., 2018). Through looking at the social life of images, we can see those utterances in dialogue with one another. Such a conceptualization of the image liberates it from a sole owner that has a unilateral meaning for it and emphasizes its continuous social life of (re)production and (re)interpretation. It also broadens our lens of analysis from looking at one image as a site of analysis to situating this image among other images that circulate within a certain dialogue. Any image, no matter how original, is an utterance in a broader dialogue. It borrows from previous meanings, symbols, and images, and the new meaning it constructs is dependent on how it affirms, supplements, or refutes the previously constructed meanings. Also, once that image enters public space it continues to accumulate different meanings in its social life as it travels and transforms, opening up for further voices and perspectives. Thus, one could interpret the meaning in an image as a response to meanings that have been communicated before the image, and as an anticipation of meanings that will be expressed in response to the image.

Art historian Deborah Haynes (1995) applies Bakhtin's ideas to visual analysis. Her work emphasizes three main concepts from Bakhtin's work that informs a dialogical interpretation that is also informed by a moral dimension. The three concepts are *answerability*, *outsideness*, and *unfinalizability*.

2.3 Dialogic Knowledge Circulation

Answerability or responsibility refers to how the creative act of production is a response to an obligation to act, and is one that expects in return a response to it. It is an act that is answerable in a particular time and place. An author produces an image with an expectation of an answerable other who would see and respond to it. Bakhtin argues that an attitude of faith and trust in an answerable other is essential in life and in art. In a broader sense, answerability refers to Bakhtin's understanding of the I–other relationships as grounded in the idea of answerable deeds. For him, to fully exist in life is to act. Each person occupies a position in life and from this position experiences and acts on their oughtness. Each person's position defines their obligation. The concept of answerability offers a way of articulating the profound moral obligation and responsibility that we bear towards others. This moral dimension is an integral part of the creative process of production. From my position as a social actor, I can produce images that renounce my responsibility, or ones that invoke trust and responsiveness in people around me, including those who are different from me. The concept of answerability brings back the focus on the author as an acting agent with a cultural function, a focus that was ignored in the shift of the late 1960s that focused more on the artefact or on the viewer alone (Haynes, 1995).

Outsideness is another concept that explains the creative process of the author. For an author to create a representation, she needs to be able to distance herself from an immediate way of seeing and be able to place herself from different social positions. Outsideness does not mean indifference, but it means the ability to create a new way of seeing and thinking about the world by being able to see an event from outside while simultaneously co-experiencing it in an embodied way. With the concept of outsideness, Bakhtin highlights the bodily aspect in experiencing and the mobility in between an embodied inside experience and a distanced outside position in the process of creation. It also highlights the interrelationships of different bodies in space in a phenomenology of self–other relations (Haynes, 1995).

Unfinalizability is the third concept, and it deals with how creation is an active ongoing process of everyday life that produces not a finished world but a range of possibilities. Both the creation process and the artefact are unfinalized and open for viewers who will engage in the dialogue (Haynes, 1995). This highlights the open-ended quality of interpretation that allows others to enter into dialogues with images (Haynes, 1995). This could be understood in contrast to a monologic view of creation where there is only one meaning and that meaning is established and finalized by the producer, for example authoritarian governments' images claiming a single and final truth.

I apply those three concepts to the different stages of an image's social life, seeing each as an utterance with an open meaning and open life trajectory to the future as well as to the past. Following Bakhtin, an utterance is inherently responsive:

> There is neither a first nor a last word and there are no limits to the dialogic context (it extends into the boundless past and the boundless future). Even past meanings, that is, those born in the dialogue of past centuries, can never be stable (finalized, ended once and for all) – they will always change (be renewed) in the process of subsequent, future development of the dialogue ... Nothing is absolutely dead; every meaning will have its homecoming festival. (Bakhtin, 1986, p. 170)

Image interpretation is therefore a process of unfolding the multiplicity of voices in a given image in a given social and historical context. It is also a process of exploring the openness or affordances of an image for dialogue. There are images that are produced as a monologic authoritative voice that denies the existence outside of itself of other consciousness with equal rights and equal responsibilities to participate in the dialogue. The monologue is finalized and deaf to others' response; it assumes the ultimate truth and the final word (Bakhtin, 1984a). This could be seen in authoritarian images, providing one, final voice, that does not expect or tolerate a response or an alternative interpretation. That does not mean that it can prohibit reinterpretation, critical appropriation, or destruction altogether, but it can be said that it constrains interaction with the image and poses risks on those who do. These monologue voices can be, however, completely challenged in times where spaces open up for new forms of transgressive and unrestricted dialogues. In another line of Bakhtin's work (Bakhtin, 1984a, 1984b), he looks specifically at the space of the carnival as a space that brings people together from different walks of life, breaking away from the dominating authority and order of things. He analyses carnival festivals during the Middle Ages as those temporary spaces of liberation from established norms and hierarchy. The idea of the carnival could apply to specific contexts such as those of protests and revolutions, when the otherwise untouched image of authority is brought down and symbolically or physically destroyed, opening up spaces for democratic dialogues (Awad, 2021).

Both Bakhtin's and Marková's dialogical perspectives have an ethical dimension in their focus on the interdependencies among the self and others. Marková (2016) recognizes in *The Dialogical Mind* the role of others around and within the self in shaping one's way of thinking and acting. Bakhtin emphasizes the interconnectedness of the creative process and life, offering a dialogical theory that is more of a moral philosophy of acting than a theory of aesthetics (Haynes, 1995). Bakhtin's interpretation of the creative act of authoring emphasizes the profound moral obligation we bear towards others as our acts are always answering the other. In other words, we are always responsible, answerable, and obligated towards other human beings in and through the creative process. Bakhtin's work helps us to look at how moral values are inscribed in the creative process and in the artefact and how their meaning is dependent on an open dialogue that continues to take shape in the future: 'Nothing conclusive has yet taken place in the world, the ultimate word of the world and about the world has not yet been spoken, the world is open and free, everything is still in the future and will always be in the future' (Bakhtin, 1984a, pp. 165–166). However, dialogues are not as open and free as Bakhtin presents them. His work ignores power dynamics and the unequal possibilities of different social actors to engage in dialogue because of structural constraints. Structures of power constrain the ability of certain individuals and groups to produce representations that are visible to others, and thus constrains their ability to live and act in an answerable and dialogical equal relationship with others (Haynes, 1995). Bakhtin's approach assumes that we all are equally free to act, ignoring privileged social positions and how self–other relationships are shaped by ideological factors and embedded within certain social structures of power. The power aspect is integral to understanding the internal (within the individual) and external (in between individuals and in society at large) dialogue that takes place throughout the image's social life. This dialogue is often a contested one that is shaped by negotiations of meaning, struggles over representation, and politics of visibility.

2.4 Image Politics

The conception of images as cultural artefacts that are used for social action, and are an integral part of dialogic knowledge circulation, presupposes a public space where societal dialogue takes place and where individuals and groups exercise agency by negotiating meaning in that space. This public space is where the politics of everyday life take place, and where images – alongside and intertwined with written and spoken language, and physical and social structures – shape this public space. From this perspective, images are intrinsically political, always taking part in knowledge circulation and the representations of people and ideas in everyday life. The processes surrounding image production, circulation, and interpretation are all political processes of collective elaboration of meaning (I. Rogoff, 1998) and sites through which ideologies are produced and negotiated in public space in any given society (Sturken & Cartwright, 2018).

Power is often associated with direct physical coercion or constraint; however, power in relation to visual culture is a symbolic and cultural power in relation to representation, as in the power of marking, classifying, and representing a person or an idea within certain regimes of representation (Hall, 1997a). Within visual culture, stereotyping, for example, is a key practice of symbolic violence. Post-colonial scholar Edward Said (1978) shows how European stereotypical images of the 'Orient' and different practices of representation (scholarship, exhibition, paintings) produced a racialized knowledge of the 'other' (Said, 1978). This ties visual representation to knowledge production and its relation to power as elaborated in the works of Michel Foucault (1974) and how images could be a site of negotiation of meaning and dominant ideologies in a society as elaborated in the works of Antonio Gramsci's (1971) and his conception of hegemony. The symbolic power of representation is not only with the powerful; everyone is part of the distribution and circulation of this power – though not on equal terms (Hall, 1997a). The circulation of images forms part of this knowledge production and contestation, and it does so within a dynamic public space with unequal power distribution.

One way of understanding this public space is through Frankfurt school critical theorist Jürgen Habermas' conception of the public sphere. He used the term to describe the social life space where public opinion is formed and negotiated, a space that mediates between the people and the state (Habermas, 1974). This is the space where opinions, arguments, and more generally discourses circulate. He looked specifically at the space enabled through the development of mass media, such as newspapers, radio, and television, and the circulation of spoken and written discourses in those spaces. His conception could be elaborated further to also address images, looking at how images, alongside language, form the intersubjective political dialogue in this public space (Doerr, 2017). Habermas originally presented that space as a liberal space where reasoned, rational, and consensus-oriented dialogue takes place and where information is accessible to the public and the public has the chance to respond to this information with different opinions, thus allowing for a rational debate between multiple interests. In an ideal form, this would require a reasoning public, a rational consensus-oriented dialogue, and a free and equal public space.

2.4 Image Politics

However, it is hard to recognize that space in public life and visual culture. Spaces for dialogue do not provide the equal free space that Habermas or Bakhtin – as discussed earlier – describe. Habermas' conception of public sphere especially ignores how factors such as social class, ethnicity, and gender inhibit who is seen and heard in those public spaces (Fraser, 1985). Also, those spaces often do not facilitate reasoned, rational, nor consensus-oriented channels for communication. Social media platforms are a clear example of spaces for polarization in many instances rather than consensus or perspective taking – that is, the ability to see the world from the position of another person.

An alternative way of looking at dialogue in public space today is to incorporate philosopher Jacques Rancière's theorization of everyday politics. He describes the public dialogue as a contentious one, with unequal power dynamics, where the less powerful is often not recognized or visible in the public space (Rancière, 2013). To look at the politics of images and why images in the public space are inherently political, I will draw on Rancière's conceptualization of politics as the distribution of the sensible; the distribution of social roles, subject positions, and visibility in society. According to Rancière, politics revolve around what is seen in the society and what can be said about it, around who has the talent to speak and ability to see and be seen, and around the possibilities of space and time.

This political lens to images opens up questions about who is visible and who is made invisible as a political subject, and how do individuals and groups – through images – reconfigure the distribution of the sensible? It highlights the social role of images in the production of political subjects; what Rancière refers to as the ethical regime of images. Images produced by minorities – such as the blue bra image discussed in Chapter 1 – to call for recognition and visibility, provide an example of an interruption in the distribution of the sensible. This interruption modifies the aesthetic and political field of possibility by modifying what could be seen in the society and what could be said and done about it and thus creating new modes of sense perception and novel forms of political subjectivity (Rancière, 2013). A powerful image from this perspective can be one that disrupts the relationship between the visible, the sayable, and the thinkable, one that can present a rupture with the taken-for-granted logic of meaningful situations.

To analyse the power of an image to do such a disruption, we need to consider the image's material properties as a cultural object and commodity, as well as the affordances inscribed into it through the intentions of people surrounding it and social practices that shape the image's social life within a certain context. Images themselves do not have powers – or lives for that matter – but individuals inscribe symbolic power onto images through their use. Symbolic power here refers to the capacity to intervene and influence actions of others through the production and transmission of symbolic form (Thompson, 2005). There is no inherent symbolic power in an image. It is thus more meaningful to analyse the 'potential' power of certain images rather than a stable 'given' power and interpret how an image can afford certain interpretations and actions, while inhibiting others. The affordance of an object is continuously constructed in the cultural and historical context rather than predetermined (Gibson, 1979). Looking at the power of the image through affordances places the potential power not solely on the material object of the image, nor on the social actors alone, but on the relation between the image, the social actors, and the cultural context and environment.

It is important to not overestimate the power of images and what we can do with them. They are tools that have the potential to mediate certain social processes and could be used in different effective or ineffective ways by social movements and by authority. I would be wary of statements such as 'the image that toppled a regime' that gives the image an unrealistic force, while ignoring years of civil society grassroot movements' political action towards changing social structures. It is not productive to overemphasize images or visuality or surveillance as the exclusive vehicle of political tyranny, that by destruction of it we can achieve liberation and political victory. This perspective can mislead political action into an overemphasis on the struggle over representation, ignoring the structural material inequalities that lie behind those representations. Images can sometimes be an attractive 'easy' political tool that people can use to claim political action and victory, but at the end of the day, no substantial changes on a structural level have taken place. I will come back to this point in the final chapter.

So, to put the potential power of the image in a more concrete and psychologically relevant lens, I dedicate the next chapter to look at the affordances of the image in influencing how we see, think, feel, and remember. Instead of asking *what do images do?*, I ask *what do we do with images?* How do people through image production, interpretation, circulation, and destruction act on themselves and others around them? And how does this action afford images with the potential power to shape our practices of looking, our opinions, and how we feel about and remember different events?

CHAPTER 3

What We Do with the Image

Figure 3.1   On 9 August 1945, dense smoke rose in the shape of a mushroom, forming a cloud over the Japanese port of Nagasaki after the United States detonated an atomic bomb with the name 'Fat Man', the second ever used in warfare, after Hiroshima a few days earlier. The two bombs remain as the only use of nuclear weapons in an armed conflict and together led to the death of more than 200,000 people and the end of the Second World War.
Source: This image was taken by Charles Levy as part of his official duties and is now part of the US National Archives and Records Administrations. *Source*: The image is in the public domain and is retrieved from the Library of Congress (www.loc.gov/item/98506956).

The image shown in Figure 3.1 became an iconic marker of the nuclear age. It shows scientific advancement and power. It triggers the fascination of scientific development, coupled with the fear of what humans are capable of and willing to do. The image marks a moment of silence when time stopped; it is the moment just after indiscriminate destruction that remains hard to trace. The mushroom cloud has become an iconic historical image of the nuclear age.

What makes an iconic image that influences how we think, feel, and remember human history? Interest in the power of the image and its impact on us has intrigued many different investigations such as *What Images Do* (Bäcklund et al., 2019) or *What Do Pictures Want?* (Mitchell, 2005). However, images have no inherent power that allows them to 'do' something. Their power is always interdependent on how different individuals and groups act with and respond to images in specific time and space. Images, as cultural artefacts, are material objects that people modify and transform for their goal-oriented actions (Cole, 1996) as they inhabit an 'intentional world' made up of 'intentional things' (Shweder, 1991). People act on themselves and others using images, and in so doing, they inscribe images with affordances that trigger or inhibit certain actions, thoughts, and emotions.

To unfold these affordances from a psychological perspective, I will address four key – and quite broad – psychological and social processes facilitated through images: *seeing, thinking, feeling,* and *remembering*. I will present each of those processes in this chapter, but it is important to remember that they are not independent of one another. They are interdependent and relate together individual, relational, and societal levels of analysis. For example, to be able to see and interpret an image, we rely on our visual perception, cognition, past experiences, and memories. These processes are influenced by how we have been socialized to see and what we have learned to pay attention to. This happens within an environment that shapes our seeing and a social space that makes certain things visible while others are invisible.

3.1 Seeing

A simple answer to the question of what we do with images, is that we construct representations of ourselves, others, and the world, and in so doing we create visibility, mediating what is seen and how it is seen. This answer might not be so simple to tackle theoretically though, as it covers broad areas of study such as visual perception, neuroscience, visual culture,

3.1 Seeing

and politics of visibility. In line with the book's pragmatic approach, I combine knowledge from those different areas to construct a bigger picture of what it means for images to mediate what we see and how we see. The way we see and experience the world combines a biological process of sensory mechanisms that operates our visual perception and enables or limits what we see, and a social construction process where vision is a cultural activity shaped by who we are, how we were socialized, and the time and space we live in.

Using this pragmatic approach, I challenge the assumption of a clear distinction between 'inner' and 'outer' processes of seeing, between vision and visuality. Vision usually refers to what the human eye is physiologically capable of seeing, while visuality refers to the way in which vision is constructed in various ways: 'how we see, how we are able, allowed, or made to see, and how we see this seeing and the unseeing therein' (Foster, 1988, p. ix). Even though there are differences between the two in terms of how they can be studied, they are interrelated and dependent on one another. Vision is as much corporeal as cultural (Rose, 2016); it involves social and historical aspects, just as visuality also involves bodily and psychological aspects (Foster, 1988). This requires a dialectical approach to visual culture that looks at the social construction of the visual as well as the visual construction of the social (Mitchell, 2005).

To approach seeing as an embodied and culturally situated process, and to tackle how images mediate and are mediated by these processes, I will focus on three interrelated levels of investigation. First, I will present how we visually perceive images on the individual level, then I will move on to the relational level of how we use images to construct visual representations of ourselves and others, to finally present the societal and political level of how images create spaces of visibility and invisibility.

3.1.1 Visual Perception

In understanding *what we do with images*, it is not only when we produce or transform images that we engage in social action, but it is also when we see images that we *do* something. As Alva Noë (2005) argues, perception is not something that happens to us or in us, but something that we do; it is a thoughtful activity that involves capacities for action and thought.

The psychology of visual perception has traditionally focused on the reception of immediate information through the senses, with an understanding of visual processing as a 'coding process' based on a stimulus (e.g. an image) activating the senses and their neural correlates allowing us to see in a certain way, while paying less attention to the cognitive constructivist processes mediating sensation and perception (Forrester, 2000). When we see a photograph of a person, we do not 'just' receive the information from the image through our eyes to be decoded by our brain; we also rely on previous knowledge, experience, and other information from the surrounding environment to make sense of this image. How we see the image will be influenced by our familiarity with the person portrayed, our bias towards certain visual cues in the image, and the expectations we have of the image genre and where it is placed. Is it yet another image of that actor in an ad, is it a shocking news image presenting us with something unexpected, or is it a photograph of a family member? Even the mere recognition of the image being that of a person presumes knowledge of what is a person and what does a person look like, or 'should' look like, and what is photography.

As neuropsychologist Richard Gregory (1997) argues, there is no unmediated vision; seeing always involves a process of decision-making and interpretation where the brain searches for the best possible interpretation of the available data, as it converts random dots and shapes into objects familiar from experience. Philosopher Alva Noë (2005) would take us a step further, arguing that perception is not limited to processes happening in the eye and the brain; it is also an embodied skilful activity on the part of the person as a whole. Cognitive neuroscientist Jan Lauwereyns (2012) would go yet a step further to argue that to properly understand perception we need to investigate what happens inside our head and what happens in our entire body and outside it in our surrounding environment. By this, he proposes an interdisciplinary approach of visual perception that brings together knowledge from the enactive view of perception (e.g. Alva Noë), the philosophy of the embodied mind (e.g. Maurice Merleau-Ponty), the ecological perspective of perception (e.g. James J. Gibson), and the cognitive neuroscience of perception. I follow Lauwereyns' approach towards a holistic view of perception that acknowledges the bodily, cognitive, and environmental influences shaping what we see and how we see.

Following this approach, active perception works at the interplay between imagination and reality. We are rarely aware that what we see is a construct, not a veridical representation of reality or internal visual representations duplicating the world inside our head (Lauwereyns, 2012). There is choice involved in seeing, in where we select and aim our gaze. We look for meaning, seeking information of high value; something interesting, important, funny, beautiful that informs where

3.1 Seeing

our gaze focuses. Our gaze does not only affect what we see but also what we are blind to. Classic cognitive psychology experiments show how we can be surprisingly blind to objects right in front of our eyes (Neisser & Becklen, 1975). In one study, participants were asked to watch a video of players passing a basketball around and to count the number of passes one team makes, meanwhile a gorilla passes through the video. Half the participants do not notice the gorilla and are surprised to see what they have missed when the video is played again (Simons & Chabris, 1999). These studies show to what extent our looking could block out salient information that does not match our goal or intention of looking (Lauwereyns, 2012).

This means that among all the images we are exposed to everyday there are certain ones that will catch our eye because they convey certain meaningful information or because they drive our motivation, desires, or fears (Lauwereyns, 2012). Eyes in an image, for example, are known to create a gravitational pull for our gaze (Mather, 2014). Studies have also shown that people tend to show increased viewing time when looking at attractive faces (Leder et al., 2016; Maner et al., 2003) and when encountering aesthetic objects such as street art in an everyday setting (Mitschke et al., 2017). This selectivity and bias in what we look at makes us prone to different prejudices and cognitive biases that make us see what we want to see, rather than reflect critically on the different images surrounding us. We also know from social psychology that human thinking is highly selective and strategic. We mould our attention to serve our own purposes and interest; one could search for the terms *selective attention, confirmation bias*, or *cocktail party effect* to see how selective one could be in the many stimuli we are presented with in our environment. Yet, biased viewing is not necessarily bad: it allows us to look strategically and act fast, providing us with shortcuts that narrow down the search area and reduce the effort required to pay attention to every detail (Lauwereyns, 2012).

Biases are not only driven by our goals and desires in looking, they are also influenced by the affordances of the environment surrounding us. The attributes of the environment can afford – as in give potential for or inhibit – certain forms of action and engagement (Gibson, 1979). This does not mean that the environment causes certain ways of seeing, as in a stimuli–response relationship, but rather that it gives the potential for them in a dynamic reciprocal influence between a person and their environment. The affordances, for example, of a framed museum image are quite different from a street poster image. We are socialized to see those two images differently, interpret them differently, value them differently, and act towards them differently. A poster in an urban environment could be easily not seen or ignored in the usually cluttered street landscape that is filled with many other stimuli. However, if noticed, it affords quite a variety of human action towards it: one can look, scratch, write over, or ignore it altogether. An art museum space, on the other hand, is designed to position the image at the centre of the attention of the spectator; you are guided towards it and invited to view it with appreciation. Of course, one can also ignore an image at a museum, but one cannot – at least not within the legal parameters – alter or destroy a museum image. When the renowned Mona Lisa painting was covered with cake by an environmental activist in 2022, the attempt only managed to make a symbolic act of destruction to the artwork, which is protected with bulletproof glass and guarded within the walls of the Louvre Museum in Paris.

3.1.2 Visual Representations

Other than our intentionality and selectivity in seeing, we also actively construct visual representations of ourselves and others through images. We create images to embody the abstract and invisible ideas we would like to see with our own eyes (Lauwereyns, 2012). The most basic communicative function of an image is that it represents objects, people, or ideas and makes them visible in a certain form. Representation here refers to the use of symbolic systems such as language, marks, and images to produce meaning (Sturken & Cartwright, 2018). An image could make an absent object present, give shape to an abstract idea, or create fictional characters that embody generalization (Lonchuk & Rosa, 2011). Thus, images provide the figurative nuclei of social representations (Moscovici, 1984) through the process of objectification and anchoring (discussed in Chapter 2), in which abstract representations (e.g. the nation state) become concrete and familiar (e.g. the mother figure) in everyday dialogic knowledge exchange.

Many examples from everyday life illustrate this function. When we represent ourselves through a profile picture on a digital media platform, we do not simply use a picture that mirrors how we look in that moment, rather we pick an image that communicates something that is more than our features, an image that communicates an idea about us (e.g. professional, fun, or unique). We also share images online such as comics or digital memes that reflect a feeling, an opinion, or an experience. Authorities also use images to position themselves in society; the image of an authoritarian leader is meant to represent broader meanings such as

authority over space, surveillance, and dominance. And, arguably the most strategic of all, is advertising agencies using images to create emotional associations with a brand. Brand culture is a distinctly postmodern phenomenon of producing human subjects through images, products, and imagined lifestyles, which promise a certain identity (Sturken & Cartwright, 2018).

Visual representations provide one way of making identities, social relations, and social differences visible in a society. Images provide a social and political tool to humanize or dehumanize and *other* different groups of people. Paintings and photography have been used by colonial powers to produce the human subject of colonialism; the 'ideal orient other', who is uniform, radical, exotic, and unchanging (Said, 1978). Photography was especially utilized by British explorers to express and articulate the ideologies of imperialism and justify the actions of the colonizer (Ryan, 1997). Those visual representations do not just belong to a colonial historical past but endure in modern Western culture and have a psychological and emotional influence on the perception of the *other* today (Jahoda, 1999).

Those same tools have also been used to resist misrepresentation and dehumanization. Social critic and feminist scholar bell hooks points to the significant role the camera played for black communities in the United States before racial integration (hooks, 1995, 2001). The camera gave a tool through which one can participate in image production and create counter-hegemonic visuals that would challenge racist images of blackness that dominated the visual culture. Using images is central to decolonization, enabling communities to construct images of themselves that transcend the limits of the colonizing eye (hooks, 1995, 2001).

3.1.3 Visibility

Visual culture is governed by power dynamics that dictate what can be seen and who gets to represent whom. This relates us back to the concepts of visibility and the distribution of the sensible (Rancière, 2013) discussed in Chapter 2; who has the power of visibility and the access to representation. In authoritarian societies only authority-approved images can have access to circulation in state media and public spaces. There are also more implicit ways in democratic societies that determine who has privileged access to circulation and visibility, whose life is covered and humanized in global news, and which content gets filtered by digital media algorithms.

Visibility involves who looks, and their ways of looking, and how images are constructed for a certain position of looking. This has been referred to as the gaze, which is different to the notion of gaze in neuroscience, which refers to the eye and head position that position us to gaze at a certain object bringing it to our foveal vision (Lauwereyns, 2012). In visual culture and feminist studies, the concept of gaze is used to tackle social difference and power relations and how they could be analytically explored through thinking about who is able to see what and with what effects (Rose, 2016).

The relationship between visibility and power is complex and requires us to take a step back and see how this dynamic has evolved over time. Sociologist John Thompson traces visibility and power back to ancient and medieval societies, before the development of print and other media. In those times, the visibility of the people in power (e.g. the king) relied on the physical appearance of the ruler at public events such as royal marches and parades, where the masses could get a glimpse of their ruler, and the ruler would display their superiority and power through those performances (Thompson, 2005).

This builds on Michel Foucault's (1977) idea that ancient societies were societies of spectacle, where the exercise of power was linked to the public manifestation of the superiority of the few in power made visible to the masses, whether through a royal parade or a public execution. This form of visibility and power changed around the sixteenth century as new forms of discipline and surveillance came into play. The army, educational institutions, hospitals, and prisons moved the 'spectacle society' to a 'disciplinary society' where instead of the visibility of the few in power to the masses, it became the visibility of the masses to the few. This new relation is exemplified by Foucault's example of the Panopticon, where surveillance is implemented through individuals' awareness of being 'seen' or watched all the time, being the subject of continuous visibility; that even when they are not watched, they act as if they were being observed – they have internalized the gaze of the power.

Thompson (2005) argues that Foucault only gives part of the picture with his Panopticon model, ignoring an important aspect that relates visibility and power, that of communication media. The Panopticon enables the many to be visible to the few, but media enables the few to be visible to the masses. When print and later on radio and television became a possibility, rulers had a further chance to display their image without needing physical appearance and an assembled audience. The new media facilitated a 'mediated visibility' where a ruler can manage and disseminate their image to the masses through those channels of communication. This development posed new risks for leaders: mediated forms of communication were not only used to promote rulers but also to attack and denounce them.

New media subjects those in power to a new kind of visibility. Consider recent cases such as the Watergate scandal, where the hidden practices of those in power were brought to the public eye, or the many cases of Black Lives Matter where image and video evidence circulated, exposing police behaviour. New media is thus further defining the relationship between visibility and power, making those in power, rather than those over whom power is exercised, the main focus of new visibility that poses fragility to the previously protected image of authority (Thompson, 2005).

Is it reasonable to argue then that today's growing accessibility to production and circulation of images through technological tools and digital media has democratized access to visibility? It certainly offers new ways for challenging dominant representations. However, one should be cautious about presenting digital media space as a democratic space that gives equal opportunity for all voices. Not everyone has access to the internet or tools for image production around the world, and among those who do have access, the digital space does not offer the same platforms for visibility to all. Visibility on digital media is governed by the companies owning the platforms, governments, and algorithms mediating the circulation of content.

The image of the nuclear mushroom cloud (Figure 3.1) is a clear example of an image of power; it is an image that gives visibility to the American technological and military power. It is not one that gives visibility to the aftermath of the bomb or the atrocities it caused to human life and nature. Despite the many initiatives to document and communicate the impact of nuclear bombs on humans and nature, when searching for 'nuclear bomb' on a Google Images search in January 2025, the first hundred images that come up are mostly of the infamous mushroom cloud (sixty-five images) and the structure of the bomb (thirty-four images) and only one single image of the nuclear destruction of Hiroshima.

3.2 Thinking

The common idea that an image is worth a thousand words assumes a privileged way by which images – as opposed to language – communicate to us. This could be because words that can summarize an image are often indeterminate and ambiguous (Mitchell, 2005). To distinguish how images affect us differently is a difficult task as we live in a multimodal world where we make sense of language and visual communication in our environment in relation to one another and through one another. Therefore, it is important to think of how language and images work together in our environment to shape our thinking, rather than seeing them as two completely separate forms of communication and knowledge circulation.

There are, however, some differences in how we interpret a message that is communicated through visual means versus linguistic means. Intuitively, there is a difference in experiencing an idea through reading about it, seeing and hearing someone explain it, or seeing an image capturing it. Images, in comparison to words alone, can evoke deeper elements of human consciousness (Harper, 2002). Neuropsychological research indicates that significantly larger areas of the brain are devoted to interpreting an image in comparison to language (Mather, 2014). Studies also show that images can elicit more emotional responses compared to written text that elicits more analytical responses; however, imaginative language can also elicit emotional responses similar to those of images, and neurological studies show that reading narratives, for example, can activate the same parts of the brain as visual images (Hill, 2004). Perceiving images requires flexible interpretation of visual cues, which is different to reading language which relies on arbitrary learned associations (Mather, 2014). Written language relies on discrete meaningful unites that prompt systematic processing and are interpreted relatively slower than images. Images are interpreted more wholistically and by instantaneously relying on more heuristic processing, thus they can provide a shortcut to fast decisions (Hill, 2004).

Visual and verbal forms of communication also present information differently. There is argumentation and narrative structures to verbal communication, while visual communication relies on associations triggered by certain visual signs and symbols (Müller, 2008), which makes visual meaning more dependent on context and the individual's memory and experience informing their associations. The way we use and interpret images and the associations we make out of what is visually represented affects how we think and how we form attitudes towards different people and topics. Images here are not understood as an external stimulus in our environment that affects thinking but as an integral part of our thinking from a distributed cognition perspective. Distributed cognition refers to how our cognition is not limited to mental processes inside the brain but that these processes happen across our brain, body, social interactions, material spaces, and cultural artefacts around us (Hutchins, 1995). This situates images in relation to thinking, as one of the resources in the environment around us that shape and guide our thought, and one that we use to regulate and expand our psychological capacities of thinking and remembering (Vygotsky, 1978).

Thinking through images requires flexibility and openness in interpreting the multiple meanings and associations they could afford. Psychologist Frederic Bartlett (1958) referred to this as an 'open' system of thinking that he argued is the more common way of thinking that is used in everyday life and in artistic contexts, as opposed to 'closed' or formal system thinking which psychological research has focused more on (Wagoner, 2017). In closed system thinking, all relevant information for solving a problem is already present and not changing, and there is one 'right' answer (e.g. a mathematical equation). Open system thinking, on the other hand, relies on a constructive process for interpretation where new information is sought after. Open thinking is what we commonly use in forming opinions and interpreting topics of social interest, where several interpretations are possible (Wagoner, 2017). While closed systems thinking require a series of steps to reach a conclusion, everyday thinking is based on a 'jump' in which the thinker finds cues to make meaning.

This everyday form of thinking is the most common in encountering images around us. We engage in a cognitive and affective process where we interpret and give value to the signs and symbols in an image, associating the visual representations to different meanings, attitudes, and feelings. This meaning-making process is influenced by the context we experience the image in, our attention to the various details of the image, and our own social position, experience, and memory. The openness of this thinking process makes it also a dialogical and argumentative one, where we engage in a dialogue with the argument that we interpret the image to be making.

This process varies in depth based on what images capture our eyes, and in which images we take their meaning for granted, and which images intrigue us to think reflectively about their meaning and our position from that meaning. The common idea that images have a charm that 'grabs' our attention is challenged – as I argued in the introduction chapter of the book – by the abundance of images today, that it takes more for an image to trigger our attention and reflection. The visual culture, especially digital media scrolling culture, promotes less reflective thinking. We scroll down hundreds of images of products in online shopping; we scroll down social media timelines to watch the lives of friends, acquaintances, and strangers we follow. Even dating is turned into a scrolling experience where we swipe through many images using only a few minutes if not seconds to decide who is a good match and who is not, while drawing on generalizations, stereotypes, and possibly prejudices in making our choices.

This speed is especially relevant in investigating the effect of images, especially those that we do not pay attention to. Images, as opposed to language, do not require a viewer to intentionally stop and read and comprehend text, but they impose themselves on our surroundings; there is something implicit about their effects even when we don't attend to them. We can be continuously seeing an image and normalizing it, even though we are not very aware of our exposure to it. One example is how our ideas of physical beauty and body sizes are very much influenced by the thousands of images we see in advertisement and entertainment media.

3.2.1 Forming Attitudes

Whether we attend reflectively to images or not, they do present us with ideas that form our everyday knowledge and our attitudes. Images communicate social representations and, as Moscovici argues (1984), social representations are rarely neutral; they often hold some form of attribution and causality. These attributions affect people's positive or negative attitudes towards the subjects and objects presented in an image, and who is blamed and who is sympathized with. The image of the Nagasaki nuclear mushroom cloud (Figure 3.1) does not show who caused it, or what it caused in its aftermath; the focus is mainly on the fascination of the bomb itself. The image was first perceived from a Western viewer position as a 'triumphant' end of war image signalling a new atomic era in human history but later interpreted as a dystopian image (Christensen, 2021). Images of Nagasaki survivors, on the other hand, show another picture; they pose accountability, showing the aftermath, attributing the cause of suffering to the actors dropping the bomb, and positioning the survivors rather than the bomb as worthy of visual attention. Campaign posters of anti-nuclear war movements also shift the focus to the vulnerability of the human race, animals, and nature in the face of nuclear technologies showing images of the Earth, the human foetus, or as in Figure 3.2, a mother and a child, symbolizing the future the nuclear bomb is threatening.

What the image shows and the value it attributes to that shown has an influence on our attitude and possibly behaviour towards different social issues. The rhetorical study of images shows how certain images can persuade and influence certain beliefs, attitudes, and actions of the viewer (Hill, 2004). Media psychology has been especially interested in the

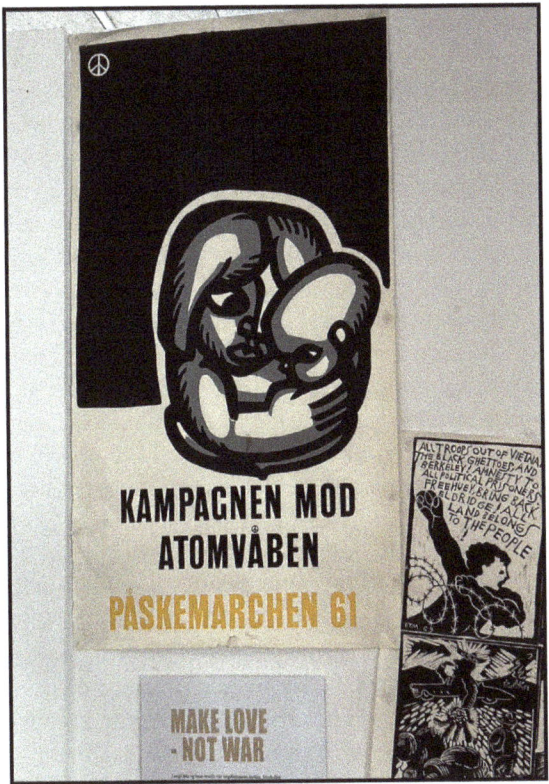

Figure 3.2 An image of an anti-nuclear weapons campaign poster.
Source: Displayed at the Cold War Museum in Rebild, Denmark. Text reads: The campaign against nuclear weapons. Easter March 61. Source: Photographed by author in October 2021.

influence of advertising images on consumer behaviour, the influence of TV and gaming on children, and the influence of political campaigns on voting behaviour (Forrester, 2000). An effective image in that sense is one that persuades the viewer to act in accordance with the message communicated. This could be one way of assessing images, but it poses the risk of diminishing the interpretation of the image meaning to whether it achieves a direct desired effect, leaving out the multitude of ways people interact and internalize meanings.

Research shows that mere repeated exposure and familiarity to certain images can change people's attitudes towards what is represented in them (Zajonc, 1968). Images can create continuous 'presence' of a certain viewpoint, making it more salient and memorable (Perelman & Olbrechts-Tyteca, 1971). While we might often act in accordance with our values and political ideologies, we are also prone to be unintentionally moved by repetitive subtle political cues around us (Ferguson et al., 2009), that trigger us to act with affect rather than conscious thought (Comstock & Scharrer, 2005; Marcus et al., 2000). A symbol, especially a patriotic one such as a national flag, can affect viewers' attitudes in less conscious ways because of its association with affective values of patriotism that are ingrained through socialization and education in certain contexts (Billig, 1995). A study shows that the repetitive use of patriotic imagery in news reporting may increase rather than decrease public polarization of American viewers regarding foreign policy issues (Gelpi et al., 2013).

However, those images that persuade us through repetition, simple cues and associations, and fast attention grabbing rely on peripheral routes of persuasion, which often result in a relatively temporary and low involvement change of attitudes that is based on simple acceptance or rejection of the cues in the image (Petty et al., 1983). Another approach to assess the psychological influence of an image is to investigate which images invite the viewer's reflective thinking and engagement with different interpretations and argumentations. If an image invites us to think reflectively and to have diligent consideration, it has a higher chance of having a longer-term effect on our thinking. This criterion, I argue, is more relevant in identifying powerful and intriguing images. They 'grab' our attention and invite us to pause and think. This approach would still investigate the 'effect' of an image, not as a direct one corresponding to an intended message, but one that varies based on how each individual internalizes the meanings from an image, and how they externalize those meanings in relation to their thinking, feelings, and actions. This process will always vary based on a thinking person who has certain experiences, associations, memories, identities, and social positions.

3.2.2 *Constructing Narratives and Positioning Social Actors*

One way in which images can invite reflective thinking is by posing an argument for us to dialogue with. Differently to how we argue using language, argumentation by images involves using visual representations to position different social actors including the viewer. Earlier, I presented the framework of the social life of images as involving different social actors taking up different social positions of producer, viewer, and censor in relation to the image. The term 'social position', in comparison to 'social role', was used by Bronwyn Davies and Rom Harré in their positioning theory (1990) to highlight the dynamic aspect of social encounters where we continuously take up different positions based on the context of an interaction or a dialogue. Social positions are relevant here not only in relation to what action a person takes towards an image but also towards how images are used to communicate with, argue with, and position different social actors in relation to different topics. Positioning theory has a primary focus on how positions are established in discursive interactions and how those positions are ascribed certain rights and duties based on a normative moral reasoning (Harré et al., 2009). This could be applied further to images, looking at how visual representations in images involves a positioning of oneself and others in response to different social issues (Awad & Wagoner, 2018). Argumentation in an image could be achieved by the choice of who is represented in the image, how they are represented, what their attributes are, and in what context. Positioning of social actors comes with certain expectations of rights and duties, which are not restricted to explicit rules and laws, but they are often based on norms and therefore are open for change and contestation in dialogue.

Through positioning in images we also tell stories about ourselves and others. Narratives provide versions of reality that rely on convention rather than empirical verification for their acceptability (Bruner, 1991). Narratives do not only rely on language but images also often borrow from and feed into social narratives (Riessman, 2008). In the anti-nuclear weapon campaign poster (Figure 3.2), the image communicates a narrative about a mother and a child, where they are positioned as vulnerable social actors, having the right to protection. Representing them as such positions the viewer, as a witness to this vulnerability, as having the duty to protect the vulnerable, whether by adopting an attitude against nuclear weapons or by actively campaigning against them. Another example is the famous graffiti image of 'Thank God it's our bomb' painted in Berlin. The image uses the quote from an editorial by Irving Brant in the daily newspaper *PM*, published shortly after the first bomb on Hiroshima. The image shows the American popular symbol of 'Uncle Sam' riding the atomic bomb as it is heading down. Unlike the mushroom cloud photograph in Figure 3.1, the graffiti image painter clearly positions the actor who dropped the bomb, who has the power and the duty to stop the use of the bomb, and invites the viewer – especially the Western viewer – to reflect on their privileged position.

A powerful image can create visual dialogues and argumentation that provoke perceptual, emotional, and representational tension (Marková,

2003). Thinking with such an image is not a mere process of identifying the referents in the image; rather, it is to enter a dialogue with the meanings suggested in the image as the viewer interprets it in a particular spatial and temporal context. Therefore, the utterances the viewers produce in response to an image are not just a reply to 'what the image says' (as if the image can speak), they are arguments which respond to the arguments they attributed the image to be saying and to the feelings and positions the image provoked (Lonchuk & Rosa, 2011).

3.3 Feeling

Thinking and feeling through images are interrelated, as we have discussed; forming attitudes, arguing, and positioning through images involve cognitive as well as affective processes of meaning making. Since images' meanings rely on associations and open thinking processes, and since they manage to affect us by their presence in our environment without us necessarily paying attention to them, it is reasonable to argue that images' influence relies heavily on their emotional appeal. The affect of images comes from their emotive vividness and memorable character (Joffe, 2008), their ability to tie together networks of associations and identities, especially in online digital spaces (Carah, 2014), and their capacity to connect individual emotions with collective community emotions (Bleiker & Hutchison, 2008).

Images have the potential to pose an immediate appeal to our emotions, as they have the capacity to absorb human emotions and reflect them back as a demand for reflection (Mitchell, 2005). This capturing feature of images can be seen in how protest images and symbols can mobilize and gather people for a cause (Awad & Wagoner, 2018, 2020). This appeal can be also seen in banal everyday social media use where people use images from movies or memes to capture a very specific situated feeling – 'this moment when' – that is hard to express in words, and that resonates with others who share the same experience. This appeal could be further investigated spatially, in how images influence how we feel in certain places; how we feel included, 'at home', or 'out of place' from certain visual cues (Awad, 2017).

Negative stereotypical images surrounding us in the environment can influence our self-perception and sense of belonging. Different social psychological experiments have investigated this, building on the concept of *stereotype threat*, which explains how when individuals are exposed to a negative stereotype of their in-group, they tend to display decreased performance on a task relevant to the negative stereotype (Steele & Aronson, 1995). For example, a study showed that women who are exposed to gender stereotypical television ads scored lower on a maths test than a control group who viewed neutral ads (P. G. Davies et al., 2002). Another study shows that female students showed higher comprehension in science after viewing counter-stereotypic textbook images of women scientists than when they were shown stereotypical images of men scientists (Good et al., 2010).

One should be critical, however, of looking at those findings as a causation mechanism as the influence is a reciprocal one that is moderated by many factors. For example, the salience of the threatened identity will influence how the person internalizes the images; a feminist who is aware and critical of those stereotypes could respond differently to the positioning and argument posed by the images. Also, how this identity intersects with other identities of the person such as their social class and ethnicity will also influence how effective the 'threat' might be. In another stereotype threat study that puts into account the identity strength, researchers looked at the consequences of radical right-wing propaganda images on immigrants (Appel, 2012). The study found that the ethnic identity strength could have a moderation role, acting as a protective factor against identity threat.

3.3.1 Affective Symbols

Images' capacity to speak to our emotions lies in how images capture an elaborate idea or feeling and present it in a concrete and immediate form. This is especially evident in investigating visual symbols. As mentioned in Chapter 2, images can present us with more than *just* signs, they can become symbols (Bartlett, 1924) that embody more than one meaning and carry an underlying sentiment that makes them affective. This can be seen in how certain national symbols such as a flag image or ideological symbols such as a cross or a communist's hammer and sickle can shape people's emotions and mobilize them behind a cause.

Looking at recent protest movements such as the Tunisian and Egyptian uprisings of 2011, as well as Black Lives Matter following the killing of George Floyd, one can clearly see certain images that became the protest symbols. Those protest symbols moved many people beyond mere recognition, to affectively engaging with them and joining action towards a common goal (Awad & Wagoner, 2018, 2020). The power of those images is in how they transformed police violence from a state-controlled act that is invisible to the public into concrete visual evidence that circulates and mobilizes resistance (Khatib, 2013). The images condensed the elaborate and long-term forms of oppression into one concrete affective symbol that people could relate to.

An example of a recent affective symbol in relation to the climate crisis is that of the image of a turtle with a straw up its nostril. The image comes from a video documented by a team of researchers off the coast of Costa Rica and became an emblem of an anti-straw movement (Robinson et al., 2015). The turtle image in a way simplified a complex problem and mobilized action towards what is a very small fraction of the ocean pollution problem, let alone the climate crisis. The image managed to overcome some of the psychological challenges that hinder people from mobilization for pro-environment action (Scott et al., 2021). First, there is a challenge in relation to how the climate crisis in many parts of the world remains invisible and is experienced as physically distant and with a delayed impact, which leads to psychological distancing. Second, we have cognitive limitation on quantitative reasoning (e.g. the millions of ocean pollutants) and abstract ideas (the overall impact of those pollutants), and we have a finite pool of worry, which make us focus on our immediate environment rather than all the wrongs in the world. The image of the turtle made the psychological distancing more proximate, the numbers and abstract ideas more concrete with one example, and most importantly it spoke to our affect by seeing the suffering of one turtle. Social psychological studies have shown that people tend to react more strongly when exposed to individual humanized faces of a crises and are more moved when invisible issues are made tangible and visually noticeable (Scott et al., 2021).

3.3.2 Humanizing the Invisible

When we use images to give visibility to a certain group of people, we choose how to construct their visual representation in ways that humanize and familiarize them, or in ways that de-individualize them and possibly also dehumanize them. This has consequences on how viewers are able to empathize, relate, and engage in perspective taking, that is, the ability to see the world from the position of another person. To be able to engage in position exchange, individuals need to recognize basic similarities between themselves and others (Gillespie, 2007); however, this is challenged by polarizing discourses and images that emphasize only the 'crucial' difference 'that matters more than any similarity and makes all common features seem small and insignificant' (Bauman, 2000, p. 176).

Photojournalism plays a key role in how people and events are covered and subsequently how people think and feel about what is covered. This gives photos a substantial political power through their capacity to frame reality by giving visibility to certain aspects of an event (Butler, 2010). For example, in the case of Abu Ghraib prison in Iraq, the news of the American soldiers torturing and sexually abusing inmates was made known to the American audience long before the publication of the photographic documentation in 2004, but it was only after the photos were published that there was a major shift in public opinion against the incident (Butler, 2010).

In news coverage of refugees, research shows that the dominant visual framing of them as anonymized and de-individualized groups of people reduces viewers' ability to attribute uniquely human characteristics to those depicted (Azevedo et al., 2021). A typical iconic image of illegal migrants is that of the refugee boat. The image shows unknown and unknowable people, making individuals almost invisible. The affective power of the boat image becomes less about the people in it and more about the loaded boat being a sign associated with the threat of invasion and infection (Falk, 2010). Psychological studies of the 'identifiable victim effect' show that migrants with identifiable faces invoke politics of pity, while images of indistinguishable large groups of migrants invoke politics of fear (Bleiker et al., 2013). The visual de-individualization hinders the viewers' capacity to take the perspective of those presented in the image and empathize with their position.

The idea of using images to dehumanize a group of people precedes photojournalism and digital media. In *Images of Savages*, Gustav Jahoda (1999) shows the enduring psychological influence of the drawings and vivid descriptions of the 'other' that early European explorers and travellers came back with in the eleventh, twelfth, and thirteenth centuries (before there was a European identity as such). These culturally unfamiliar images were assimilated through a cultural transition process (Bartlett, 1932) and anchored through culturally familiar comparisons (Moscovici, 1984). The distant 'others' became understood as legendary creatures, monstrous races, and wild men of the woods with animal and child-like characteristics (Jahoda, 1999). Those images have had an enduring emotional appeal that shaped a certain perception of the 'other' as opposed to the physical appearance and mode of life of Europeans – which were perceived as criteria of full humanity. The transhistorical persistence and continuity of those images could be traced in the nineteenth-century display of 'exotic people' in the so-called ethnographic exhibitions popular in Europe and America and also in advertisement images (Jahoda, 1999). In mid nineteenth century the image of the savage became not only for representing the exotic distant non-European but also for representing the lower class, the criminal, the mentally ill, and women. Even when the 'savage' image was no longer supported by the majority of political and scientific establishments, the image still endured in popular culture, serving emotional and ego-protective needs (Jahoda, 1999). Ethnocentric images rely on stereotypes that reflect more of the in-group's motives, wishes, guilt, and fears rather than the actual characteristics of those represented (LeVine & Campbell, 1972). Those motives can be clearly seen in the colonial visual construction of the 'ideal orient other' (Said, 1978) that is incapable of self-governance and therefore justifies the actions and ideologies of imperialism (Ryan, 1997).

3.4 Remembering

Arguably the most powerful aspect of what we do with images could be to shape *what* we remember and – more importantly – *how* we remember. The power of images in shaping our personal and collective memories brings together the cognitive and affective aspects of images already discussed, as well as the politics of visibility and the endurance of certain ways of seeing across time. Our memories are constructive and affective (Bartlett, 1932); we are more likely to remember images that moved us emotionally (Stones & Bygate, 2009) and produce images of people and things that matter to us.

In our personal lives we have photographs of ourselves and people around us that we cherish and display and others we conceal or forget about. When we lose a loved one, we look at images that we can remember them through and display in our environment to continue to *see* them. We choose a photograph that freezes a moment that represents the person in our eyes. It represents what we love about them and how we want to remember them. A photograph can give us this frozen moment to cherish and to represent the person's whole life, even when we know it only represents an idealized snapshot of it. Photography here becomes a way of appropriating that which is being photographed and a way of an imaginary possession of a past (Sontag, 1977). The photograph helps us recall the past by freezing its representation at the most powerful moment (Zelizer, 2004), thus indicating some sort of mortality, and functioning as a significant tool in social, cultural, and familial memory preservation (Barthes, 1981).

The social practices surrounding family photographs and travel images show how images are used as memory objects as well as tools for commodity production and inscription of social identities (Tagg, 1988). This is evident even more with the development of technologies facilitating the taking and sharing of images. One could say, when observing the amount of mobile phone cameras taking images of a famous tourist destination or a celebrity at a concert, that the act of imaging takes over the actual experience. Instead of witnessing a moment in real life, people are seeing it through their screens as they are keen on having their 'own' image that 'documents' they were there and gives them the cultural capital that comes with that. What is captured thus becomes a documentation of the act of viewing itself (Dilley, 1986). Cognitive psychologist Linda Henkel (2014) has shown that taking pictures instead of immersing oneself in an experience can in fact hinder one's memory of the event – what she labelled as the *photo-taking impairment effect*.

The use of images as memory objects is closely tied to individual and collective identity formation. Family photography can reflect people's thinking and emotions and serves as a private form of memory reservation and family identity construction (Rose, 2010). Edwards and Middleton (1988) show how family photographs are meaningful semiotic and cultural artefacts used by parents as mediators of the past, narrating to their children the family's history through images, elaborating on stories that are not necessarily depicted in the images. In this process, they argue, children learn how to remember without actually having to remember. This also makes photograph destruction a weapon in family conflict situation and separation, where a person tries to reshape family history by promoting certain photos while concealing or destroying others.

Private family and travel images do not always stay confined to the personal space, and the boundary between the private and public sphere is blurry especially in how some of those images travel to museums and are used to collectively 'remember' a community's past and ways of living. As a community we share a collective memory that is closely tied to our collective identity. Collective memory is understood as the shared representation of the past among members of a social group such as a generation or a nation (Wertsch, 2008). It is an affective relationship a community has with its past that feeds into the group's identity and imagination of their shared future (Halbwachs, 1992). The resources for remembering the collective past are usually unequally distributed among the members of a group and their cultural artefacts such as narratives and images (Wertsch, 2008). Through looking at those artefacts we can see how the collective memory is negotiated and how it unfolds within a specific spatial framework (Halbwachs, 1992).

Images of the collective past can be seen in family photography, imperial expeditions, news images, paintings in history books and museums, and in memorials. All these shape how we remember our past; who were our heroes, our victims, and our enemies? Images simplify events such as wars into certain representations and symbols that trigger certain reconstructions of memories (Bartlett, 1932). Therefore, similar to family photographs, public images can be used as weapons by those in power to regulate a community's memories, choosing which events and people to be glorified and which to be concealed out of sight and forcibly forgotten.

Memory is a socially situated practice (Bartlett, 1932; Wagoner, 2017) that is culturally mediated through signs and tools (Vygotsky, 1978). From this sociocultural psychological perspective, memory is social, dynamic, and embodied. When we remember we do not draw on a literal recall of a static stored collection of images, we engage in a creative process of reconstruction. This reconstruction is influenced by who we are today and the demands of the present time, and influenced by where we are and how does our environment give affordances or constraints to the recall of certain memories. This means that remembering is both personal and social, and it is always open for reinterpretations and adaptations to fit our present and future concerns and circumstances (Wagoner, 2017; Wagoner et al., 2019).

Images surrounding us in the environment – whether accurate or inaccurate, drawn or photographed, doctored or original – have an influence on us if they are spread wide enough to become our anchor to remembering certain people or events. We might be more critical today of the idea that photographs are clear evidence of what has been, given advances in digital imaging and image manipulation, but we are often less critical of how images show one way of seeing and remembering among multiple other ways; they show one snapshot that often misses much of the details or depth of what is represented. Images are in many instances arbitrary, conventionalized to be meaningful to entire groups, and simplified to be capable of transmission (Fentress & Wickham, 1992; Zelizer, 2004).

Images that become iconic powerful ones for collective memory are often ones that capture an event in a powerful moment. Like the mushroom cloud image, it is the moment just after its dropping. They are also images that simplify and objectify a whole idea, generation, or crisis in one concrete visual that people can find meaning in. To take another example, what is the first image that comes to mind when you remember the terror attack of 9/11? It could be the photograph captured by Kelly Guenther after the first plane crashed into the World Trade Center and the second plane on its way to the second tower, frozen in time. It could also be another photograph taken by Richard Drew of a man falling from one of the towers.

Chances are more people would remember the first image rather than the latter. Communication and media scholar Barbie Zelizer (2004) argues that news photographers often document a sequence of images of an event, but the ones that get to represent the event in newspapers are images that strategically freeze and capsulate the event in its most powerful moment. Unlike with language and narratives, an image tells a story best through strategically freezing its potentially strongest moment, the moment most suggestive of what has happened before it and what is about to follow. One of those powerful moments, she argues, is often the 'just before' second, the image that captures the 'about to' moment. Both images we have mentioned mark the moment just before death, rather than after, as the most significant in the sequencing of events surrounding human demise. However, the second image was not received well, as this was not the way many people wanted to remember the last moment, especially family members of the victims, which led many newspapers to stop publishing similar images (Zelizer, 2004), I refer to this as *community censorship*, which I will discuss in Chapter 9.

It is especially in such times of crisis and contention in society that negotiation of visual documentation becomes evident. Which images accurately document an event and from whose perspective become key questions. Also, which images we need to protect ourselves and others from, because they are images that unsettle and disrupt our view of the world and our position in it (Forrester, 2000). The decision of what is made visible and how will always have consequences on how people respond to the event and relate to others (Zelizer, 2010).

Community censorship, editorial decisions, and people's engagement with images are all factors that shape which images become iconic after an event. Another factor is government censorship and official shaping of a country's collective memory. Since the Egyptian revolution of 2011, there has been contestation over the memory of the revolution and its documentation. Activists' photographs, street art paintings, and online images documented the narrative of the revolution and commemorated those who lost their lives for the cause. After 2013, the army government produced its own counter-images promoting the people and the army as 'one hand' against the old system and the Muslim Brotherhood and promoting the 2013 coup as the 'second revolution' (Awad, 2017; Awad & Wagoner, 2018). Here the social lives of the protestors' images were quickly cut short from the public space, and could only continue their lives in online spaces and archives, while the images of the government got the prominent place in urban space and national media.

Community and authority censorship influences what is available in our environment as remembering resources and analysing those practices can show the monopoly or dialogue allowed around representation and visibility. However, even in the most authority-monopolized visual cultures, there are always resistance and counter-images, and there is always a process of reconstructing meaning even out of the most monological authority images that do not afford tolerance for different interpretations. In an earlier study (Awad, 2017) conducted five years after the 2011 Egyptian revolution, I studied how pedestrians perceived different images representing the revolution from the activists and from the government/army side. Participants' interpretation of the images and their narration of what is represented in the image were influenced by their political position, their own experience of the events, and their position regarding who produced the image.

3.4.1 The Act of Not Forgetting

It is especially when there are attempts to censor certain representations of an event or a group of people that the effort to 'not forget' become evident. A collective memory persists as long as its content is of active concern to a group of people (Halbwachs, 1950/1980). As bell hooks (1995) argues, it is when the psychohistory of a people is marked by loss, and their histories are denied, that documentation can become an obsession, and images could become their way of entering history without words. The documentation of the Egyptian revolution in online archives and books became an important ongoing duty for many of the activists. The documentation was not only aimed at not forgetting the uprising that has happened in the past but to also not forget the future that the activists imagined and worked for. This is captured in a graffiti piece by activist Keizer, that reads:

فاكر بكره اللي ما جاش؟

Translation: *Do you remember the tomorrow that never came?*

Going back to the mushroom cloud image (Figure 3.1) I started the chapter with, the image, produced by the powerful actors, documents the history of the nuclear age and shapes a certain collective memory of 'the' atomic bombs. The image, like most human history, tells the story from the 'hero' perspective. As novelist Ursula K. Le Guin (2019) eloquently says in *The Carrier Bag Theory of Fiction*, the story told of our civilization is not one of humanity, it is the story of the killer, the story that tells 'how the mammoth fell on Boob and how Cain fell on Abel and how the bomb fell on Nagasaki and how the burning jelly fell on the villagers and how the missiles will fall on the Evil Empire, and all the other steps in the Ascent of Man' (p. 32).

For every image that shows, documents, and commemorates something, there is something that it does not show, something that it erases. The documentation of what those weapons caused would be regarded as an unpatriotic endeavour for the American commemoration (Sontag, 2003). The image is a spectacle of a tragedy that does not show the 'deathly silence' of the bomb that many survivors recall, the ghastly stillness coupled with massive instant deaths that descended over the time and space of the burned Nagasaki, or the blinding flash of an explosion that lives on and continues its explosion in the bodies of *hibakushas* (atomic bomb victim survivors) (Barad, 2017a). The images of Nagasaki and Hiroshima as 'the' images of nuclear bombs are themselves erasing an important 'before' – the first actual atomic bomb dropped in New Mexico, home to the Indigenous peoples of the Southwest, on 16 July 1945 – and an important 'after' – bombs dropped afterwards in the name of nuclear testing (Barad, 2017b).

The mushroom remains as the visual symbol of the explosion. A symbol of a cloud between heaven and earth, and – perhaps not accidental – the symbol of the mushroom as the ultimate *pharmakon* associated with life and death, with food and poison, capturing the fascination and anxiety of human control over life and death (Barad, 2017a). This is not the only way of remembering; the act of not forgetting the rest of the picture persists through survivor accounts and images of loss and destruction. These images not only reshape how we remember the past of what happened but also serve as a reminder of the duty to not repeat it in the future.

PART II

The Social Life of Images
An Analytical Framework

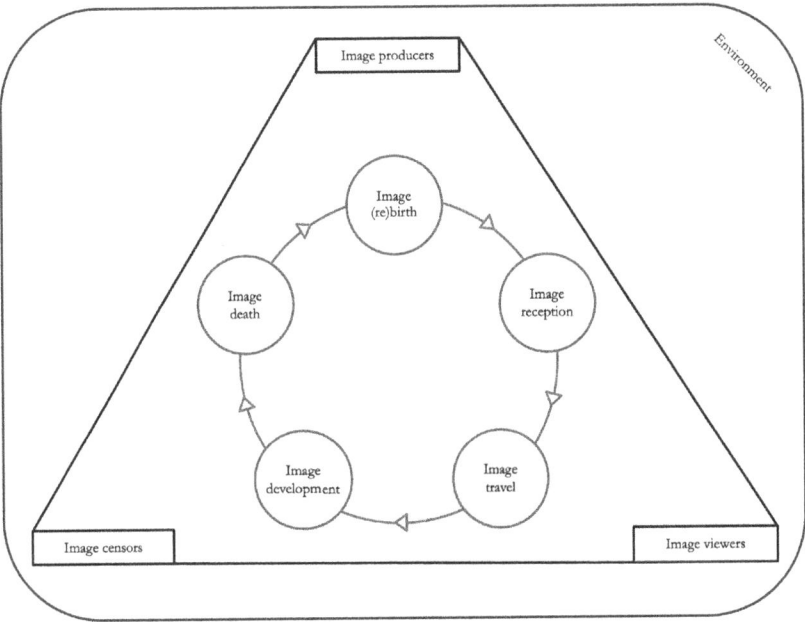

Figure II   The social life of images' analytical framework.

In Part I, I presented a conceptualization of images as signs and tools with social lives that influence ways of seeing, thinking, feeling, and remembering. In Part II, I elaborate on the social life of the image as a framework to analyse images as an object of study as well as a method for studying psychological and social processes and contested dialogues in society. In the following chapters, I follow the social life of the image from birth to circulation, transformation, and possible death. The life of the image is

75

presented as circular and as one that can divert into multiple trajectories rather than a single linear trajectory from birth to death. Each chapter will focus on one life stage of the image and an example from a specific genre such as protest posters, caricatures, graffiti, political campaigns, photojournalism, and social media memes.

If one has all the resources and time to study a certain image, one could start from its first appearance and follow every development of it, as well as how it is received by different viewers in different contexts. However, this is rarely the case, as most of the time we have a limited access into one space where the image circulated or to some participants who could share their experience with producing or viewing certain images. For this, I present different methods in the chapters that could tackle various image genres and different aspects of the social life of images.

Figure II sums up the analytical framework. The circular social life of images is presented as interdependent on different social actors who take on varying social positions of *producers, viewers,* and *censors,* as they do social action through images. A social act is an action that cannot be completed by a single person in isolation; it requires several actors' contributions and interactions to be completed (Mead, 1934). Thus, there is a dialogical relationship between those three positions where for example the act of viewing an image is also an act of considering the perspectives of the producer, other viewers, and possible censors of that same image. Also, the act of censoring an image is an act of expecting and preventing the possible future viewers and an act in response and opposition to the producer. Those positions are also changeable, rather than static social roles. They change based on how different people position themselves regarding an image; an image producer could become its own censor and an image viewer could become its next producer as they reproduce it and share it in a new space.

The actions of those different positions shape the life of an image from the moment of *birth, reception, travel, development,* and possible *death.* Those processes reflect a certain *contested dialogue* in the society surrounding the topic the image tackles. This dialogue can only be understood within a certain *environment,* that is, a specific time, place, and context. The different power structures within that environment afford or constraint certain social actions and shape which social positions have the privileged access to represent themselves, others, and the society at large, and who gets to censor other representations. The environment also affords certain ways of seeing and certain forms of interpretation.

Through this social life framework, I set the focus on the negotiation and tension between those different actors and how that tension constructs and transforms meanings in everyday life. It is also that tension that drives social change. Here, social change is understood as a communicative process between social actors taking up different positions in relation to an issue of mutual interest (Marková, 2003). Investigating images through this approach opens different ways of understanding processes of change and acts of resistance through the use of images.

CHAPTER 4

The Birth of the Image

Figure 4.1 Image of the Ancient Egyptian queen Nefertiti wearing a gas mask.
Source: Ahmed Hayman.

In the early days of the 2011 Egyptian uprising, a 24-year-old activist was moved by the active role of Egyptian women in the front lines of the protests. To represent this, he created an image of the Ancient Egyptian queen Nefertiti wearing a gas mask. This image became one of the most iconic images of the movement and the activist became known by his graffiti name: El-Zeft. The image had a rich and transformative social life. It started as a stencil sprayed around the area of Tahrir Square, then developed into a poster, an online image, an Amnesty campaign image, as well as a body tattoo image. In the image in Figure 4.1, El-Zeft holds a poster version of his graffiti with the text 'women's voice is a revolution'. This was captured by photographer and visual storyteller Ahmed Hayman, who kindly allowed me to reproduce it here.

The interest in the birth of the image is an interest in the moment a social actor produces an image and places it in a specific context for a specific purpose. The intentionality in the act of image production and placement is relevant to understanding how individuals and groups act using images and how images are used to achieve certain social actions such as representation of one's ideology, argumentation, or mobilization of others. Given the dialogical approach to images presented earlier, the birth of the image is understood as an instance in a dialogue that relies on previous images, signs, and discourses in its creation. The birth of the image does not mean seeking an 'original' version of an image, that never existed before that moment, but rather seeking the beginning of the circulation story of a certain image in relation to a specific topic and context, while acknowledging the past lives and previous signs this image is drawing upon.

This chapter will focus on the production process and the social position of the image producer. The image producer could be, for example, an artist creating a new image, a social media user posting a photograph they took, an activist spray painting a protest symbol on a wall, a company producing a billboard advertisement, or a government launching a poster campaign. I will use in this chapter examples from my research on image production in the context of the 2011 Egyptian revolution. I have interviewed activists, graffiti painters, and caricature artists who have used images to express their opposition to the government and to represent their political and social critique. The purpose of my research was to understand the broader visual production of the movement at the time. Their stories and life trajectories were diverse, they each had a specific intention behind their production, a different idea and production process, and their images lived on in different ways in urban and online spaces, despite the risk of censorship and imprisonment.

El-Zeft – whose graffiti name means asphalt or tar in Arabic, and is also used to express frustration with a bad state of being – was one of the activists I interviewed. My analysis of the birth of the Nefertiti image (Figure 4.1) included looking at who El-Zeft is, his activism, the conditions and motives behind his image, and the meanings he intended by producing this image. The analysis of the birth of the image also involved looking at the moment of production, its placement in the urban space of Tahrir Square during the context of the protests, and the before-life of the image. The before-life of the image involves looking at the previous instances and signs the image has borrowed from. Using Bakhtin's dialogical theory introduced earlier, we can interpret the image not as a novel creation that never existed before in other forms but rather as an 'utterance' in a chain of a contested dialogue about the revolution and its representation. El-Zeft appropriated an ancient Egyptian local symbol of a revolutionary queen and combined it creatively with the gas mask, which represents a contemporary global symbol of protest and opposition subcultures. The final creation became El-Zeft's own production, populated by his voice. His image shows the intentionality in combining different signs to produce new meanings. The image shows a relationship between the signifier and signified that is not arbitrary or conventional but one that is transformative and arising out of the sign maker's cultural, social, and psychological history and framed with the specific environment in a certain time and space.

After its moment of production, El-Zeft's image lived on to have a long social life in posters, digital images, tattoos, and face masks in Egypt and abroad. The poster in Figure 4.1 is El-Zeft's own reproduction of his stencil graffiti into a poster design. El-Zeft was one of the activists who shared his designs online for others to use freely, as long as it was not for commercial purposes. This influenced the circulation and use of his images for different – mainly political – purposes. The meaning of the image was elaborated through the different reproductions of it to represent women in the Egyptian revolution, advocate for the rights of women in the Arab region, and for the fight against sexual harassment (for a tracing of the image's social life, see Awad, 2020b).

The social position of an image producer – or image author or artist – has significantly changed in response to technological development. Technological tools facilitating image production, such as smartphones, computer software, and the internet, have made the position of an image producer a more accessible one for many without specialized artistic or design skills. This has resulted in an acceleration in the number of images produced and the number of people able to produce and use images. It is fascinating to think that in one hour today, more images are shared on social media platforms than those produced in all of the nineteenth century (Sturken & Cartwright, 2018). In 2014, there were 60 million photographs uploaded to Instagram every day, 350 million images uploaded to Facebook, and 400 million photos sent to Snapchat (Rose, 2016). This creates a significantly different relationship between individuals and images and the use of images as a tool for expression and social action in everyday life.

El-Zeft expresses this in the interview; he does not identify as an artist. At the time of the interview in late 2014, he was a 24-year-old who had recently graduated with a bachelor's degree in engineering. At the beginning of the Egyptian revolution in 2011, shortly after protesters occupied different main squares around the country, street art emerged as a form of revolutionary expression that shaped the occupied public spaces. El-Zeft found it fascinating to be able to put what was on his mind on a wall for others to see. He was inspired by graffiti artists drawing on the West Bank Wall in opposition to the Israeli government's treatment of Palestinians but did not imagine he could do graffiti himself. As he joined the protests, he asked other activists who did graffiti about how he could do it. He learned from another activist that with simple photo editing software he could create images and produce layers for stencil spray painting. And since then he started producing his own images and became among the most known of the Egyptian revolution graffiti painters.

It was also only after the revolution that Hend – another activist and graffiti painter – started producing images. Hend, at the time of the interview in 2014, was a 33-year-old single mother with a bachelor's degree in construction engineering. She says that after the revolution she felt like 'I can say my opinion on the wall too!' Hend's style was different from El-Zeft; she reproduced famous images from Egyptian movies while transforming them to give a protest message:

> I like drawing and using Photoshop. There was a sit-in in Tahrir Square, and I decided to do my first graffiti. Before the revolution, there were few people who did graffiti and mural art for the sake of art or advertisement. But after the revolution it was more about opinion expression ... Everyone expressed their opinion in graffiti with their own style. For me I am into cinema and old movies, so I take a certain scene and line from movies and do my modification depending on the current events ... my images are always political with a sense of sarcasm ... I do action with graffiti instead of just objecting in front of a television screen or on social media. So, I hope it does have an impact.

With Hend, El-Zeft, and other image producers I interviewed there was a strong emphasis on what the image production served for them. While many expressed wanting their viewpoint to be seen and interacted with by people in the street and wanting to have an impact on those who view the image, there was a more personal psychological purpose that many shared. Expressing themselves through putting their mark 'out there' in the world was in itself carrying a sense of relief for many. In a time where opposition voices are silenced and media channels only communicating the governments' official narrative, putting one's political stance out there in the urban space gave the affirmation of 'we are here, we still exist, and our opinion exists', as graffiti painter Keizer expressed it. That motive was for many worth the security risk it takes to express oneself. The work of those image producers contributed to the visual production of the revolution, which carried its collective memory and travelled in between urban spaces, online media, books, and documentaries. The significance of those visuals served several psychological and social functions that included creating visibility for the cause, constructing a group identity that mobilized others to join, commemorating those who lost their lives in the protest and holding those responsible accountable, and positioning different social actors in relation to the revolutionary cause (Awad & Wagoner, 2018).

4.1 The Image Producer

An image producer is a dynamic social position – rather than a static social role – of acting by producing, appropriating, or sharing an image. This conceptualization highlights the agency and intentionality in the process of image production. The position could be taken up by different individuals and is changeable based on the context. For example, I take up the social position of an image producer when I am a witness of an event and take a picture of it and then share it on social media, but I am also simultaneously taking up the social position of a viewer of other images produced of that same event and might be even a censor by reporting images that I find not suitable to represent the event.

While traditionally news images were produced by a photojournalist and an art piece by a painter for a targeted audience that takes up the role of viewing, those positions are more hybrid today. Technological advancement has enabled the viewer to take up the position of producer at times. News outlets now seek images produced in the moment of the event by people – what is commonly referred to as 'accidental journalism', 'user-generated content', or 'citizen journalism' – where the ordinary person assumes the position of the author of the latest news. This development has dramatically redefined the producer and viewer positions in relation to news, offering both liberating and damaging qualities as it challenges the dominance of mainstream media and at the same time redefines the traditional journalistic construct of experts (Sturken & Cartwright, 2018). Changes are also evident in protest settings, where every protestor on the street is a potential image producer and broadcaster of the political cause, creating an alternative coverage of those events and breaking away with the government's control over media and visual representation in the public space (Khatib, 2013).

Image production, in that sense, is used as an act of resistance. An act of resistance can be understood here as an intentional social act that articulates change, one that is oriented towards an imagined future, and one that opposes dominant representations and affirming one's own position on social reality (Awad et al., 2017). Resistance through image production can create disruption to the distribution of the sensible: making that which was made invisible by the powerful visible and recognizable (Rancière, 2013). This understanding of resistance to power builds on an understanding of power as omnipresent and distributed, not centralized or localized (Foucault, 1974). This distribution is not equal; in some places and with some social actors, power is far weightier, thicker, and concentrated than in/with others (Bayat, 2013). It is those dynamics that made the visual production of the Egyptian revolution in the streets powerful; the graffiti images were a clear violation of the authority's dominance over urban space and what is allowed to be done and seen there. Urban space in authoritarian societies is a space that is only allowed to be used passively, as a passer-by (Bayat, 2013).

4.2 Image (Re)production and the 'Unique' Original

In regarding the image producer as every social actor producing or reproducing an image in a specific context for a specific purpose, we run the risk of losing the distinction between production as a creative process resulting in a unique original image and reproduction as the mere repetition of a previously produced image. If I claim that I am an image producer because I reproduced El-Zeft's image in this book, it runs the risk of wrongfully claiming the creative process, authorship, or skill of El-Zeft in his design or of Hayman in his photography.

The dialogical focus could make those distinctions blurry, positioning us all as actors in a dialogue producing difference instances of the image. Rather than ignoring the unique original image or the creator that first produced it, the dialogical lens sets the focus on the dialogue taking place through a certain cycle in the social life of an image, while acknowledging the past and possible future lives of the image. An important part of acknowledging the past lives of an image is addressing the producer who first came up with the unique combinations of the image I am reproducing and afforded it with certain uses and meanings. The dialogical lens also

4.2 Image (Re)production and the 'Unique' Original

revisits what we mean by uniqueness, originality, and the creative act of production.

Recent perspectives from sociocultural psychology (Glăveanu, 2014) and evolutionary psychology (Muthukrishna & Henrich, 2016) move away from the idea of creation as a process undertaken by a few independent talented minds in isolation from society, whose creations are then passed on to the masses. Creation is rather understood as an inherently social and collective process, involving intra-psychological and interpsychological processes in interaction with other people and other artefacts (Vygotsky, 1978). Social networks, information transmission, and cultural ideas we are exposed to all contribute to our mind's development and our ability to create. More often than not a new creation is actually a new recombination or development of different previous ideas meeting together in a new context (Muthukrishna & Henrich, 2016). This is of course not referring to stealing ideas or plagiarism, nor does it undermine the individual position of an image producer. It rather acknowledges creation as a distributed social cognitive process that happens outside as well as inside the individual mind (Glăveanu, 2014).

We cannot meaningfully separate the image producer from their environment, the social networks they are part of, and the material and symbolic artefacts they are exposed to. The intentionality of the producer, their trajectory and experiences, their perspective and purpose for image production, and their production process are very important in understanding their image. Also, as important, is understanding that they are not the only person involved in the process of production. Even an image that is created in a seemingly isolated setting is created in relation to some form of a dialogue with previous ideas, imagined viewers, and future uses of that image. To create, or to 'author' in Bakhtin's term, is to express ourselves and shape our perception in a process that involves other people and nature (Haynes, 1995). Bakhtin argued that the *other* and the relationship to the *other* is an essential ingredient in any creation. Creation is an ongoing process and an ethical act towards others that produces an unfinished world with a range of possibilities (Haynes, 1995).

El-Zeft's image of Queen Nefertiti and the gas mask puts together two local and international known symbols. That does not mean that El-Zeft did not produce a creative new image. His image was born by him combining the meanings of those earlier symbols, populating them with his own activist voice, and placing them in a specific moment of protest. Each new production is a creative development of previous ideas, signs, and tools. Sometimes the reproduction of an image in a new context can reinscribe it with new meanings and let us rediscover its boundaries in its new material setting (Haynes, 1995).

The image production process cannot take place without the material affordances of the environment, whether it is a spray can, a printing machine, or a digital technology. Marxist and cultural critic Walter Benjamin (1935) wrote about the development of image reproduction in the early twentieth century in his essay 'The Work of Art in the Age of Mechanical Reproductions'. His essay tackled a significant moment of change in relation to technological advancement and mass photography. Written during the Nazi regime in Germany, his essay provides a critical look at the changes of the value, physical qualities, and political function of art in response to the technologies of print and mass production. Print technologies have allowed the original authentic painting that was only seen by the few to be reproduced and seen by a much larger number of people and in very different places and contexts than where the painting was originally produced.

Benjamin predicted that advancements in image production would challenge the emphasis on an authentic singular original as a commodity in the capitalist system. He argued that a reproduction of an art piece will always lack in terms of its presence in time and space – its aura – because it does not have the authenticity and unattainability of its original unique physical existence in the place where it was produced. Nevertheless, he saw reproducibility as potentially freeing the art practice and allowing the image to circulate in a much broader context, and thus enabling it as a tool for politics that could be viewed by the masses.

Tools for image production and reproduction today, especially in relation to digital images, challenge the idea of an original image even more. One example is what is known as digital memes on social networking sites, where an image becomes viral and is reproduced repeatedly by different people who use a variety of captions and edits to often communicate a relatable feeling or situation in a humorous or ironic way. How can we then assess the creation process and who is the 'producer' of online digital memes? Building on Benjamin's ideas, one could argue that even in replication, the image acquires a new presence every time it is produced in a new context by a new social actor.

As much as technological advancements have given individuals more venues to create collaboratively and share different images, they have also produced a hyper-individualized emphasis on each person's unique original image. The accessibility has, in its own way, created a new form of commodity production for identity construction. There are many social media platforms (e.g. Instagram) that are based on the consumer or viewer being the producer of content, creating a form of obsession – at times – with self-representation as an individualized project of constructing and negotiating an identity through image production and dissemination. In this context, authorship becomes about producing one's own image of certain places or events, as a tool for cultural and social capital.

Another development that challenges even further the idea of authorship, creation, and reproduction is artificial intelligence (AI). How do we tackle AI-generated images? Who is the author and what is the creative process involved? Is there still a possibility to credit and value an original digital media image producer? New tools such as non-fungible tokens provide new ways for valuing and selling digital 'originals', acting as a digital certificate of authenticity. The potential and the risks of those developments are still to be discovered. One distinction that should remain relevant is an ethical one. A dialogical reproduction is one that acknowledges rather than conceals previous productions and producers whether human or AI. It is not one that claims originality and ignores previous social lives of an image.

4.3 Does the Producer 'Die' When the Image Is Born?

Does the 'original' image producer 'die' as the image is reproduced and transformed throughout its social life?

Literary critic and semiotician Roland Barthes (1978) in his essay 'The Death of the Author' argued that there is no ultimate meaning determined by the author for receivers to uncover. For him, it is the context and the viewers that influence the interpretations. He argued against the traditional practice of looking into the intentions and the biography of the author to interpret a work, because as we focus on the author, we impose a limit on the work and close its interpretation. He announced the 'disappearance' of the author as an authority over the work's meaning; the birth of the reader comes at the cost of the death of the author. He argued that a work's unity lies in its destination rather than in its origin and therefore focused on the processes of consumption (Barthes, 1978).

Literary critic and historian Michel Foucault (1979) in his essay 'What Is an Author?' argued similarly that the concept of an author is becoming less relevant. Instead, he proposes using the concept 'author function' rather than 'author'. This makes the focus less on the author as an individual person and more on the author as a function of a discourse that informs a set of expectations and patterns of circulation (Foucault,

1979). With this argument, he too announced the 'death' of the author and, alongside other authors such as psychoanalyst Jacque Lacan, focused on the role of the viewer and the nature of the gaze and spectatorship.

These ideas, originally dealing with literature, marked a shift in the late 1960s' approach to literature as well as artworks, from an interest in the artist and their biography to either the art object or the viewer. Bakhtin's work, however, remained dedicated to looking at the triadic relationship between the creator, object, and viewer. He looked at the position of the producer as an acting agent with an important cultural function (Haynes, 1995). Similar to Barthes and Foucault, Bakhtin acknowledged that the meaning of an artwork remains open and not limited to what the author intended. He emphasized this with his concept of the 'unfinalizable' state of a creation (Haynes, 1995). The ongoing openness of creative work means that ideas live on and are never limited by the author's intentions. He also moved away from a 'private craftmanship' of an author, to looking at the creative act as a socially situated and dialogical process that always involves an 'other' (Bakhtin, 1981). Yet, he insisted that looking at the author's biography is important. He emphasized how the process of creation is shaped by different factors such as the producer's world view, aspirations, and their critical response to earlier works. The producer's biography helps the viewer gain insight into the producer as a person and to try to understand them within their historical time and their social, cultural, and economic position (Haynes, 1995).

I argue that the author is never dead because their inscription remains in a way throughout the image's social life. Whether we are talking about a painting, a photograph, or a digital meme, the author is relevant to the social life of the image. To acknowledge the histories and social lives of visual artefacts, we do need to acknowledge the different social actors that originated them in different contexts and populated them with their voices and meanings, even if those meanings are not stable or sustainable as intended. The social position of an image producer tells us about the power dynamic behind the production, circulation, and reach of different images. It tells us about the chances an image has for visibility and why some visuals manage to be seen and sustained in our visual culture and others do not have a similar chance of visibility.

I second art historian and artist Deborah Haynes' warning of what Barthes' and Foucault's ideas could mean for the death of marginalized and minority voices (Haynes, 1995). From a feminist perspective, she argues that the intersectional identities of producers are relevant to understand a work of art and to situate it within its cultural and historical time.

Also, from a sociocultural psychological perspective, the agency of the producer and its constraints within a certain context and environment inform possibilities for meaning construction and possibilities for knowledge transformation. Also, from a non-relativist perspective, studying images as forms of knowledge means that the source matters and not all meanings are relative to only how they are viewed and interpreted. Images provide representations of the world, sometimes posed as 'truth', or at least as a version of truth, and therefore the producer is one that holds a certain social responsibility towards others. There are different producers constructing different versions of realities and not all realities are relatively credible, ethical, or true. I agree with Barthes and Foucault that the producer does not dictate the meaning or hold authority over how an image can be interpreted. However, the producer does populate the image with a certain voice that shapes its affordances for interpretations and the variety of ways it could be seen; then, along the image's life, that voice could be developed, countered, or transformed altogether. Images are thus multivoiced and need to be interpreted through the multilayered dialogues between the producers, viewers, and even censors within a specific environment.

4.4 Methods: Interviews and Photo Elicitation

If the producer is not dead, then how can we methodologically approach their voice and meaning in relation to an image? One can investigate the meanings embedded in the image body itself (Chapter 5), one can look into the environment and social context that shaped the possibilities of production (Chapter 6), and one can attend to the voice of the producers themselves as they make meaning of their visual production. This voice could be out there in secondary data such as something they have written or said in relation to an image they produced, or if accessible one could interview a producer to unfold those different meanings in dialogue.

Investigating the social life of images can involve the analysis of a variety of images, a variety of social actors, and a variety of social instances of an image's life trajectory. In most cases, it would be impossible to methodologically approach all those aspects. I propose instead, based on available data, to take a point of departure in one aspect of the social life of an image, and through the focus on this one aspect one could explore the other aspects. In this chapter, I take my point of departure as the production stage and the social actor of the image producer and, through the eyes of the producer, I explore other aspects of the images' social life.

One relevant method for this purpose is qualitative interviews and photo elicitation. I have used this method in relation to the topic of protest street art and caricature production in the context of Egypt. Through the perspective of the activists and artists who produced the images, I investigated the lives of those images starting from the inspiration and intention of the producers, the process of production and placement in the urban, print, or online spaces, and the expected reception and impact of those images from the perspective of the producer. This research focus was later supplemented by an investigation of the response to those images by pedestrians and the government, as well as the government's own image production (see Awad, 2017).

Semi-structured in-depth interview is a qualitative method that – within psychology – is commonly used within a variety of theoretical approaches such as phenomenological, narrative, and discursive psychology among others. The purpose of conducting interviews is not to come up with a generalized result from a big set of data – as one would do with a survey, for example – but rather an in-depth situated understanding of thought processes, experiences, and meaning constructions with selected few participants in a specific social context. For further details about the process of conducting and analysing qualitative interviews, refer to *An Introduction to Qualitative Research* (Flick, 2018) and *Doing Interviews* (Brinkmann & Kvale, 2018).

Semi-structured interviews normally follow a question guide that has the main topics and questions a researcher wants covered, while leaving room for flexibility in the dialogue and for the participants to bring in their own new angles to the topic. In the appendix, I provide an example of an interview guide that I used different versions of in my interviews with image producers. The questions are organized so that they cover the key areas of the producer's background, creation process, dialogue with others, the image's social life, image interpretation through photo elicitation, and finally the producer's broader viewpoints. The flow of the questions is also meant to progress from the psychological and personal trajectory to the public dialogical engagement, and from the past and present to future-oriented thinking and imagination.

The photo-elicitation section of the interview is meant to take the conversation from general talk about images to focusing on specific preselected images. I have used photo elicitation as a tool in combination with different methods such as interviews, focus groups, or surveys. In interviews and focus groups, it can help unfold how people think and feel about an image and make meaning of what is represented in the image alone and in dialogue with others. In surveys, it can help with testing out different visual symbols in different cultures, seeing if they evoke similar interpretations and emotions, and how image meanings could be transferable across contexts.

Photo elicitation refers to the idea of using photographs as part of a research method to elicit different thoughts and feelings. Douglas Harper argues that photo elicitation can evoke a specific kind of information, feelings, and memories in response to the particular form of the visual representation. This has a physical basis, he argues, as images utilize more of the brain's capacity when processing images than when processing words alone (Harper, 2002). Also, using images in an interview, as psychologist Paula Reavey (2020) argues, can steer participants away from ready-made, rehearsed, and generic narratives of experience; they can facilitate access to more specific memories and feelings that are otherwise not accessible or narratable. The method could also help us explore how the feelings evoked by the image might be connected or disconnected from how the participant feels in the present time, and therefore allowing engagement with emotions through time (Reavey, 2020).

Images used in a photo-elicitation interview could be preselected by a researcher or brought in by the participant based on a prompt before the interview. For example, one could ask the participant to bring to the interview the images that mean the most to them in relation to their childhood. A researcher could also ask a participant to take certain images for a period of time before the interview, sometimes referred to as a *photo-voice* method. For example, psychologists Alan Radley and Diane Taylor have examined how hospital in-patients and homeless people talk in interviews about photographs they have taken using cameras supplied by the researcher (Radley, 2010; Radley & Taylor, 2003).

In my interviews with Egyptian activists, I preselected and brought to the interview images from their own work that I wanted to have a dialogue with them about. This helped me view the images through their eyes, taking me through the process from idea generation to implementation and placement. It also facilitated exploring the participant's own emotions towards the images and how they see them in the present versus when they created them. Some participants remembered specific stories that occurred in the making of the images and pedestrians' reactions to them. Some reflected on new ways of seeing their own image and how they might do it differently in hindsight. The images in a way brought the past, present, and future perspectives of the participant in relation to one another. The participant reconstructed memories and emotion in relation to the time they produced the image and their imagination of the future of the image and how it would be received. Those memories were brought into the present moment of the interview and reflected upon retrospectively in relation to what had actually happened since then. Alternative futures were also brought into the conversation through what the participants have imagined, what has happened, and what alternative actions could have brought different futures.

In some of the interviews, I also included other images that have a certain resemblance to the participant's images and might have provided inspiration, or images that were produced in response to their own images, whether to reproduce its meaning or to counter it. This was useful in hearing their perspectives on the possible uses and 'misuses' of their images. I also picked other images that simply belonged to the same societal dialogue in a sense – for example, other political images tackling similar topics through a similar genre such as that of political street art – to hear how they dialogue with other image producers.

There were often ethical and risk concerns about doing interviews with producers of images that are deemed by government as political opposition that should not be allowed. There are thus security risks for those producing the images, reproducing them, and researching them. This required trust from both the participant and from my side to be able to meet and share thoughts. For this reason, I often found participants through snowball sampling – where participants I interviewed would connect me to others who would be willing to join the study. Some of the activists I met travelled to live abroad after 2013 to avoid the risk of arrest, some stayed but stopped producing images because the stakes were too high, and some continued cautiously especially on digital media rather than in urban space. There was also often some dilemma with anonymity in writing about the interviews. Some activists preferred that I use their graffiti name, so in a way concealing their real name and at the same time acknowledging their work and perspectives. I did that in most cases, though it still had the risk that once their real identity became known, my research no longer makes them or their opinions anonymous. In some cases, where I was able to keep in contact with some participants, I showed them what I have used from the interviews and what I plan to publish, to hear if they have any concerns and whether my analysis resonated with their experience.

4.5 A Caricature Image: The Woman in the Green Dress

I started this chapter with El-Zeft's graffiti image (Figure 4.1) and its reproductions. I would like now to look at a caricature image that provides an example of a response image or a counter-image to a known historical

4.5 A Caricature Image: The Woman in the Green Dress

symbol in Egyptian culture, that of a woman in a green dress that is commonly used to symbolize Egypt as a nation. I will draw on my interview with Andeel, the image producer, and his motives for deconstructing that symbol and how his experience, background, and political ideas inform how he appropriated and intervened with this symbol, creating new ways of seeing in the visual culture.

Andeel is an Egyptian caricaturist and digital creator. The images he creates and the opinions they represent were behind his firing from the newspaper he worked for in 2013 and later for his exile outside Egypt. I met Andeel in 2022 for an interview while writing this book. I was interested in knowing about him as an artist and to follow with him the social life of one specific image: the woman in the green dress. I first came across the image when I was doing research on the representation of nationhood in political caricatures in pre-independence Egypt around the 1930s (Awad, 2020a). The image was, and continues to be, a recurrent symbol that is used in many different forms especially in national newspapers.

Andeel was a child when his drawings were first published. He describes his home growing up as one of cultural production. His mum is a poet and his dad is a storyteller and translator. They sometimes used the drawings of Andeel and his brother as covers for their books. He first learned about caricatures in high school, where he got a side job in a newspaper that he describes as belonging to the 'fake opposition press' that was common in the time of President Mubarak. Fake opposition parties and press were an integral part of Mubarak's regime, helping to present an image of democracy and free speech, but in reality they worked in collaboration with the regime and had clear guidelines on the framework and limits of their 'opposition'. His job was to simply draw what the editor-in-chief asked him for.

It was not until he later got jobs in 'proper private oppositional newspapers' that he had the mentorship to develop his skills as a caricaturist. In 2011, as he recalls: 'The revolution happened! And the space just opened up much more for expression, and with the internet, there was more direct communication channels with the viewer that I wanted to explore.' However, this was short-lived, as in 2013, right around the time of the coup and El-Sisi's government taking over, his whole team was fired. This team then got together and decided to start an online opposition newspaper: *Mada Masr*. *Mada Masr* still survives today despite the Egyptian government blocking internet access to it and the continuous arrest and questioning of its members. The transition of Andeel's images from print to online was not easy: 'That was a messy experience.

I understood the visuals of the paper from working in newspapers, but now I had to understand the visuals of digital media for the website. How can I turn what I am imagining into a code and a digital design?'

It was only then that Andeel saw himself as a proper caricature artist because he was producing images that freely represented his own views:

> This developed my ideas a lot because I felt more responsibility towards what I produce. My images became an outcome of a thoughtful process, knowledge, and a viewpoint. Not just drawing what I think I 'should' be drawing. My style developed also as a result of knowing that no one is revising or censoring what I produce. This liberated me a lot. I started using different techniques, especially with the full migration to the internet.

The social upheaval of the revolution, the changed medium of production, and the new space for freedom impacted Andeel's development and the topics he was interested in tackling:

> When the revolution happened, like many others, I became engaged with certain broad topics that I think are key in the context of Egypt, such as freedom, violence, and governance and the principles and philosophy behind it. Those broad topics are reflected in smaller everyday life practices that I show through my images.
>
> One broad topic that occupies me is that of populism. How is the idea of the *Egyptian people* constructed and how do Egyptians see themselves as a nation? How does this conception of a nation come with certain assumptions about shared characteristics of the people? How was this image constructed historically, and was it imposed top-down? And how do people respond to this image constructed of them and construct themselves according to that image?

The image of the woman in the green dress was one of the images that caught Andeel's attention in relation to ideas of nationhood. She is a character commonly used in images to symbolize Egypt as a nation. Representing nations through an imagined abstract visual form is common practice for many nations, and choosing a woman for this is not unique to Egypt – see, for example, the French 'Marianne'. The social life of the image of the woman in the green dress extends to at least the 1870s (Baron, 2005). The characteristics, age, and dress of the woman have varied over time (see Figure 4.2). From the 1920s the woman was often drawn in contemporary European dress rather than earlier conservative and peasant dress with a headscarf or a face cover; this coincided with a time where the veil was becoming less common among Egyptian women, especially those living in cities (Baron, 2005).

4.5 A Caricature Image: The Woman in the Green Dress

Figure 4.2 An illustrative collage of different caricature images that were captured by the author from the newspapers available at the library archive of the American University in Cairo.
Source: (a) from *al-Kashkūl* newspaper, issue no. 321, 8 July 1927; (b) from *al-Kashkūl* newspaper, issue no. 347, 6 January 1928; (c) from *al-Kashkūl* newspaper, issue no. 345, 23 December 1927; (d) from *al-Kashkūl* newspaper, issue no. 526, 12 June 1931.

In my earlier study (Awad, 2020a) of political caricatures in two newspapers, *al-Kashkūl* and *al-Siyāsa al-Usbu'iyya*, between the years of 1926 and 1931, the character was frequently used. In most images, the woman was portrayed as wearing a green dress, sometimes with a white crescent and three white stars on it resembling the Egyptian flag at the time. Sometimes she was represented as a young girl, sometimes she was a woman, and her clothing varied between peasant clothing and contemporary Western style dress (Figure 4.2). The caricaturists always made it clear through the caption that she *is* Egypt. In my analysis, the image always represented some form of passivity; she is the object of politicians' negotiations, and she is powerless and dependent on those controlling her (or occupying her). Note that this period follows Egypt's nominal independence in 1922 from the British occupation and negotiations were under way to secure complete independence.

The representation of the Egyptian nation as a woman could be argued to serve different functions. It gives a concrete objectified form for the abstract conception of a nation. The objectification is in a feminine figure that fits with the 1890s' domestic ideology that women's role as 'mothers of the nation' was to teach their children patriotism and prepare them to protect and serve the country (Baron, 1993). It also fits with patriarchal notions of women's honour and vulnerability, where the viewer is positioned as the man figure who has the duty to protect her. Some images went further to suggest a form of a romantic attachment to the nation through representing her as a beautiful, sexualized woman. Paradoxically, the images of Egypt represented as a woman endured for a long historical period where Egyptian women were rarely represented in images or in political public life, and their role was confined within the domestic private sphere (Baron, 2005).

This image has endured and persisted especially in national newspapers. In a caricature published in *al-Akhbar* newspaper in October 2013, the current Egyptian president El-Sisi is drawn flying in the air wearing a *superman* outfit carrying the woman in the green dress. The 'superhero' is carrying 'Egypt', saving her in his embrace. She wears a green peasant dress and looks out to the viewer with a smiling face and a docile submissive posture as she is carried away. Below them there is a landscape with the typical national symbolism: a mosque, a church, palm trees, buildings, and birds. To see the image and a further analysis of it check historian and illustrator Rim Naguib's article (Naguib, 2020). Her analysis shows clearly how such caricatures communicate the gendered nationalist narrative of Nasser and El-Sisi's government, where the feminine, subordinate, and

4.5 A Caricature Image: The Woman in the Green Dress

passive nation is seeking the protection and salvation of the masculine military leader.

Andeel was quite acquainted with this image growing up. He describes how those caricatures would usually represent a relationship between the woman and a person addressing her in the image, such as the president. The message is usually calling upon the reader for a certain action in some abstract nationalistic tone such as 'May God bless those who build and protect Egypt.' Those images are always positive, says Andeel, and the woman is always beautiful, thin, and happy. This, he thought, needs a more realistic reconstruction, his own parody reproduction of this nationalistic symbol. In his caricature (Figure 4.3), Egypt is a tired older woman, weighed down with all her troubles and responsibilities, and her life trajectory shows on her body and rheumatic disease showing on her joints. Her dress is not green or colourful; like most village women her dress is black. Instead of the official or the citizen who usually addresses Egypt, this time it is a young oblivious kid, who grew up hearing and internalizing propaganda messages and repeating them mindlessly. He extends his arm

Figure 4.3 Andeel created this caricature in 2013 and posted it on different online platforms. He kindly gave me the permission to reproduce the image for the purpose of this book.
Source: Andeel.

to performatively address Egypt saying 'oh Egypt, come up, and get strong'. She looks at his performative excitement with dismissiveness, and responds, 'shut up, you jerk!' Behind them, the usual Egyptian symbols are squeezed in to fit, following her body line to make sure they are all there and apparent: the mosque, the church, the palm tree, the buildings, and the pyramids, because 'no good nationalistic caricature can pass without those symbols', Andeel says sarcastically.

Andeel created this image shortly after the army took over the government in 2013. It was his response to an ongoing nationalistic narrative that presented the coup d'etat as a heroic rescue of Egypt from the Muslim Brotherhood and from collapse. He created it in response to hearing again many of the classic clichéd nationalistic statements of 'Egypt is coming back to us', 'it is time to build Egypt', 'we need to protect Egypt from internal enemies', and the like. Andeel expresses that he wanted to comment on this dialogue by reminding people of the naivety of nationalistic imaginaries and to present a more realistic image of the situation in Egypt.

The boy's call out to Egypt: 'oh Egypt, come up, and get strong' is a quote appropriated from a song by Sheikh Imam. Sheikh Imam was a known Egyptian protest singer; together with poet Ahmed Fouad Negm, they made songs criticizing the Nasser and Sadat regimes, and were imprisoned in the 1960s and 1970s. To Andeel, however, they represented a protest art that he found problematic. They used nationalist sentiments that were not that different from the regime's discourse; for example, in their songs, they too feminized Egypt as a beautiful young village girl. Even though their songs were used a lot during the 2011 protests, Andeel found their discourse to be lacking in terms of transforming ideas, and at times also problematically romanticizing imprisonment and sacrifice for the nationhood. The use of the quote in the image plays on this paradox of those statements that are supposedly coming from protest history but are still deeply rooted in a problematic nationalistic discourse.

In composing the image, Andeel sarcastically squeezed in all the clichéd symbols of what is Egypt: 'I don't think I thought consciously about it while drawing it, but I wanted to express that feeling of the chaos of all those symbols and how I saw them growing up.' In composing the look of the woman, Andeel drew his inspiration from his own grandmother:

> Moving away from those idealized images, I wanted to bring an image of a real woman. My grandmother was a village woman who took care of like eighty family members. She had no time to dress up or joke, and she certainly would not have tolerated those nationalistic metaphors and slogans. The weight she had to carry showed up on her body, her sickness,

4.5 A Caricature Image: The Woman in the Green Dress

and her grumpy face. She wore nothing aesthetic; it was always just black. This is the majority of the Egyptian village women. This does not match with the women that I grew up seeing in caricatures; those images were more of the wishful thinking of the artist and represent in my view the obsession of fascist regimes with the ideal perfect citizen, an imaginary image, an ambition.

In relation to classifying this caricature, as well as other images produced by Andeel, he would rather not classify his work as political art. He says that his images can intersect with a certain political moment, and they can be political in the sense that anything else in the world is part of politics. However, he has reservations about the genre of 'political art' where the image is given by default a certain worth or value because it expresses a political message relying on clichéd statements such as 'down with the regime' or 'power to the people'. He thinks the label limits how we can critically assess whether the image actually constructs something meaningful, and creates a repetitive genre of images:

> Political art many times has this repetitive style of representing the evil-looking dictator. I like to draw El-Sisi as this cute figure, like a teddy bear, because this liberates me of this cliché … also because it responds to something that I find more interesting: that this is how he sees himself and this is how people who love him see him. And these are all very powerful aspects in creating his powerful image with its political and psychological influence. Ignoring those aspects would make us not understand how his supporters see him as the symbol of many things they want and wish for.

Finally, in discussing with Andeel the lives and afterlives of his images, who sees them, and how they circulate, he says that his imagination of the viewer position has changed over the years. When he was trained in traditional newspapers, there was always the idea that the reader is ignorant or at least has less ability to understand the material produced by the newspaper. With his images travelling to online media, he got to 'meet' the viewer and read their reactions and see how they share and appropriate his images. This liberated him from the idea that there is one defined audience for his images.

One main viewer that Andeel is especially focused on and shapes how he produces images is his future self. He always imagines how he would look back at his images in five or ten years and what would be his reaction. It does not have to be that his future self likes the image, he says, but he is keen on how the image can help him reflect back on his trajectory at the moment of production and how he responded to the historical moment that triggered the image. The image can help him see where and in which direction he had developed since he created it.

CHAPTER 5

The Body of the Image

Figure 5.1 Lifejackets piled up on a beach in Lesbos, 2015.
Source: Anna Klitgaard.

In Figure 5.1, bright orange lifejackets are placed in a disorderly way on the ground in abundance. In the distant background there is an open horizon and a slightly turbulent sea. On the side, there is a tree offering a temporary shadow. The presence of the lifejackets points to an absence of those who wore them, leaving an uncertainty of who are they, where did they come from, and where they are heading? The image could afford feelings of relief for reaching a safe shore and the hope – as well as the uncertainties – of the potential futures of the wearers of the lifejackets.

This photograph was taken by Danish journalist Anna Klitgaard at the Greek island of Lesbos in 2015. She kindly gave me permission to use it here. Anna followed the journeys of refugees through Europe as they settled and thought they had found new homes. However, none of those she followed really found home; they either left or were deported. For her, this image shows 'a vest for each human being who made the crossing, a testament to hope ... that was soon turned sour. Lifejackets, piled in their thousands on the beaches, became a symbol of the failed and unfair asylum policies of Europe ... there was nothing lifesaving about them.'

In this chapter, I move from the birth process of an image and its producer to the meanings and emotions an image can afford through its contents and form. By the *body* of the image, I refer to the characteristics of the image, its visual features, pictorial composition, and material form, and how these together afford certain meanings and interpretations of the image in a specific moment in its life trajectory. Using Gillian Rose's (2016) classifications, this chapter moves the analysis from the site of production towards the site of the image itself. While the body of the image is the focus here, this is not done in isolation regarding the other aspects of the social life framework. In analysing how the image looks, we also reflect on how images are looked at by different people (Chapter 7), the environment of the image that influences its interpretation in a specific time and space (Chapter 6), and the influence of the cultural and psychological history of the image producer (Chapter 4). The capacity of the image to convey meaning, as W. J. T. Mitchell (1994) argues, relies on a complex interplay of social practices surrounding visuality, apparatus (means or media of image production and circulation), institutions, subjects (producers and viewers), and the image's pictorial form. Those circuits of visual meanings are what make image meaning possible, not through a causal or sequential determination, but through interactions in this circuit (Evans & Hall, 2007).

The image interpretation model I present draws on the dialogical approach and the sociocultural theoretical lens presented earlier (Chapter 2). This informs the analysis of images as cultural artefacts that are both signs for meaning making and material tools for social action. Looking at the image as a sign means that we can attempt to interpret it, looking for the different meanings it can afford, and what thoughts or feelings it might provoke. This involves an understanding of image interpretation as a process of sign making and meaning making. This interpretation is always situated in a certain social position of an interpreter in a certain social and cultural context that influences this interpretation. The interpretation is done with the awareness that this meaning is not stable, or necessarily corresponding to how the producer intended or to how viewers will see it. This means that interpretation does not seek a 'preferred' or 'right' meaning but is rather an exploration of different possibilities and affordances. The meaning of an image is unfinalized, as Bakhtin (1986) would argue, and it changes as different social actors interact and dialogue with it. Analysing images as also tools for social action incorporates an interpretation of how they are shaped by the material conditions of production, and how those conditions afford certain social actions and interpretations while inhibiting others.

The model also builds on well-established methods for image analysis that come from different theoretical traditions. I combine ideas from social semiotics, critical discourse analysis, and iconography for their emphasis on the ideological aspect of images and how meanings are made in social action and interaction with others relying on socially available resources that change meaning in their use across time (Kress & Leeuwen, 2021). I also draw on Gestalt psychology's interpretive approach, which marks one of two distinct approaches within the field of psychology of aesthetics (Tinio & Smith, 2017). The other approach is one that draws on cognitive behavioural psychology and often uses experimental and neuroscience methods to analyse the image as a stimulus, having inherent measurable structural features that can evoke universal responses across people, time, and space (Tinio & Smith, 2017). The Gestalt approach, on the other hand, does not look for universalities but investigates how the interplay between the wholes and the parts of an image create subjective aesthetic value in certain contexts. In this approach, attention is brought to the relation between the artist, the image and the viewer, and how, as John Dewey (1934) argues in *Art as Experience*, active engagement between the artist and the viewer can be made possible through the image itself.

One aim with this interpretation model is to bring together the relevant elements from those traditions and make them applicable to the analysis of the variety of images in contemporary visual culture. The main object of analysis for the psychology of aesthetics and for iconography has been artworks. As mentioned earlier in the book I move away from a clear art/non-art distinction and focus more on images that are accessible in everyday life, with no preference for the 'original' meaning of an artist – as some iconographers would – or a finalized meaning. Another aim with the image interpretation model is to provide a concise and accessible language for interpreting images. Image analysis traditions sometimes use many complicated terminologies; this could be necessary to describe complex meaning systems, but it could also sometimes give a sophisticated description to something that is not particularly interesting or meaningful

(Rose, 2016). Instead, I exercise what Michael Billig (2013) advocates for in relation to using clearer language in explaining complex processes.

5.1 Layers of Interpretation

> [A] picture, then, is a very peculiar and paradoxical creature, both concrete and abstract, both a specific individual thing and a symbolic form that embraces a totality. To get the picture is to get a comprehensive, global view of a situation, yet it is also to take a snapshot at a specific moment – the moment when the click of a camera shutter registers the taking of a picture, whether it is the establishment of a cliché or stereotype, the institution of a system, or the opening of a poetic world (perhaps all three).
>
> (Mitchell, 2005, p. xvii)

Mitchell's quote eloquently shows how image interpretation is a complex task that cannot be carried out by just looking at the concrete representations nor by only understanding the abstract meanings. I present in what follows an interpretation model that is based on four layers that capture the concrete, abstract, situated, and embodied dimensions of the body of the image. These four layers are meant to go from the specific, descriptive, and immediate site of the image to the broader levels of interpretation that incorporate the broader social life of the image. The layers are not meant as separate chronological steps that should be followed in a linear process; they are interrelated and interdependent on each other. The specifics can inform how we understand the abstract, and the social and abstract can inform how we see the specifics. The interpretation model does not provide a single signifying system that can produce the same interpretation independent of the interpreter, image placement, and context. Instead, the different layers of the model provide a dialogical tool for exploring the meanings and affect of an image, with the recognition that the process will always vary based on who is interpreting, their ways of seeing, and when and where they are seeing.

5.1.1 First Layer: What Is Shown and How Is It Shown?

At this layer, the focus is on the concrete contents of the image and their composition. In Anna's photograph (Figure 5.1) we see lifejackets, a tree, the ocean, and waves. It is important to reflect on those contents and how they are portrayed at this concrete level to be able to distinguish between what the image actually shows and what meanings we might automatically jump to when we see what is in an image. This could help one see details that are not noticed otherwise when one jumps quickly to other layers of meaning and associations. It is important, however, to remember that even in the most descriptive attempt at basic contents, we cannot avoid engaging in some minimum level of associations and interpretation at the other levels of interpretation. The compositional details of an image always indicate certain meanings and connections and rely on certain common knowledge for their identification. The focus of this level is close to what compositional analysts would attend to; it also corresponds roughly to what in semiotics would be referred to as 'denotation' (Barthes, 1978) or the 'signifier' (de Saussure, 2021) and what in iconography is referred to as 'representational meaning' (Panofsky, 1970). Next, I will present some of the main aspects one can attend to at this layer: *subjects and objects*, *setting*, *framing*, *absences*, *text*, and *genre*.

5.1.1.1 Subjects and Objects

One could start by looking for the subjects in an image (e.g. people, animals, or fictional characters) and the characteristics shown by those subjects (e.g. posture, facial expression, age, gender, size, or clothing). Also, one could attend to the attitude or emotion the subjects are displaying, and whether there is a communicative act displayed (e.g. pointing, touching, or talking) and who it is targeted at. Gazes are an especially relevant communicative act in interpretation – who is looking at whom and how; are they looking up, down, or on an equal level to you or to another image subject? Gazes can convey a sense of interaction (or the lack of) between image subjects, as well as between image subjects and the viewer. A subject that is shown as turned away from the viewer could convey absence of interaction and could turn a subject into an object for the viewers' visual scrutiny (Kress & Leeuwen, 2021). Images can also position us so that we are given access to the gaze of the subject shown; we stand behind them seeing – with them – what they are looking at. Other than the subjects or characters of an image, one could attend to the different objects shown, their nature (e.g. manufactured items, nature, shapes), and how they are organized. In Figure 5.1, lifejackets take up more than half of the photograph, but it is their organization – or lack of – that shapes the composition of the image – they are scattered and in abundance.

5.1.1.2 The Setting

This could include the environment where the subjects and objects are placed (e.g. a windy outdoor, a quiet dark basement room, a blank background design). The colours, shades, and tones could also inform the setting of the image: What is the colour saturation (e.g. intense and vivid or closer to neutral)? How light or dark are the colours? Are the different colours harmonious or contrasting? Are there any effects the colours are making (e.g. showing distance, depth, time of the day, ethnicity)? Are the colours affecting how realistic the image is (e.g. by using same colours one would see in the same objects in real life)? The setting also involves motion in an image: Are there any signs that give us a sense of direction in the image (e.g. arrows, lines, gazes, wind blow, process pointers)? Are objects/subjects shown as static or in dynamic or dramatized positions? The setting also includes how the image is organized. Subjects and objects could be cluttered in a certain part of the image or distributed. The use of empty spaces, shapes, and lines could also give a sense of smooth flow in an image or clear divisions and boundaries. In Figure 5.1 there is a contrast between the lifejacket concentration with the tree that is closest to our viewing position and the openness of the distant sea in the horizon. Finally, the setting could affect the naturalistic modality of the image; the greater the congruence between what is represented and what one can see in real life, the higher the modality of the image (Jewitt & Oyama, 2011).

5.1.1.3 *Framing*

This is closely related to the organization of the image and deals with how meaning is conveyed by using borders, angles, and distance. For example, subjects or objects can stand out using closeness, size, or colour. Borders and angles of an image set the limit to what we see and what is left out (e.g. visual angle, cropping, close-up). The angle can also shape what is in focus, inform a certain perspective, guide the eye, and position the viewer (e.g. the viewer can be positioned as peeking from the side of a room). Distancing the different subjects or objects from the viewer can also serve similar functions. A close-up on a certain subject could suggest intimacy or familiarity. Stuart Hall (2019) shows that this is a typical manipulation strategy used in press photographs of politicians in parliamentary sessions. A 'bird's eye' view can create certain meaning potentials such as power or detachment. Framing can indicate how the elements of an image are given separate identities or grouped as belonging together by the use of empty spaces, lines, and contrasting colours (Jewitt & Oyama, 2011).

5.1.1.4 *Absences*

This is related to what the border has cut out, but it could also be an absence of an expected subject/object in an image (e.g. an empty living room sofa with a turned-on TV, or footprints indicating absence). In Figure 5.1, the lifejackets could indicate absence of the people who wore them: Who wore them and left them there? Where are they now?

5.1.1.5 Text

Is there any text on or around the image? How is it integrated within the image and what function and meaning is it serving? (e.g. speech bubble, descriptive text). How does the text look (e.g. font, colour, organization)? Is it descriptive of what is in the image, complementary, or detached or contradicting with what is shown visually?

5.1.1.6 Image Genre

What is the material form of the image and how is it affecting the different aspects already described? Images that belong to the same genre share certain features and styles. Whether the image is a photo, graphic design, painting, or an AI-generated image affects how we can see the details of it (e.g. sharp lines, brushstrokes, pixels, spray paint). Image genre and material form will be discussed further in Section 5.1.2.

5.1.2 Second Layer: Image Meanings in the Immediate Environment

This layer of interpretation deals with what the content of the image, as embedded in the immediate environment (specific material form and sociocultural context), means. We engage in a process of meaning making and associations to unfold the different possibilities – or affordances – of the image for certain meanings and emotions. In visual semiotics terms, this layer would be moving the analysis from denotation (what is represented and how?) to connotation (what ideas and values do those representations stand for?) (Barthes, 1978) and, in iconography terms, it would be setting the focus on iconographical symbolism (Panofsky, 1970). I add at this layer also the psychological affordances of the image in relation to seeing, thinking, feeling, and remembering (discussed in Chapter 3) and the image's social life.

Engaging with this layer of analysis involves a hermeneutic circular interpretation process that is in dynamic movement between this layer and the other layers. This dynamic movement is emphasized in Gestalt psychological interpretive approaches. It is about attending to how the parts of the image explored in the first layer inform the whole and how the whole of the image gives meaning to the parts. There are several aspects that could be explored at this layer in relation to *associations, social positioning*, and *immediate environment*.

5.1.2.1 Associations

Exploring associations in an image can help us understand what ways of seeing and knowing does the image draw on and construct. Here, we ask: What meanings do we associate with the specific parts of the image? And what are the overall meanings communicated by those items together? This involves a reflection on what meaning systems and social representations we draw upon to make those associations. In Figure 5.1, to interpret the lifejackets as those of refugees and the sea as that of the Greek shore, what background information are we drawing on (e.g. the photographer's anecdote, our previous knowledge of the refugee situation in Europe at that time, our previous exposure to similar images of lifejackets)? It is important to make explicit what knowledge the interpreter is drawing on to be able to construct further meanings of the lifejackets. Like with the first layer, we also explore what meanings we associate with the different compositional elements and why. Colours, shapes, settings, borders, and other aspects mentioned at the first layer could all convey certain meanings. As Kress and Leeuwen (2021) argue, image composition is rarely ever free of ideological dimensions – even basic shapes such as a square could be used to communicate order and structure versus the use of a circle to communicate an organic process, or a triangle to convey directionality and action. Organization and framing of an image can also invite certain ways of seeing and certain positions and expectations of who the viewer is.

5.1.2.2 Social Positioning

Interpreting social positioning (see Chapter 3) in an image involves analysing how the image positions its subjects and its viewers and the meanings those positionings carry. Positioning often relies on – and presupposes the viewers' knowledge of – certain narratives, discourses, and collective memories. What stories do the image presuppose that we know to be able to understand it? And how are the different subjects positioned in this story? Images can give a snapshot of a story that suggests to the viewer what happened just before or what is about to happen. In Figure 5.1, the photograph is a snapshot of a longer journey that Anna covered of the refugees' route in Europe. What do we know and remember about the rest of the story that informs how we perceive and feel about this image?

Positioning can evoke certain emotions based on how the image is framed and how the subjects are presented. The subjects could be positioned in a humanizing way that affords empathy; they could also be positioned in relation to one another in a way that privileges one subject over the other, or positioned as a homogenous unidentifiable crowd, which constraints the viewers' empathy. Emotions could also be conveyed through the different compositional elements: Does the use of colour, contrast, or lighting afford a specific mood or evoke certain emotions? Is the image genre or style inviting certain ways of relating to the image (e.g. black and white photography and nostalgia)? In Figure 5.1, it is the absence of the subjects and the abundance of empty lifejackets that can bring the affective dimension of the image to a viewer who is aware of the refugee crisis. The absence could evoke emotions in relation to uncertainty from a refugee-sympathetic position or emotions of a 'coming threat' from an anti-refugee position.

A positioning analysis also involves the social actors surrounding the image production, viewership, and circulation. Who created it and for whom? Are there people who censored it? In Figure 5.1, what meanings can we interpret of the image knowing that Anna is a photojournalist and knowing why she was on the Greek island? Also, does the image presuppose a certain gaze that suggests who the viewer 'should' be? How is the viewer positioned in relation to the subjects of the image? Does Figure 5.1 position us as witnesses to the refugee crisis and therefore having an obligation to take social action and help? Viewers of images are not only positioned in the internal structure of the image but also by the structure of its immediate environment and image placement. For example, a huge portrait of a leader in the street positions us as relatively 'small' viewers looking up at the image. An image can also symbolically position us as equal to the subject even when in fact it has considerable power over us (Jewitt & Oyama, 2011) (e.g. politicians' close-up images on social media).

5.1.2.3 *Immediate Environment*

Situating the image in its immediate environment involves looking at the media, genre, and the material placement of the image, as well as the specific time, space, and social context that shape the meaning of the image. With this latter aspect, Figure 5.1 can be understood in relation to when and where Anna took the photo within the context of this specific so-called refugee crisis in Europe, and the knowledge of this context informs certain interpretations. The environment also involves other images, language, and discourses surrounding the image. Images rarely stand alone isolated from other visuals and language. An image can be a part of an album with other images, a newspaper with certain news coverage, a social media post that is positioning it in a certain way as an argument or evidence. When I first saw Anna's photograph (Figure 5.1), it was on her professional page. I could see it as part of a bigger series of her photography and with information about her and the goal of her work. This relates to what in discursive and social semiotics traditions could be part of an intertextual or a multimodal interpretation of the image. A further interpretation of this aspect can go from the immediate environment surrounding the image to broader discourses and narratives that circulate in the public space that make meaning possible, which bridges to the third layer of analysis.

5.1.3 Third Layer: Image Meaning in the Extended Environment

At this level, interpretation moves from the specific site of the image and the immediate context of the image to the broader social, historical, and cultural contexts, societal structures, and social practices that shape the meanings of the image. Meanings are accumulated and transformed in the different moments of image production, circulation, and consumption and become meaningful within certain social processes and historical moments (Lister & Wells, 2011). This interpretation can help us understand how the image persuades, produces claims of truth, or presents 'natural' ways of things (Rose, 2016). The tradition of iconography addresses some of the aspects of this layer with its analysis of the broader contextual knowledge that makes cultural meaning come about historically (van Leeuwen, 2011). Art historian Erwin Panofsky (1970) offered some tools to analyse the signs in an image through a grasp of their historically specific intertextuality and how they were used in different works. He also addressed this layer through what he labelled iconological symbolism, which refers to the underlying sociocultural principles that reveal the basic attitudes of a specific time, nation, religion, or philosophy. Visual semiotic tradition has focused more on the image's contemporary cultural meanings (first and second layers) but has also addressed the conventions that underlie the relationship between the signified and signifier. It is especially within social semiotics that those conventional meanings are analysed through looking at ideologies and deep social assumptions. Different terms have been used to address certain aspects of this wider system of ideologies, including dominant codes (Hall, 2001), referent systems (Williamson, 1978), or mythologies (Barthes, 1973). Barthes (1973, 1978) explored 'myths', which are collective representations or beliefs that make certain aspects appear 'natural' rather than socially and historically constructed and he has also explored 'third meaning' that holds the image's additional power and that is hard to locate because it is not situated within the structure of the image itself.

Next I suggest broad conceptions and aspects that one could engage with at this layer that include *societal dialogues*, *power relations*, and *absences*.

5.1.3.1 Societal Dialogues

In the second layer of interpretation, we considered the surrounding images and language in the image's immediate environment and the dialogue in between its different social actors. Here we address broader societal dialogues and debates that the image could be interpreted as part of. This relates to what semiotician and psychoanalyst Julia Kristeva (1980) has referred to as intertextuality: the ways in which works of literature (or art more broadly) do not exist in isolation but are interconnected and influenced by each other and by broader discourses in society. Her concept connects semiotics (how signs attain meaning within context) and Bakhtin's dialogism (the ongoing dialogue between different works and authors).

Here, we address the broader level of dominant discourses or schematic narrative templates that the image could be borrowing from or responding to. Schematic narratives are generalized collective-level narrative forms that shape certain collective identities and memories (Wertsch, 2004). For example, does the image feed into a dominant hegemonic discourse or a schematic narrative, or does it refute and construct a different one? Also, what are the social representations (Moscovici, 1984) that provide a normative and common-sense ways of seeing the image? What are the norms, conventions, and attitudes associated with those social representations? Are there coexisting, diverse, and contradicting social representations that the image is drawing upon in relation to the same social object portrayed? Moscovici conceptualized this coexistence of multiple meanings as cognitive polyphasia, which forms a central motivation for societal dialogue (Marková, 2003).

One could also address the previous images that the image is in dialogue with, supporting, or refuting. It is impossible to find every previous or subsequent relevant image, but one can look at what examples make qualitatively meaningful connections and what possible sources of images could help explore the borrowing, transformation, and dialogue in relation to an image.

The broader dialogue also involves the social actors involved in the broader context of the topic of the image. The photograph of the

5.1 Layers of Interpretation

lifejackets (Figure 5.1) relates to a broader discourse on war and immigration that involves politicians, refugees, and debates about their deservedness of help, and people in the host countries and their attitudes in relation to immigration. This connects the image to other images that were used as historical analogies to identity common aspects and bring familiarity into the dialogue, such as those of Second World War refugees. The photograph also falls more specifically within discourses of immigration from the 'East' to the 'West' with all the historically enduring psychological perceptions about the 'Eastern other' discussed in Chapter 3. This connects it to other images and metaphors that represent the crisis as a 'plague' or a 'flood' within a schematic narrative that positions the refugees as invaders and the water as the border through which the invasion takes place.

5.1.3.2 Power Relations

Situating the image within broader social and historical dialogues helps explore the different social structures and power dynamics relevant to the knowledge the image is producing. This could include questioning: What are the social structures and institutions enabling or limiting the production and circulation of an image and its visibility platforms? What are the social positions of the different social actors involved and how do they affect who gets represented and how? Do certain social positions and certain social classes afford certain ways of seeing, that differentiate how different viewers can engage with the image? Here, Bourdieu's (1984) concept of habitus could be of relevance, which I will discuss in Chapter 7 in relation to acts of viewing.

5.1.3.3 Absences

While in the first layer I tackled immediate absences in an image (e.g. empty chair), here I question what ideas, subjects, or objects are made invisible through certain images – what is concealed from vision. In relation to refugee images, this could be seen in how certain coverage focuses only on representing the burden and 'threat' the refugees might cause in a host country, rather than the threat of what they are running away from in their own countries.

5.1.4 Fourth Layer: Symbolic, Affective, and Embodied Dimensions

There is something about images that cannot be anchored in language; something in the psychological encounter with certain images that cannot be pinned down by a structured meaning system. At this layer, I explore the potential affective and embodied way in which individuals and groups subjectively experience certain images. In every encounter with an image, the historicity and life trajectory of the image meets with the socialization and life trajectory of the viewer, and at times this can trigger an affective embodied response from the viewer – the feeling that they were 'moved' by an image.

It will always be a challenge to capture what an image *does* or means to someone affectively and the subjective intensity of that affect in relation to what personal memories or experiences that person might have. It is especially challenging when it is also sometimes beyond a person's conscious cognitive comprehension but is experienced bodily in response to certain images. For example, a person can feel comfort with certain images or can feel repulsion and immediately look away from some. Images can afford an embodied response of connection, resonance, and empathy, sometimes in ways that the viewer can not immediately explain. The same image can trigger opposing emotions in different people. Roland Barthes (1981) used the concept 'punctum' to refer to the specific, often subtle, detail of an image that resonates with a viewer in a way that can evoke a unique personal emotional reaction. A punctum may not be immediately obvious or universally understood but has a particular significance for the individual viewer. This significance makes an image memorable for the person and affords a deep personal affective connection for them.

At this layer I address the *hyper-generalized affect* on the individual level and the shared affect of *collective symbols*.

5.1.4.1 Hyper-generalized Affect

In the second layer, I addressed emotions that certain representational aspects of the image can evoke. Here it is more relevant to talk about the affective, embodied, and sensory experiences that are beyond the representational level that an image can afford engagement with. I draw here on cultural psychologist Jaan Valsiner's (2008) idea of how certain signs can create a hyper-generalized affective semiotic field; where a person 'just feels something' but cannot put one word or one direct explanation on the feeling evoked. Here the image manages to internalize an abstract feeling; one that overgeneralizes to the person's general feeling about themselves and the world. In my research on graffiti, I found that based on the person's social position, where they grew up, and their relation to underground culture, graffiti images in certain places could easily evoke a sense of connectedness and freedom or a sense of fear and danger.

The hyper-generalized affect occurs in the encounter between the semiotic and material properties of the image – described in the earlier layers of interpretation – and the first-person experience. The image could trigger a certain memory, resonate with a certain thought, or bring a certain association from the person's life trajectory. These connections involve conscious and unconscious dynamics. For instance, I encounter an image in a subway station of a child on a beach that catches my attention with a sense of discomfort. This is a premediated affective and embodied response to the image. I then recognize that it is an advertisement for a vacation destination in Greece, an association that does not hold much interest on the cognitive level for me. However, the image also triggers other associations at the periphery of my consciousness – it might be reminding me of my son at that age, who is now nearing adulthood. This is an affectively laden memory that is connected to several emotions of longing and reminiscence and connected to many personal memories with conscious and unconscious affects. The image also triggers another association from the shared social context: I am seeing the image at a time where news images of refugees dying on the shores of Greece and Turkey are circulating, including the image of the child Alan Kurdi whose body was found on the mediterranean shore in Turkey as his family were trying to reach Europe. In the moment, I do not think about it, but later I start reflecting on this latter association and the difference between tourists who travel by choice to a world that is accessible to them and those who travel by displacement; those who are pushed from behind. This reflective and conscious thought is influenced by my academic socialization and how the sociologist Zygment Bauman (1998) used the metaphors of tourists and vagabonds to distinguish between those who are privileged to inhabit the globe and embody the mobility prospect of globalization and those who are supposed to be chained to place. While the first group – represented in the advertisement – move because they want to, the second group move because they have no other bearable choice; they move because the places they are supposed to be chained to are unbearable. The hyper-generalized affect of discomfort I experienced when I encountered the image could be triggered by a combination of those associations – and probably others I am less aware of – with varying degrees of consciousness and reflexivity.

5.1.4.2 Collective Symbols

The generalized emotions an image can afford are always subjective, relying on individual as well as collective emotions, memories, and experiences. However, I am especially interested in the generalized emotions an image can afford on a collective level – when can a visual become a psychologically powerful one for solidarity, or protest, or hate, and how does that affective affordance vary across time and space? Also, when do those visual symbols lose their affective power throughout the image's social life, for example due to overexposure and saturation or commercialization?

Not every image goes beyond communicating a meaning through its signs to transforming into an affective symbol. An affective symbol is constructed when a specific sign in an image become an independent symbol, travelling across time on its own with an accumulated meaning that triggers certain emotions and memories. A symbol is a sign that accumulates and condenses several elaborate meanings and evokes an underlying sentiment (Bartlett, 1924). Images holding a symbolic affective value are often ones that have managed to condense certain surrounding images, narratives, discourses or events in a way that resonates with certain groups of people. A symbolic image has a history that has accumulated the meaning, as well as a potential future, as visual symbols are often attractive for appropriation and reproduction for the meanings they can carry and travel with and for the emotions they can evoke.

On the collective level, we can identify certain contexts, histories, and collective memories that can afford certain visuals to become affective symbols in a certain cultural setting. For example, depending on one's social and political position regarding the refugees, the lifejacket photo (Figure 5.1) could evoke certain specific and generalized feelings. For a person with an anti-immigration position who is also exposed to different images and news about the magnitude of the crisis and the security and cultural threat it brings to Europe, the image could evoke a generalized feeling of fear and the need for protection. For a person with a pro-immigration position and with the knowledge of and sympathy with the many who lost their life in the water and the failure of host countries to support, the image could evoke a generalized feeling of despair and pessimism, coming from a feeling of 'this story does not end well'.

The affective power of the lifejacket image comes precisely from it being part of broader contested dialogues and emotions. These dialogues include many other images, news, and narratives of refugee boats, border controls, questions of who deserves help, and whose life and safety matters. This transformed the lifejacket into an affective symbol of this crisis embodying many of these meanings and emotions for some. The lifejackets transformed from objects on the shores to visual symbols travelling in between news images, protest posters, paintings, and social media images. One example of this is the art installation of Chinese artist and activist

Ai Weiwei, where he used 3,500 refugee lifejackets that he has received from Lesbos Island to create an installation barricading the windows of Kunsthal Charlottenborg in Copenhagen, which is an exhibition space for contemporary art. According to the exhibition's website, Ai Weiwei aims with the installation to raise awareness about the social and political reality of the humanitarian crisis. The name of the installation (Soleil Levant) comes from Claude Monet's painting *Impression, Soleil Levant* from 1872, which captured the political and social reality of its time.

5.2 Methods: Constructing a Dataset for Visual Analysis

There is a methodological challenge in applying the different interpretation layers on large sets of image data and on images from different genres, mediums, contexts, and environments. Also, since images have continuous social lives, it could be challenging to set a boundary for the visual dialogue under investigation. Whether looking at one image or a set of images, following a method of image interpretation often comes with its own challenges. The methodological tools and techniques are only helpful to a certain extent. There is a further skill of interpretation that goes beyond a certain list of steps that one needs to learn by doing and by being open to explore multiple ways of seeing and experiencing images. As cultural theorist Stuart Hall (1997b) argues, there is no single or correct interpretation; a good interpretation is about making a plausible interpretative argument and justifying this interpretation transparently in detail and in relation to the specific context.

It is assumed with the interpretation layers presented in this chapter that the dataset is a manageable group of images that one could engage with in depth (later, in Chapter 7, I will present other methods that deal with big image datasets). The interpretation process starts in the specifics of one image then moves on to connect it to the broader meanings and other images it engages in a dialogue with. This involves choices in terms of how far one should look to trace the life of the image and other images that came before and after that image, that one could argue forms a dialogue in a certain space. There is always a need to create a boundary for where the research will look. I propose that this boundary could be established based on different criteria, as I will list next.

5.2.1 *Visual Symbol-Specific Dataset*

A dataset could be based on following a specific visual symbol's social life in a specific context. The symbol could be seen as especially relevant or holding some affective value in relation to a topic, and therefore following the different uses and appropriations of that symbol could be meaningful. The example of the Nefertiti wearing a gas mask in Chapter 2 is an example of such inquiry. Based on my broader research in the context of the 2011 revolution and its visual production, the Nefertiti in a gas mask was identified as an affective symbol that had a rich transformative social life, and therefore And therefore I traced its reproductions to analyze how it was appropriated and transformed in the urban and digital space (Awad, 2020b).

It is challenging to find every reproduction of an image, but some tools could help. There are search engines such as Google Images and TinEye that can do a reverse image search to find where an image came from, where it circulated, and different modified versions of it. There are also different computational tools that can help with mining visual datasets based on specific keywords or cues. Images, for example, can be sometimes associated with certain hashtags on social media. In the context of the Egyptian revolution, I also relied on consulting the image producers themselves and their knowledge of reproductions and transformations of their images, and I also consulted different activists and researchers who were documenting protest images and graffiti.

5.2.2 Producer-Specific Dataset

Another way of constructing a relatively easier dataset is to focus on one image producer and analyse all their images. This could be, for example, an activist, an artist, a movement, an organization, a newspaper, or a political party. The example presented in Chapter 7 uses this strategy, where we followed the visual production of a Danish political party, looking at all images it has produced in three specific mediums: newsletter, urban campaign posters, and its Facebook account. This was informed by a research question investigating how this party visually constructs an exclusionary national identity. The research question also informed which timeframes are meaningful to focus on.

5.2.3 Space and Time-Specific Dataset

In this strategy, the dataset is built from a specified space with a certain timeframe: digital platform, a wall in the city, an archive, a newspaper, or other physical or digital spaces. This dataset gives a clear framework for where to look and could be combined with another criteria; for example, images from a specific producer in a specific space. In street art and graffiti research, this could be based on an interest in the longitudinal tracing of interaction on one wall (Awad, 2021; Hansen & Flynn, 2015). Like other strategies, the choice needs to be meaningful in relation to the research question. For example, in investigating how popular education informs Americans about 'non-Westerners', Catherine Lutz and Jane Collins (1993) analysed photographs published in the *National Geographic*. Here the *National Geographic* is both a space-specific dataset and a producer-specific dataset, that they argued constitutes an appropriate data source since it is one of the most culturally valued media shaping American understandings of the outside world, and it was – at the time of the study – the third most popular magazine in the USA based on subscriptions.

5.2.4 Topic-Specific Dataset

Another choice criterion, often used in combination with one or more of the previously listed criteria, is a topic-specific dataset. This could be addressing a research inquiry into a specific debate or event. For example, in a study investigating the response to and representation of the coronavirus pandemic, Constance de Saint Laurent and colleagues (de Saint Laurent et al., 2022) analysed a dataset of digital meme images (genre specific) on Reddit social media platform (space specific) between January to May 2020 (time specific) addressing coronavirus (topic specific). Again, justifications of why this genre, space, and time make meaningful choices in relation to the research question is key. The size of the dataset can inform what is suitable to be done in terms of analysis. Sometimes the interpretation method process presented earlier could be applied to all of the datasets. At other times, it might be more suitable with large datasets to start with a quantitative content visual analysis first, then based on findings select a few images that could be qualitatively interpreted in depth.

5.3 A Street Poster: Refugees Welcome ... Terrorists Welcome

I end this chapter with another example from the context of refugees in Europe. This example is centred on a specific genre: urban posters and stickers; a specific space: the city centre of Aalborg in North Denmark; and a specific visual symbol: the fleeing family. Since 2015, I have been living in Aalborg – this coincided with the refugee humanitarian crises in Europe and Danish debate about receiving Syrian refugees. Driven by my interest in the topic and my interest in urban images, I started taking pictures of urban images I encountered in the city centre relating to the broad topic of refugees and immigration. This was not part of a systematic data collection procedure but rather a practice of curiosity and a qualitative inquiry that takes everyday life materials as rich data for interpretation and analysis that could help us understand broader societal issues (Brinkmann, 2012). There are, however, different methods developed for such inquiries, where walking is used as a methodological and political practice for the psychological interpretation of social environments (Hayes, 2003) – see, for example, psychogeography (Bridger, 2010).

Of the images I collected between 2015 and 2021, there were twenty-eight photos of posters and stickers dealing with the topic of refugees, eighteen of which included the visual symbol of the fleeing family which I will discuss here. My guiding question was simple: how are the pro- and anti-refugee attitudes visible in the visual landscape of the city space? Later, regarding the fleeing family visual symbol, I started looking at how the fleeing family visual symbol is used to mobilize solidarity with or fear of the refugees. These inquiries are part of a broader interest in visual political dialogues in the public space and how they are inscribed onto city spaces as different social actors use images to position themselves and others within the debates.

Most images were not signed or branded to show the producer, except for ones produced by the Amnesty International humanitarian organization and Generation Identity, which is a European youth far-right group. The images were all collected from the centre area of Aalborg. Aalborg is a small city in Northern Denmark. There are around 12,000 people living in the city centre area, and it has an overall municipality population of around 219,500, 89 per cent of which are of Danish origin and 11 per cent are immigrants or descendants, according to Aalborg municipality's webpage in 2021. The images correspond to a broader debate in Denmark in relation to immigration policies, which intensified with the Syrian humanitarian crisis.

The images that include the fleeing family visual were all graphic-designed images used in both pro- and anti-refugee posters. The visual shows a silhouette image of a family (a man, a woman, and a child) running (Figure 5.2). I will focus on the interpretation of the two top images: the 'Refugees welcome' image and its counter-image: the 'Terrorist welcome' image. The rest of the images will be used as examples to show the social life of these images in the urban space and the material interactions with them.

On a first layer of interpretation, in both images we see three subjects; there is movement in their posture, they are all running in one direction,

Figure 5.2 (a) The graphic design of the pro-refugee poster; (b) The graphic design of the anti-refugee poster by Swedish Artist Dan Park; (c) August 2017, text reads: Refugees welcome, bring your families; (d) April 2018, text reads: Refugees welcome, no one is illegal; (e) August 2016, text reads: Refugees welcome, bring your families; (f) December 2015, text reads: Terrorist welcome, bring your weapons; (g) February 2016, previous poster scratched out; (h) August 2016, text reads: Terrorist welcome, bring your weapons; (i) June 2018, text in Danish translates to: Invasion, no thank you!
Source: Author's photographs of posters.

and the child is holding the hand of the woman. The further details of clothing and objects in the two images differ. In the first one, the clothing seems generic: the man wears a shirt and pants, the woman a shirt and a skirt or a dress, and the child a shirt and shorts and what seems to be a hairband. In the counter-image, however, the man now has a beard and a turban and holds in each hand a sword. The woman's face is moved to look back at us rather than in the running direction; we can now see that she wears a headscarf but her face has no features, just a blank white circle. She carries a rifle in one hand and the child still in the other. The child wears an explosive belt (commonly worn by suicide bombers) while holding what seems to be its control switch in its hand. Both images are surrounded by text. The first reads: 'Refugees Welcome, bring your families' and the second reads 'Terrorist Welcome, bring your weapons'. In the first one there is a star surrounded by a circle on both sides of text, while in the second one this is changed into a star and crescent (historical symbols commonly used to refer to Islam).

On a second layer of interpretation, the three subjects portrayed in the two images are typical portrayals of a family. While in the first image it could be a generic family, in the second image it is clearly a Muslim family with the beard, turban, headscarf, and the star and crescent symbol. Incorporating the text into our understanding of the image gives quite clear messages. The first one is an image of a fleeing refugee family, and the image communicates a welcoming message from a host country's perspective. The second one identifies that same fleeing family as terrorists rather than refugees. In the text, this is done by simply replacing the word 'refugees' with 'terrorists'. However, the 'welcome' part is left, which emphasizes the ironic response the second image is making to the first one, furthered by changing the 'bring your families' to 'bring your weapons'. The context for meaning is clearly associated with the debate in Danish society about receiving Syrian refugees, and whether this is a humanitarian responsibility or a cultural and safety threat to the country. The meaning of the second image is interpreted through the first image and other similar images; it presents a clear counterargument. It also poses a change in the possible narrative of the image. In the first image, given the posture of the family and their movement, it conveys a narrative of the family running away from some threat that we cannot see. The counter-image manages to change that narrative; through the weaponization of the running family, the narrative is changed to them running towards something, to them becoming the threat, rather than running from a threat.

I could not identify who designed the first image. It is available for free download and use on several open platforms online and through different pro-refugee initiatives across Europe. The second image is a readaptation done by Swedish artist Dan Park. Park is a controversial street artist who has been arrested several times for hate speech. Park's poster has been reported to the police in Sweden and Denmark. In one report, the Danish police established that there were no grounds to charge the artist or his supporters with making threats or inciting terror; however, those involved with hanging the posters on electrical boxes and city walls were fined 1,000 Danish kroner (The Local, 2015).

On a third layer of interpretation, the images are not only part of the specific debate of whether Denmark should receive Syrian refugees or not, the debate extends to the divide between the so-called West and East, the terrorism discourse especially since the 9/11 terror attacks in 2001, and global humanitarian solidarity. The second image fits into a broader invasion schematic narrative that is commonly used by far-right groups in Europe, where the foreign – especially Muslim – 'other' can infiltrate and destroy the nation (Nissen et al., 2021). The image portrays the 'ideal orient other' in Edward Said's (1978) terms, the one who is radical and undifferentiated, holding medieval weapons and ready to attack once let in. Both images rely on normative social representations for their arguments. The first one uses the fleeing family as the anchor to the legitimate group deserving help, and the second one uses generalizations to equate refugees, Muslims, and terrorists.

On a fourth layer of interpretation, the fleeing family, whether weaponized or not, has become one of the visual affective symbols in many of the images about the refugee humanitarian crisis in Europe. The different images – whether for or against refugees – can afford a generalized feeling of urgency, fear, and threat. That generalized feeling, based on the image and who is viewing it, can afford a sense of empathy with the family for the threat they are running from, or a sense of threat from the family as they are running towards the viewers' home country.

Following the different posters across time showed how the image possibly provoked some pedestrians enough that they intervened and scratched part of it out (e.g. the word 'terrorist'). This is an interaction that this genre and urban placement affords. Following the image across geographical contexts also showed how it was further transformed for different purposes. After incidents of sexual assaults in 2015 in Cologne, Germany, similar posters were designed in protest. These posters adapted the text to 'Rapefugees not welcome, stay away.' The family subjects were changed to being three men with turbans and beards holding knives and running after a woman. The images were also later adapted into digital memes (Dafaure, 2020) and used in German right-wing political mobilization communicating broader racial and gendered discourses about migration (Pępiak, 2019; Roth, 2020).

The fleeing family, the weaponized family, and the mob attacking the woman show a contested social life of an affective image that started in support of refugees. The examples show how the images are used as political tools to advocate for certain arguments in a contested societal debate. The transformations of the modified images gain power and meaning by their reference to and adaptation from the first image. In Bakhtin's (1986) words: 'every utterance must be regarded primarily as a response to preceding utterances of the given sphere .... Each utterance refutes, affirms, supplements, and relies upon the others, presupposes them to be known, and somehow takes them into account' (p. 91). The symbolic power of the later images builds upon their use of irony and 'double voicedness': 'using someone else's words in order to express one's own intentions and meanings that are hostile to others' words' (Marková, 2003, p. 63), thus backfiring by using the opponent's symbolic weaponry (Wagoner et al., 2018).

CHAPTER 6

The Environment of the Image

Figure 6.1   Berlin-based artist Prizmu's stencil art piece of 'Fuck Wars'.
Source: Author photograph with permission from Prizmu.

Among the many cluttered posters and paintings in Figure 6.1, graffiti and multimedia Berlin-based artist Prizmu added his stencil art piece of 'Fuck Wars'. The image appropriates the title design and the Ewok character from the popular *Star Wars* films and pop culture fiction. In the *Star Wars* universe, the Ewoks are fictional species of small furry mammaloid who are presented as a primitive tribe that fight the technological empire. Part of understanding this image is to situate it within the medium of urban art, more specifically in the genre of stencil and paste-up graffiti, and to look at its specific placement in the urban environment. A significant part of the meaning of this anti-war image comes from its placement on the remaining part of the Berlin Wall in Germany, and the symbolic meaning of this wall. The social life of the image is shaped by its life on the wall, the other images that came before it and the ones that come after it and continue to cover it, as well as the wear and tear to its material properties. A further interpretation of the image comes from the time and socio-political space that the image exists in. What are past and ongoing wars that the image is speaking of? What are their consequences? And are there Ewoks fighting against the powerful empires?

I captured this photograph on 12 January 2017 from the remaining part of the Berlin Wall. I reached out to Prizmu for permission to use since the photograph includes his graffiti image and he kindly agreed.

Images cannot exist on their own. They are environmental, in the sense that they always have a context and are delivered through a medium (Manghani, 2012). The image's life unfolds within a specific time and physical and social space, which shape the context in which we view the image. By context here, I refer to the connected whole that gives coherence to its parts and situate a social act within its environment in a specific historical moment (Cole, 1996). Situating the image is important for understanding its production, interpretation, transformation, censoring, and all the life trajectory of the image. The environment is especially relevant to understanding the viewing context of the image, which involves different aspects such as the geographic location, the time period, institutional setting, and cultural and religious framework (Sturken & Cartwright, 2018). Similar to all human thinking and behaviour, our interaction with images cannot be understood in isolation of the time and space in which the interaction occurs. The spatial aspects of images help emphasize how we not only inhabit our culture but also how we reconstruct it and alter the very structures by which we organize it (I. Rogoff, 1998).

Since images cannot exist on their own, their interpretation should always incorporate an 'ecology of images' (Sontag, 1977). Similar to ecologists' interest in the interrelationship between organisms and their environment, an ecology of images considers the image in relation to its environment of production and viewership, as well as its interaction with other images (Manghani, 2012). To situate an image in its environment is to acknowledge the specific context it unfolds in, while acknowledging also that its social life extends to other times and spaces before and after that instance. We can, for example, analyse the specific time and space of a graffiti image in a specific urban space, while also looking at how its life extends back to a popular image with a different context and different geographical location (e.g. the Star Wars reference in Figure 6.1) and how its life extends forward as it is photographed and transformed in online spaces. In this chapter, I will discuss situating the image within the immediate material environment where the image appears, which includes the *medium*, *genre*, and *placement* of the image. Then, I will discuss the broader *time* and *space* surrounding the image, which includes the extended historical, social, cultural, and political context that the image exists within.

6.1 Medium and Genre

Images need a medium to reside within just like an organism resides in a habitat (Mitchell, 2005). The distinction between different mediums and genres has become more blurred today as images move from one environment to another. There is a move from medium-specific content to convergence between different platforms, where content flows across them, which complicates distinctions between new and old media, and top-down corporate media and bottom-up participatory cultures (Jenkins, 2006). Different media technologies are also dialectically and historically linked, meaning that ancient and archaic media (e.g. paintings and sculptures) provide the framework for our understanding of television and the internet, and our understanding of these early media depends on the new inventions of communication means (Mitchell, 2005).

The medium is not only important to understand the materiality of image production and circulation but also to understand the social practices surrounding the materials (e.g. brush, computer) and the things people do with them, as well as the complex social institutions and history of practices that facilitate those technologies and techniques (Mitchell, 2005). The specific means and technologies used in image production shape the way the image will be viewed and interacted with, affording certain practices of looking and engagement in everyday visual culture (Sturken & Cartwright, 2018). For example, the material technologies and techniques of a physical image can include the surface of production (e.g. wood, paper, wall), the substance of production (e.g. ink, paint), and the tools of production (e.g. brush, pencil, spray can) (Kress & Leeuwen, 2021). There are also different established social practices and techniques within the same medium; for example, within digital photography there are portrait images, self-portrait, news images, and family photos, among many others.

To interpret an image as facilitating certain meanings and engagement, we must consider the specific affordances of the medium and genre of the image. The concept of affordance brings together the potential power of an image in relation to the different social actors surrounding it, social norms and practices, and the environment where it is placed. Affordance can be understood through psychologist James J. Gibson's (1979) ecological approach. His work explored how perception and thinking interrelate with the environment; he used the concept of affordance to explain how our surrounding environment can 'afford' us to act and engage in certain ways. Affordance of an image then is about the material properties and appearance of an image that give potential for or inhibit us to engage with it in certain ways. This does not mean that an image 'acts', causing us to react in a certain way, as in a stimuli–response relationship. Rather the image, through its material form and how it was produced and placed, affords or gives potential for certain responses. Different viewers might then respond to those affordances differently in a dynamic reciprocal influence between the person and the image. Affordances are normative and continuously constructed in the cultural and historical context rather than predetermined (Glăveanu, 2012) and creative engagement with images often involves generating novel affordances and uses of images.

This relates to the conceptualization of images as tools (as well as signs) that acquire meaning through their different uses in their social life. In *The Social Life of Things*, Arjun Appadurai (1986) highlights how material objects are integral to human life and social structures and institutions. The material object's significance does not precede its social life but rather is actualized through what we do with it. Similarly, anthropologist Nicholas Thomas (1991) emphasizes that the significance of an image lies in what is done with it rather than an inherent meaning. The images' material qualities and their affordances are mobilized in when and how we engage with them.

Looking at different image media and genres can help unfold the variety of material prosperities, social practices, and visual technologies that make images how they are, and can show what different uses and engagements they can afford. Those aspects vary greatly based on whether the image is a photograph, digital image, emoji, social media meme, graffiti, or oil painting, to name a few. There is dedicated literature addressing each of those media that one could engage with when interpreting a specific set of images. In the following sections I will tackle some aspects in relation to photography, digital memes, and urban images, to discuss how those afford different interpretations and engagement with the image.

6.1 Medium and Genre

6.1.1 Photography

Some would argue that an unedited photograph is distinct from other painted or designed images, in that it always captures a moment that is 'real', a moment that corresponds with some external reality out there in the world (Giardetti & Oller, 1995). However, this affordance for credibility is challenged by viewers who are increasingly aware of photo manipulation technologies and photo framing, where even without editing an image, the choice of a specific angle and focus can shape the 'reality' the image claims to be representing.

Within photography, there are different styles and practices that afford different social actions and power relations. The 'mugshot', for example, is a specific genre of portraiture photography, with a clear power relation between the person represented and the institution (e.g. prison, school, adoption centre) producing the photo (Tagg, 1988). The composition of such images has a repetitive pattern of the face in sharp and illuminated focus, the body isolated with a narrow space around it, the pose reflecting the person's subjection to an unreturnable gaze, and the body gestures limited to holding a board with a name and a number. Since the nineteenth century photography has been of major significance to institutional interests as a method of surveillance and control (Tagg, 1988) and to serve the interests of powerful nations to monitor and document 'alien' populations (Robins, 1996).

The development in technologies of photography and the growing accessibility of tools to take and share photos have expanded who takes photos and for what purposes. Consider the 'mugshot' in comparison with 'selfie' photographs. The latter are taken by the person themselves, through a smartphone, with the ability to take many shots until one perfects a certain portrayal, that could be then shared on social media. The pose, place, and angle of the image are all in the hands of the selfie taker who also chooses where to post it and how publicly visible it is. Unlike the gaze of the mugshot, the selfie is about the gaze of the photo taker, looking back at the viewers, allowing them to see a certain aspect of their life. What we see around the face of the person are usually the social, cultural, and economic status markers that they choose to display. The selfie, in that sense, is a commodity that communicates social status. The mugshot and the selfie afford different agency positions for the person represented and different possibilities in the use, circulation, and interpretation of the images. Analysing the choice of pose, gesture, gaze, expressions, props, and costumes in photos could shed light on different practices and social norms – see, for example, the work of psychologist Halla Beloff (1988) and her analysis of distinct gendered patterns of self-representations. Such analysis could also show how our notions of self and social identity are tied with our practices of self-representations especially in a time where self-portraits, edits of them, and selfies are a common cultural practice in online space (Forrester, 2000).

The access to tools for self-representation does not guarantee, however, an equal space for visibility and recognition. In the context of the refugee humanitarian crisis in 2015, images of refugees taking selfies with smartphones were looked upon with suspicion by some. Several of those images were taken up by news agencies and appropriated in critical digital memes on social media. One example is a selfie photo of a group of young men as they pose happily after reaching the island of Lesbos in a rubber boat from Turkey. The image was met with a lot of critique; the refugees were not in the 'right' social position to engage in the social practice of selfie taking. The image also contradicted with the stereotypical idea of who is an eligible refugee who is worthy of help. Digital memes were created of the image with captions such as 'oh I'm fleeing my home, I must remember my selfie stick!!!' or 'too scared to stay in their own countries, but happy to leave their women and children there!' (Literat, 2017).

In this example, the access to a camera is not enough to affirm one's own image in the public space and counter dominant media representations. Photography technologies have indeed created certain affordances for marginalized communities to self-represent and to take part in the politics of image production and circulation (hooks, 1995); however, those affordances should be understood in relation to the affordances of different media platforms. Photojournalism and news media have much wider platforms for visibility and continue to have a strong influence in shaping people's emotions in relation to world happenings (Butler, 2010; Sontag, 2003) and in producing affective debates in relation to the refugee crisis (Kjeldsen, 2018; Olesen, 2020).

6.1.2 Memes

Another interesting digital image genre that has its own affordances is that of social media memes. A meme usually refers to an image that has developed into some form of a template that people communicate through it different attitudes and feelings. People alter the text accompanying the image or part of the image itself to appropriate it for the purpose they want to communicate. Media scholar Bradley Wiggins (2019) conceptualizes image-based internet memes as an artefact and a genre of online

6.1 Medium and Genre

communication in digital culture. Memes are a form of ideological practice that involve agency through their creation, interpretation, transformation, and sharing. Much earlier than their social media use, the concept of memes was introduced in biologist Richard Dawkins' (1989) evolutionary theory. He used the term to refer to cultural transmission; the process of imitation of ideas from one brain to another, just like genes carry from one body to another.

Dawkins' cultural memes (such as slogans, popular songs, fashion) seek replication for the selfish purpose of survival and serve as catalysts for cultural jumps in the evolution of human beings. However, as Wiggins (2019) argues, internet memes are not exactly a process of imitation. Internet memes are marked by their capacity to engage in arguments using visual and verbal interplay. They are not 'just' attractive catch content but a 'remixed iterated message that can be rapidly diffused by members of participatory digital culture for the purpose of satire, parody, critique, or other discursive activity' (Wiggins, 2019, p. 11). They thus become part of a shared cultural experience, as communication scholar Limor Shifman (2014) argues, and a way of connection between the personal and political realities. They characterize a form of 'networked individualism' as people use memes to simultaneously express both their connectivity and uniqueness (Shifman, 2014, p. 30).

Here it is helpful to make a qualitative distinction between viral media (e.g. a video going viral and having millions of viewers) without significant change to its content and internet memes where there is a process of modification and participation (Shifman, 2012). The refugee selfie image already mentioned went viral online, but it was only transformed into a meme when different groups appropriated the image to express certain attitudes about the refugees. Meme images are marked by dynamic social lives, where the main feature of a meme is that it transforms and takes on new lives on the internet as different social actors appropriate it. There are different websites dedicated to documenting the travel life of digital memes and tracing where they come from (e.g. knowyourmeme.com).

The accessibility of meme image making and sharing allows it to play a role in societal dialogues, as it can circulate a wide range of perspectives and sentiments regarding an issue such as immigration and refugees (Glăveanu et al., 2018). The nature of this image genre is also very dialogical in the sense that memes do not exist without building on already existing images in the visual culture and on others engaging in a dialogue by adding, refuting, or sharing arguments and sentiments on previous memes. This gives memes certain affordances to disseminate discourses and values, to normalize stereotypes and discrimination (Drakett et al., 2018), to facilitate the construction of collective identities (DeCook, 2018), and to carry cultural repertoires and practices (Iloh, 2021).

6.1.3 Urban Images and Graffiti

Images produced for the city space offer distinct affordances for interaction and engagement with people in the street. These include graffiti, street art, posters, advertisements, and political campaigns, among others. In comparison to advertisement and political campaigning billboards, graffiti and posters are culturally perceived as affording more participatory intervention, whether in putting them up or interacting with them (e.g. by cutting them off or covering them with other posters). Protest stickers, for example, are often used to promote social movements and communicate radical or subversive opinions (Awcock, 2021). As early as the French Revolution, print images and posters were used to deconstruct the sacred visual imagery of the king and reconstruct the nation and its populace (Landes, 1992).

Other than their use for subversive opinions, posters have also been traditionally used as a propaganda tool by authorities. For example, Haskins and Zappen's (2010) study of Soviet posters in the 1920s and 1930s shows how posters were used to communicate the authoritative monologue discourse of authority. Those posters, however, always involved a dialogic element as the visual expressions relied on previous discourses and culturally available symbolic resources to communicate their message. Posters also continue to be used today as a main communication tool for elections in many countries, and different methods have been developed for their study (see, e.g., Geise & Vigsø, 2017).

Graffiti and street art – especially unauthorized – offer another tool for intervention in city space that affords further interaction with the public. Broadly defined, street art compromises different forms of self-authorized paintings and writings that are applied to surfaces in the city space (Blanché, 2015). Given the accessibility of its tools and freedom of its form, street art has been an attractive tool for youth to claim city space through tagging and for activists to use it as an act of resistance (Avramidis & Tsilimpounidi, 2017; Awad & Wagoner, 2017; Khatib, 2013). Even when graffiti and street art do not have an explicit political message, one could argue that they are inherently political in the way they challenge the authority's power and monopoly over public space (Awad, 2022; Waldner & Dobratz, 2013) and in how they pose an act of dissent to dominant urban aesthetics and established institutions of art (Avramidis & Tsilimpounidi, 2017). This status is challenged, however, as graffiti has been increasingly used for commercial, commodification, and gentrification purposes, which threatens to 'neutralize' any political message the art form might have (Lewisohn, 2008).

Similar to memes on digital space, graffiti in urban space is open to dialogue and intervention, and therefore should be analysed as instances in an open and continuous interaction that could be traced through different approaches such as visual ethnography (Pink, 2021) and longitudinal documentation of city walls (Hansen & Flynn, 2015). Their analysis could also involve the interrelations between images in the urban and digital space and how they influence one another and travel in between different genres and media (see, e.g., MacDowall, 2019).

6.2 Placement

The place in which an image appears to its viewers has a strong influence on how the image is viewed and how its social life evolves. Even within the same medium and genre, a digital photograph taken by an eyewitness placed on the BBC's Facebook account has quite different affordances for engagement and believability than the same photograph placed on a discussion forum on 4chan, or the same image posted by a famous activist or social media influencer. Considering the specific geographical location and environment in which the image lives is important to understand the spatial affordances of images; how they can appropriate a space, give a certain dominant feeling of a space as inclusive or exclusive to certain groups of people, and can shape how people think, feel, and behave in certain spaces.

Placement of graffiti images, for example, forms such a significant part of the meaning of the images that many would argue that the images become meaningless when moved to a museum. The urban space provides a material place in which graffiti, as well as advertisement billboards and political campaign images, inhabit. This place is not only material space but – as philosopher and urban sociologist Henri Lefebvre argued (Lefebvre, 1991) – is also a social product that is dominantly produced by a centralized power, and continuously influenced by how its inhibitors use the space. Historian and cultural critic Michel de Certeau (1984) shows how we do not passively inhabit space, we are mediated by and mediating the environments we live in, shaping them through everyday social practices to make them inhabitable. His work highlights the bodily aspect of being in places, where we are immersed in mediation with the spaces, objects, and technologies surrounding us. Practices such as walking in the city or remembering old places that are no longer there involve a process of a negotiation of our environment, where visuals in that environment interact with our field of experience.

We identify ourselves with the places we live in and encounter in everyday life. Even when we are not always attentive to images surrounding us, they can shape where we feel familiar and included or constrained and alienated. Images can appropriate a certain place by the meanings they communicate and the consequences of those meanings for different people. In places where there is a visual monopoly over public space, images of leadership can be a continuous reminder for passers-by that they do not own that space, they can only use it passively. Other public spaces can be more dialogical in having visibility to different groups and different social and political perspectives. The continuity and insistence of those visuals around us make them influential even when we do not reflect consciously on their meanings.

The power of image placement to appropriate and construct social spaces was clear to me in my fieldwork research with activists in Egypt and Denmark. In 2016, I joined as a participant observer a group of activists in the Danish city of Aalborg. They had planned to go out at night and put up street posters advocating for welcoming refugees. This was in the wake of Europe receiving many Syrian refugees and the rise of anti-refugee sentiments in Denmark especially from nationalist right-wing groups. I was interested in seeing how they would plan to put the posters up in the city, what would be their strategies, how would they select where to place them and how. One of the activists, Joachim (a pseudonym), had just moved to Aalborg from a smaller city a year earlier for his university studies. In his first days in the city, he noticed many anti-Nazi posters in the city (Figure 6.2) communicating statements such as 'Nazi-free city' and 'no Nazis in our streets'. Joachim thought, 'that's a city I would like to live in'. He was well aware, he says, that this could be a small group of people who went around the whole city at night putting up those posters, but they managed to shape the city space with their opinion in a way that made Joachim feel he could belong in such a space. This influenced him to start doing similar urban interventions in his activism.

On the night when I joined the group, they were putting up pro-refugees posters while there were already some anti-refugee posters in the city. Some suggested that they should cover the hostile messages with their posters, but Joachim disagreed; he said, 'but we want to open a

Figure 6.2 These are some of the many street posters I took photos of in Aalborg, Denmark during 2015–2023. Text reads: (a) No Nazis in our streets (translated from Danish); (b) I hate Nazis; (c) Nazi-free city (translated from Danish).
Source: Author's photographs.

conversation rather than shut it down, we do not censor others' opinions, then we become like them. We should put our poster next to them and hope the passer-by reflects on both positions and choose where they stand.' Joachim's approach was dialogical in the sense that he wants his intervention to be an instance in a dialogue rather than a final say. However, this example overall tackles a relatively accessible medium for place appropriation, where passers-by can look, not look, cover a poster, or scratch it out. In less accessible media such as an urban billboard or news media, we do not get as much say in what is represented.

Image placements in the city, digital spaces, or inside our homes can influence what images we cannot help but see as we enter a house or a church, for example, versus images that we seek and look for. Image placement also informs how we are positioned to look: images could be placed in order for us to look up to them (e.g. an image of Jesus on a church wall), to be overwhelmed by (e.g. advertisement billboards in New York and Tokyo city centres), to be immersed in (e.g. a virtual reality experience), or to be in close contact with (e.g. a magazine portrait close-up image gazing at you).

6.2.1 Re-enacting by Placement

The placement and re-placement of an image can be significant for its affective power. An image that has lost its effect or has been neutralized in one place can be reborn and re-enacted by its re-placement elsewhere. For example, artist Ai Weiwei's re-placement of the refugee lifejackets from Lesbos Island to a visual installation in Copenhagen (see Chapter 5) re-enacts the magnitude of the humanitarian crisis and brings a geographically and psychological distant tragedy to be tangible, physical, and visible in a Danish city context.

An image can also re-enact a memory by the significance of its placement. Egyptian activists created stencil images of photographs of protestors being killed and placed the stencils in the physical location where the incidents happened to create an instant place reminder and an evidence marker of the memory (Awad & Wagoner, 2018). Also, in Berlin – as well as in other places across Europe – *Stolpersteine* or stumbling stones are created to commemorate Jewish life lost during the Holocaust. They are brass plaques planted in the streets and sidewalks of the city, in the location where the person's last known address was. The influence of what is seen in the urban space on collective memory often triggers controversy over who and what can be remembered and where should that memory be triggered. The debate in the USA over the removal of Confederate monuments and memorials is a clear example.

6.3 Space and Time

An image acquires meaning in relation to the specific time and space in which its social life unfolds. In addition to analysing what is 'in' the image and its material form, medium, and place, we need to also analyse the wider socio-historical context in which it acquires meaning, which includes the cultural, social, and political space, and the historical moment. If images are utterances in a dialogue, the extended environment helps us understand that ongoing societal dialogue that an image might be responding to or relying on to communicate a meaning. The same image of a raised red fist could be in one geographical space and historical time seen as a political act of opposition, in another a propaganda image by a ruling power, and in another a consumer image printed on a t-shirt devoid of political meaning.

A societal dialogue takes place in a certain public space, or public sphere. A public sphere in which societal dialogues and debates take place could be defined as a space – that can be a physical place, a virtual space, a social setting, or a medium – that provides a platform for information sharing and public opinion in relation to society's relevant, pressing, and possibly contested topics. Habermas (1974) has argued that an ideal public sphere can exist through the assembly of individuals in a society to discuss matters of common public interest, in a way that can mediate state power. He saw a potential in the development of newspapers, intellectual salons, book clubs, and different social circles, where public debate could take place among the liberal European and American middle classes of the eighteenth and nineteenth centuries. He imagined this ideal public sphere to be emblematic of participatory democracy, where rational discussion could flourish, public opinion be formulated, and the public interest would be prioritized over private interests. However, Habermas' vision of a public sphere was not exactly 'public', it was a sphere of white bourgeois men, excluding women, working-class people, and ethnic minorities (Sturken & Cartwright, 2018).

The public sphere where images circulate could be conceived instead as one that is marked by the struggle over visibility (Rancière, 2013). That public sphere is not a unified one, there is no 'one' public sphere in which all members of a society can debate and have their voice represented. Also, it is a public sphere with blurry boundaries with private spheres. As discussed in Chapter 1, even when we aim to analyse a debate or an image's social life that takes place on public platforms, it is important to realize the fluid nature between public and private spaces. The traditional division between public and private spheres is based on gender, race, and class ideologies that have long been challenged (Sturken & Cartwright, 2018). Critical theorist and political scientist Nancy Fraser (1990) argues that there are many publics and counter-publics that intersect, overlap, and work in tension with one another. She used the term counter-publics to refer to collectives that challenge and subvert mainstream public sphere by producing alternative forms of knowledge. This opens up meaningful ways to analyse what spheres the image circulates within, speaks to, or counters. One could look at opposition publics, feminist publics, working-class publics, different religions publics, and so on. This is not to say that these publics are homogenous within or that they do not overlap with other publics, but the purpose is rather to identify common ways of thinking, representing, and debating within different circles and communities. This could also show image transformation as they travel across different spheres, changing meaning and getting appropriated for different purposes. An analysis of the different spaces highlights the limits of what could be represented in each sphere and different ways of seeing.

6.3.1 Situating the Image within Contemporary Society

Other than the public space the image circulates within, we can also consider the historical, social, economic, technological, and cultural time that shapes our encounter with the image and we engage with it. This includes an understanding of contemporary visual culture and the place of the image within it, and how it has changed over time.

As a field of study, visual culture emerged around the 1980s as images and screens became central to entertainment and mass media (Sturken & Cartwright, 2018). Many of the field's theoretical approaches were derived from the field of cultural studies, which emerged around the 1960s in Britain and was dedicated to studying how cultural practices shape individuals and societies. The field of visual studies focuses on images within the different interconnected social realms of art, entertainment, news media, advertising, and science. Advancement in technology, especially after digital technology, has influenced a move away from traditional divisions in academic fields such as art history, film studies, and communication studies (Sturken & Cartwright, 2018).

Technological advancements in relation to the production and reception of visual culture have always been met with a mix of excitement, suspicion, and fear. Every new advancement comes with uncertainties. Some predicted that writing would destroy human memory and that computers would destroy cinema and sound recording (Mitchell, 2005). Cultural critic Walter Benjamin (1935) predicted changes in the value, physical qualities, and political function of art as a result of technologies of print and mass production. Mass media also has long been feared for its influence on society and culture, especially throughout the Cold War period (Sturken & Cartwright, 2018). Critique of mass media has especially focused on its role in producing propaganda and mass ideology especially by authoritarian and totalitarian regimes, such as the use of poster art and film by the Nazi regime in Germany. However, as Sturken and Cartwright (2018) argue, propaganda is not unique to totalitarian regimes; the role of mass media in repression of thought has a long and global history. For example, the American media industry by the mid twentieth century has established itself with a global reach and became a central mechanism in the dominance of the USA as a global superpower.

The rise of mass media has also influenced the industrialization and commercialization of culture, where art, for example, has become increasingly standardized and commodified. Frankfurt school theorists such as Max Horkheimer and Theodor Adorno applied Marxist ideas to study mass media's influence on culture in the post-war years, criticizing the capitalist and consumerist orientations of different media forms such as movies, television, and advertisement, and how they created a 'mass culture' that destroys critical thinking and exploits especially the working class as passive consumers (Horkheimer & Adorno, 2002). They argued that mass media obscures the realities of life in class society and makes conformity a tolerable and 'natural' way of living. The industries did not just create goods, like a movie or a shoe, but also created cultures and promoted certain lifestyles that continuously reproduce the capitalist class society. This reproduction is maintained as people consume different media representations and symbols that promote capitalist ideologies.

Though Horkheimer and Adorno's critique provides an important lens through which to understand the reproduction of capitalist ideas in mass media, it neglects the variety of ways in which people view media and appropriate its messages. Media in a globalized world can also facilitate active engagement and transformation of ideas. Anthropologist and post-colonial theorist Arjun Appadurai (1996) has challenged the idea that media is the opium of passive masses; he argued that active consumption of media throughout the world has in many times provoked anger and resistance rather than conformity and lack of agency. This goes in line with the critical psychological approach to images I present in this book. Unlike the classical crowd (Le Bon, 1896) and group psychology (Freud, 1922) that perceived masses as sensational, susceptible, and prey to manipulation by simplified repeated ideas that rely on visuals and emotions, critical approaches have looked at the different factors – especially in physical crowds – that can influence the attitudes and behaviours of the group, with a stronger emphasis on agency, minority influence, and identity group affiliations (Moscovici, 1976; Reicher, 2001).

The so-called information age and the development of the internet since the mid twentieth century pose new questions about the psychology of the masses, not only as active or passive receivers of visual culture but also as now co-producers of media. The overabundance of information in these new technologies also has its consequences on how people attend to and perceive what they see. As psychologist and economist Herbert Simon (1971) argues, in this information-rich world, the wealth of information means a scarcity of what this information consumes: our attention. The internet creates a new culture that changes the way we do things and why we do them, and what counts the most in this new space is what is most scarce, and that is attention (Goldhaber, 1997).

Digital media provides a central platform for this attention scarcity and poses a fundamental change to the public sphere discussed earlier. Literary critic and social theorist Michael Warner expands Habermas' conception of the public sphere to incorporate digital media developments (Warner, 2002). He conceptualizes a public as a space for discourse and exchange of ideas that involves a relation among strangers, where there is both personal and impersonal public speeches. He argues that one important aspect that constitutes a public is attention. Attention here is not just the cognitive quality of attending to something but is also the active uptake (by coming into range, showing up, and becoming a viewer of a certain medium) that makes one become part of a certain public. As we scroll through the internet, an image can solicit our gaze, communicate a 'look here', but this does not render us passive, rather it is our willingness to answer that call and attend to something that determines which publics we belong to (Warner, 2002).

Digital media has transformed the idea of masses, crowds, publics and counter-publics from physical sites of interaction like a coffee shop or a physical protest to an online space. Those mediated communication spaces could be in times as intensely personal and emotional as face-to-face interactions (Sturken & Cartwright, 2018). Digital cultures merge between cultures as lived and cultures as programmed digital spaces (Wiggins, 2019). Part of the Frankfurt School critique of mass media still applies on digital media: it reproduces capitalist cultures and lifestyles. However, digital media is distinct from mass media in that it is one of personalization, user-generated content, algorithm-shaped newsfeeds, and competition for attention.

The digital space provides new affordances for the image as an accessible and abundant tool for social action and knowledge exchange. With the cameras, computers, internet, and artificial intelligence, more people are able to be image producers and disseminators, and more spaces are open for image viewing and sharing. The accessibility means that there is also a massive increase in who produces and how much is produced, and therefore further scarcity of attention. There are more images shared today in an hour than the total images produced in all of the nineteenth century (Sturken & Cartwright, 2018). This speaks of a certain magnitude of a societal change in relation to visual culture.

The development in accessibility means that there are psychological, social, and political implications on how images mediate our relationship with others and the environment around us. Images do not stay put; we circulate them from one medium to another, change their meaning, and appropriate them for different personal and social purposes. This accessibility comes with its democratizing potential – we can see this in the growing role of citizen journalism and the growth of different counterpublics and social movements online. Social movements have always relied on available communication channels to advocate for their causes, such as pamphlets and manifestos; digital media provides today further communicative tools for social movements, that are interactive, less hierarchical, and more participatory (Castells, 2015). The technologies also allow the reversing of the top-down surveillance, allowing us to 'look back' at those in power and have more tools to reveal corruption and state violence (Thompson, 2005).

The democratizing potential of digital media has its constraints. Online spaces involve corporate ownerships, algorithms, advertisements, and other interventions that influence the circulation of ideas there. Similar to other aspects of social life, online spaces – and media more broadly – are part of the broader institutions and structures of power in society. There are clear differences in who has access to powerful visibility platforms that reach the masses. Even our taken-for-granted access to the internet and images online is not a given in every society. Communication scholar Toussaint Nothias (2020) shows how there are striking differences and inequalities in the cost of connectivity globally. Due to high internet costs, there is a growing use of services that filter the content of different websites, such as Facebook's so-called free internet. This type of access, also known as zero-rating, provides users with a text-only or 'visuals-lite' version of selected websites. He argues that the visual properties of these services show the ever-growing influence of Big Tech over journalism globally: by removing data-heavy content, these services visually construct silences, moderate the content as well as the form of journalism, and create a singular visual aesthetic that promotes certain tech companies (Nothias, 2020).

Digital media has also influenced a psychological change in what content attracts our attention and what practices we normalize. It has created a further fascination with the need to be seen and the interest in following other people in their everyday personal spaces, whether they are acquaintances, celebrities, or so-called social influencers. Here, one's image and lifestyle becomes a commodity and a source of content for the entertainment of others. This is also reflected in politics, having more politicians known for their appearances and their 'visual performances' rather than their arguments or their political actions. US president Donald Trump is one example of such a politician who acts in performative and exaggerate ways that generate viral content on digital media. Similarly, far-right politician Rasmus Paludan in Denmark is known for his viral videos and images burning the Islamic holy book (Quran) in different Danish and Swedish cities.

Politicians and leaders have always used visual technologies to promote themselves. This has been always the case with paintings and photographs of those in power. Television technologies have also been used to turn politics and news into consumable visuals, making figures such as former US president Roland Reagan known more as a visual symbol than for what he said (Postman, 1986). Digital media and its practices, however, have further influenced the prominence of visuals and representations in politics over rational argumentative verbal content, which has facilitated the popularity and appeal of politicians such as Trump and Paludan.

Middle Eastern studies scholar Walter Armbrust (2019) refers to those politicians as political tricksters, who attract by their lack of commitment to normative cultures, transcending boundaries in what they say, how they appear, and what they do. Those kinds of politicians have always existed, but now they can flourish and gain popularity more than ever. The digital space affords this kind of exaggerated performance, spectacle, and drama, it grabs attention in short sensational bites, and deviates the viewer away from taking what is seen seriously or reflectively, or going beyond it to hear what the politician's arguments and ideologies actually mean. These factors explain the growing utilization of provocative visual content by far-right groups (Awad et al., 2022; Özvatan & Forchtner, 2019; Richardson & Wodak, 2009), and their strategies to modernize traditional far-right imagery to gain popularity especially among youth (Doerr, 2021; Klein & Muis, 2019; Schober, 2020).

It appears that our current visual culture promotes these performance-based politics, that politicians who do not play this game are seen as unique cases. In a study using visual discourse analysis, sociologists and communication scholars Julia Sonnevend and Olivia Steiert (2022) show how former chancellor of Germany Angela Merkel has come to stand for the opposite in relation to attention-seeking personal profiles on social media. Her visual appearances have been consistently ordinary with no reliance on emotional aspects of representation. Despite the limited charm and deliberate dullness in her visual performances, she built a reputation for her rational decision-making and pragmatic approach, moving away from the visual political performances of contemporary digital cutlure and of the German Nazi past (Sonnevend & Steiert, 2022).

Investigating the environemnt of the image and the place of the image in contemporary society can help us understand what subject positions are desirable and popular in the visual culture, and what kind of images attract, promote trust, and have a chance for visibility in digital and material spaces.

6.4 Methods: Photo Documentation

One method that is especially relevant to exploring the environment of the image and its ability to proclaim spaces is that of photo documentation. It can help trace how power is spatialized in certain places and how this changes over time.

Photo documentation is one way of using images as a research tool, where the researcher is also an image producer and documenter, rather than only working with found images. It can be used to analyse a particular visual phenomenon, to understand social relations in a specific place, to convey a certain feel of a certain landscape, or to capture part of the sensory richness and human inhabitation of urban and physical environments (Rose, 2016). Photo documentation as a method does not belong to one specific theoretical tradition but rather is used differently by different approaches and based on the research purpose. One tradition, however, that has developed its use is that of visual ethnography (Pink, 2021).

Visual ethnography draws on different fields of study such as anthropology, visual sociology, visual and cultural studies, media studies, and human geography. It is a research practice that involves engagement with visual and digital methods to create participatory and situated new ways of knowing. In *Visual Ethnography*, anthropologist Sarah Pink (2021) presents photo documentation as one way through which we can engage in the social, material, and infrastructural environments we research and the social practices associated with them. Photo documentation can invite us to view spaces around us in a different way, seeing what might go unnoticed, and bringing attention to certain aspects of the environments we study. It is therefore important to have a reflexive stance in using this method by considering our position as photographers in particular settings; how we frame and select certain images, the purpose for our documentation, the academic, institutional, or interventionist goals we might have, and the power relations in the settings we photograph.

This method has been used for a variety of research purposes. Photographic surveys of the material environment have been used in ethnography to capture artefacts of certain significance or symbolic meaning (Collier & Collier, 1986; Gómez Cruz, 2016; Young & MacDowall, 2017). The method has been also used to capture the lived experience of participants in psychiatric settings using the researcher's own photographing (Duque et al., 2019), or by asking participants to take their own photos of the space (Reavey et al., 2019). The method is also especially helpful in tracing changes over time. Longitudinal photo documentation of city walls has been used to study graffiti and street art as instances in an ongoing dialogue over time (Awad, 2021; Hansen & Flynn, 2015) and in tracing gradual changes in a city space, such as that of gentrification processes (Rieger, 2011; Suchar, 1997). The method has been also used in combination with go-along walking interview (Kusenbach, 2003), ethnographic walking tours (Irving, 2010), and psychogeography walking methods (Bridger, 2010; Hayes, 2003) to explore the urban lived experience.

Based on the research purpose and the photo documentation tool selected, one could then consider what are useful ways to organize, archive, interpret, and present the images as part of the knowledge production. Here the images are treated in their own right as a way of knowing, rather than as mere visual documentations that need to be 'translated' into words (Pink, 2021). The interpretation process is often done collaboratively with participants, especially if the method is combined with interviews. The interpretation involves situating the moment in which the images were made and the relations between the image body and the human body of the image taker and viewer (MacDougall, 2005).

6.5 A Graffiti Image: A Thousand *Fucks*

> I saw another 'Fuck you' on the wall. I tried to rub it off with my hand again, but this one was scratched on, with a knife or something. It wouldn't come off. It's hopeless, anyway. If you had a million years to do it in, you couldn't rub out even half the 'Fuck you' signs in the world. It's impossible ... You can't ever find a place that's nice and peaceful, because there isn't any. You may think there is, but once you get there, when you're not looking, somebody'll sneak up and write 'Fuck you' right under your nose ...
> – Holden Caulfield in J. D. Salinger's *The Catcher in the Rye*, 1951

Images we take in our fieldwork can build narratives, develop understandings, and help us notice certain patterns in our environments. Researching the topic of urban images for a long time has shaped my selective attention to little posters and tags in the streets I encounter. So, in a way, other than specific research projects, the interest in urban images became part of my everyday way of seeing and walking through any urban space. Photographing different urban images has become an ongoing exercise

6.5 A Graffiti Image: A Thousand Fucks

wherever I go, leading to a huge archive that is organized by place and time. One pattern that caught my eye in my graffiti archive is the different common signs and expressions often used in the subculture of graffiti across cultures; for example, tagging behaviours and tagging's different competitive placements on trains or on the top of buildings. Also, the adaptations of common graffiti statements such as *ACAB* (all cops are bastards) across different contexts and the many *fuck* statements used in graffiti.

For more than ten years I have been photo documenting *fuck* graffiti and building up an archive dedicated to the use of *fuck* in graffiti and what subjects and images are commonly associated with it in different locations across Africa, Europe, Asia, South America, and the USA. This developed into more of an art project rather than a research project, though the lines are often blurry in working with images. I work towards developing an archive entitled 'A thousand *fucks* from around the world: what do people give a *fuck* about?'

The graffiti of 'Fuck Wars' I started the chapter with is part of this collection. Many other *fucks* graffiti (Figure 6.3) express different frustrations with and objections to different issues (e.g. cancer, nations, gender) and people (e.g. hipsters, Putin, Trump, the police). In what follows, I elaborate on one *fuck* graffito that is from a familiar research field and one that affords a further understanding of how images can inscribe and appropriate urban space.

The graffiti image in Figure 6.4 is from a series of images following the same wall over the period from 2011 to 2019. According to the different types of datasets presented in Chapter 5, this one is from a *space-specific dataset* and following the longitudinal photo documentation method (Hansen & Flynn, 2015). The layers of graffiti in this image provide a good example of the significance of the environment for the meaning of the image, both in terms of the placement in the physical environment, as well as the broader sociopolitical environment. The image is also part of a contested dialogue in the public space about the Egyptian revolution and its representation. The photograph shows one instance in this dialogue that extended from urban to digital space. For a further analysis of other instances in the dialogue on this wall, see Awad (2021).

Figure 6.4 shows a heart, with wings, and an open key chain. A speech bubble coming out of the heart reads 'unlock your passion'. The image colours with the bright orange background are in striking contrast to the layers of paint surrounding it and to the often grey city landscape of Cairo. Underneath this painting there are traces of an older mural (see the eye on

Figure 6.3   These are some of the many *fuck* graffiti images I have taken photographs of: (a) *Fuck Cancer*, Aalborg, Denmark, July 2019; (b) *Fuck Nations. Squat the World*, Chania, Athens, June 2016; (c) *Fuck Hipsters*, Berlin, Germany, January 2017; (d) *Fuck Putin*, Copenhagen, Denmark, April 2017; (e) *Fuck your Gender*, Eichstätt, Germany, June 2022; (f) *Fuck Trump*, New York, USA, August 2017; (g) *Fuck the Cops*, Geneva, Switzerland, March 2015; (h) *Fuck Politiet* (the police), Aalborg, Denmark, July 2022; (i) *Fuck Cops*, Reykjavík, Iceland, October 2022.
Source: Author's photographs.

top) that is part of what became known as the street art of the revolution. On top of this seemingly uplifting heart painting, someone spray painted the statement: 'we're locked in a counter revolution, *fuck* you and your passion'.

The environment of this image helps us understand the complex visual dialogues taking place on the wall. The photograph of the wall was captured in 2015. This is a time that followed significant sociopolitical events: the Egyptian revolution of 2011, the Muslim Brotherhood-elected president in 2012, and the military coup in 2013, followed by El-Sisi becoming president in 2014. The political public space in 2015 was shaped by counter-revolution measures to bring back control to the new government; those measures included the suppression and arrest of revolution as well as Muslim Brotherhood voices. Those political turbulences were inscribed and spatialized in the different urban spaces in the country (Nagate & Stryker, 2013).

6.5 A Graffiti Image: A Thousand Fucks

Figure 6.4 The graffiti on this wall show layers of different images and texts covering one another. A revolution street art painting is covered by a winged heart painting, that is further spray painted over with the text 'we're locked in a counter revolution, *fuck* you and your passion'. I took this photograph in the Tahrir Square area in Cairo, Egypt in May 2015.
Source: Author's photograph.

The graffiti painting's placement is on a wall in Mohamed Mahmoud Street, close to Tahrir Square in Cairo. In 2011, the street became a central location for the revolution street art paintings. It was where the Nefertiti image with the gas mask (discussed in Chapter 4) first appeared. The street also witnessed some of the violent clashes between protestors and authority forces, which were documented through paintings on the walls to commemorate those who lost their lives. Many studies have shown the role street art played in the representation and commemoration of the Egyptian revolution and how it was used to challenge the authority's control over visual representation in the public space (see, e.g., Abaza, 2014; Abdelmagid, 2013; C. Smith, 2015).

In the time of the image, the public space has been fully reclaimed by authority. No more revolution street art images were tolerated and the whole area of Tahrir Square went through a major renovation that erased many of the revolution traces (Awad, 2017). The painting of the heart does not belong to the same genre of revolution street art that was done independently by activists. The painting was part of the project Women on Walls (WOW), which is funded by the Swedish Institute and the Danish Centre for Culture and Development. Dina Saad was part of this project, and she painted the heart image as her own artistic expression of women's empowerment.

However, the placement of the image was seen by some activists as oblivious to the history of the street and the social political context, hence the response to it by the spray-canned statement. The WOW image, if placed in a different environment, could have been received as an uplifting and possibly a feminist message. In this location and time, however, it was perceived by many activists as yet another way of censoring the revolution street art. The government was continuously whitewashing any political statements on walls, and here was a funded project replacing revolution street art and its memory by new messages that are oblivious to the history of the place.

This contested dialogue took place on the wall, as well as on social media, as the graffiti image was photographed and posted on different platforms. The WOW project artists, objecting activists, and others joined the dialogue to defend or attack the image and the sprayed statement in response to it. The social life of this wall, and specifically this image, reveals something about the censoring and destruction of images. The authorities censored revolution images by whitewashing them from city walls and arresting activists. The WOW project, as well as other gentrification projects in Tahrir Square, symbolically destroyed the revolution's visual traces by commodifying them and changing their meaning. Here, in this image, the '*fuck* your passion' statement symbolically destroys the meaning of the heart image by revealing its obliviousness and misplacement.

CHAPTER 7

The Viewing of the Image

Figure 7.1 The image of the Muslim woman in a headscarf (hijab) or a face cover (niqab/burqa) has become a strong symbol of difference in Europe.
Source: This photograph is used as an illustrative example. It was taken by Engin Akyurt and is shared for free use through pixabay.com. Engin_Akyurt/pixaby.com

The image in Figure 7.1 is especially used in European far-right visual communication to mark the difference between the European identity and the foreign *other* who poses a cultural threat to European values. The image is often used to position Muslim women as a de-individualized homogenous unchanging minority group.

The image, when used by the far right, invites a European gaze that can look at this woman as an embodiment of irreconcilable and pathologic difference. As I will argue with further examples in this chapter, there are reasons why this image is a popular one for mobilizing viewers' attitudes and emotions against migration.

Image viewing is integral to the image's meaning and social life. All through the previous three chapters, the social life of the image was explored through its producer and production process, its body and composition, and its environment. However, an image's public social life is only actualized as it encounters its first viewers. It is in this encounter that the intentions of the producer and meanings inscribed in the body of the image take on their own social life as the image is encountered by different viewers in different environments. Once the image is out in the world, its life is in the hand of infinite viewers who might look at it, look away, appropriate it, reconstruct its meaning, or attempt at censoring it.

The social position of an image viewer is not distinct or separate from that of an image producer. Already as an image is produced, the producer creates it with certain viewers in mind – including their own self. The image production process involves the act of viewing an artefact as it is being created, whether it is a painting, a photograph, or a graphic design, and modifying it in relation to how it looks to the producer. The social position of the 'viewer' is not one that is set by an image producer or limited to one environment such as a museum. Today an image is produced for an indefinite range of potential viewers (Thompson, 2005), who will encounter it in its social life throughout different spaces. The viewer position is critical to some image genres that only come into being when the viewer takes their position. For example, for an image to be a digital meme, viewers must respond to it, interact with it, and share or transform it (Wiggins, 2019). This does not mean, however, that the viewer position is more significant or can take over that of the producer.

In Mikhail Bakhtin's dialogic understanding, the viewer does not replace the author; any artefact exists in a context involving both the producer and the viewer (Haynes, 1995). Both positions are necessary to fully understand the – unfinalized – meaning and the social life of an image. Both positions are also important to understand how creation, compositional elements, and placement of an image can call upon or exclude a certain viewer and a certain viewing position. As media and communication scholar Marion Müller argues, image viewing and interpretation competencies are connected with image production in a cycle that is embedded in a social, political, and cultural context (Müller, 2008).

Viewing is a process of meaning (re)construction from a specific social position, that is influenced by who the viewers are and how they see. It is

The Viewing of the Image 149

also influenced by the environment, as viewing is a situated act that is shaped by the material and social space that shapes the possibilities of viewing and affords certain normative ways of viewing and interpretation. We look in a socially and historically shaped field of exchange, where meaning is co-constructed and influenced by different factors such as culture, history, sexuality, class, ethnicity, and time period (Sturken & Cartwright, 2018). Similar to all human thinking, viewing is also a dialogical act, that involves seeing and interpreting in dialogue with the eyes of others – how we think the image would be viewed and recognized by others.

This dialogical and interpretative meaning-making process of a viewer goes against an assumption of a linear transmission between a producer and a targeted predefined audience. Early research on audience relied on the idea that meaning is transmitted in a linear process from the sender (producer) to the receivers (viewers) and tried to study the direct effect of media on its 'receivers' (Rose, 2016). This idea has also influenced the focus of psychological studies on the influence of media (Forrester, 2000). Many psychological studies investigate a causal relation between what we see and how we act, looking at the negative effects of exposure to violent media, for example, or investigating the effectiveness of advertising images in influencing buying behaviours, rather than how different individuals use and interpret the visuals differently, and how those visuals afford diverse ways of interpretation and action.

The question of how much of a passive or active viewer we are is a complex one. On the one hand, present-day viewing habits and practices (e.g. online scrolling and oversaturation of images) move the viewers away from being active reflective interpreters, to being shallow consumers who are easily swayed and polarized by the material they are exposed to. On the other hand, even when we are not consciously engaged reflectively with an image, the mere idea of perception involves some form of action. As argued earlier, in Chapter 3, perception is not something that happens to us but something that we do that involves some level of embodied and situated thoughtful activity (Gibson, 1979; Noë, 2005). Psychology of visual perception has moved away from the traditional idea of visual processing as a coding process based on stimuli reception, to looking at the cognitive constructivist processes mediating perception (Forrester, 2000). Seeing always involves some form of interpretation (Gregory, 1997) and some form of choice and motivation that shape our attention (Lauwereyns, 2012). Yet again, our visual perception is also influenced by the environment and its affordances. This does not make us passive receptors, but it does pose the question of how digital scrolling culture, thirty-second videos, attention-diverting 'pop-ups', and visual oversaturation promote certain ways and habits of viewing, while inhibiting others.

Building on a sociocultural psychological approach, I argue that images are actively reappropriated by viewers, and therefore the meaning of an image is in a continuous process of reconstruction by different social actors encountering it. Viewing is a dialogical social act of interpretation that involves reconstructing the signs in the image, constituting them with new meanings and values in a cognitive and affective process (Lonchuk & Rosa, 2011). This process redefines who the image viewers are and expands what arguments and counter-arguments the image communicates (Lonchuk & Rosa, 2011). Even the most saturated and banal images – that we might view with less attention – do not have a stable or permanent meaning: they are continuously exposed to multisensory interpretation and apprehension (Mitchell, 1986). The image of a flag, for example, could go from a banal familiar symbol in the social environment that operates mindlessly, to becoming a salient hot symbol in times of unrest and wars (Billig, 1995). In the context of the Egyptian revolution, the political and social developments following 2011 changed the meaning of the flag from opposition and protest to government support (Awad, 2017).

Given this conceptualization of viewing, I use the term viewers and the act of looking and seeing, rather than the term audience that has been associated more with the idea of a passive audience that is receiving the media targeting it. Viewers rather than audience as a concept highlights the individual situated activity and social practice of looking (Sturken & Cartwright, 2018). Arguing that viewing is not passive does not mean that every viewing is an active intentional thoughtful process or that we engage with every image we encounter in everyday life. Viewing is a learned social practice that takes place in an environment that influences how much we can attend to what. We are socialized to attend to certain images, to stop at images that intrigue us or talk to our desires, and look away from images that make us uncomfortable. We also respond to our overly saturated environment, by looking less, paying less attention to regulate all the overstimulation, moving it to the 'background' of our environment in daily life. Today's visual culture promotes this practice of skimming (e.g. through dating apps looking for potential matches, through shopping websites, and through the city that is overpopulated with images). The interesting part here is that we still 'see' those images, and they might be even more critical to investigate than the images people 'stop' at and remember, because those background images develop quickly into a common sense, a normalization of phenomenon, without intentional engagement with them. There is a fine balance here between seeing viewers as active interpretative social actors, who can constructively interpret images and counter-argue their meaning, and at the same time acknowledge the power of visibility, propaganda, and repeated exposure (see Chapter 3) in normalizing certain social representations and discourses.

To address this balance, I distinguish in the social act of viewing when people intentionally *look* and when they *look away*, and how social positions, socialization, and the environment shape certain ways of looking, a certain gaze.

7.1   Practices of Looking and Looking Away

As visual theorist Nicholas Mirzoeff shows, looking is different to simply seeing things – looking is a social practice and an act of exchange between self and others where it can establish solidarity and recognition or social dominance (Mirzoeff, 2011). The act of seeing is constituted through histories of knowledge, power, and domination (Berger, 1972). Looking is implicated in the dynamics of power; we are allowed to look at certain images, restricted from others, and we can choose to look at what is concealed in an act of defiance. This relational and dialogical aspect of viewing is always there whether we look in private or public and whether the image is personal (family photo), technical (medical image), or public (news photo) (Sturken & Cartwright, 2018).

Cognitive and neuropsychological studies show that there is intentionality in what we look at and selectivity in what we pay attention to as we look (Chapter 3). Our looking is shaped by motivation, what we find relevant, important, or interesting, and even when we choose to look our attention to what we are looking at is highly selective and biased, possibly blocking out salient information that does not match our intention of looking (Lauwereyns, 2012). Eye movement studies show that the way our eyes scan an image is often dependent on the information we are seeking to extract from the image (Mather, 2014). Research looking at fixation patterns in images shows that viewers often fixate on the most salient part of an image, areas with high density of features or high contrast. Another pattern found in this line of research is that faces and eyes in an image are often powerful attractors of attention (Mather, 2014). This could explain the emotional potency of portraits of political and religious leaders throughout history and their use to mobilize action (e.g. consider the famous First World War poster with Lord Kitchener starting straight to the viewer with a pointed finger, asking British men to join the army). In fact, our eyes are attracted to seeing faces to the extent that we often see faces in objects that do not have any, such as seeing the face of Jesus in a grilled cheese sandwich. There are groups on social media platforms dedicated to sharing such images, such as the Facebook group Faces of the World that invites members to share pictures of 'everything in this world that resembles a face'.

Even though these are some of the usual predictors of where we look and what attracts our attention, they are not always good predictors of looking, because looking is always depending on the meaning of the image to the viewer, who the viewer is, and what is the context of viewing. The image of the woman in a headscarf in Figure 7.1 would probably attract much less attention in a Muslim majority country where this is a normalized practice; in such a context the attention of the viewer could be on what the woman is looking at rather than the woman herself. Practices of looking and looking away go beyond the cognitive and neuro dynamics of looking, to also involve the subject position of who is looking and who is being looked at, and the public space that mediates the looking. Our experience and socialization shape what we consider worthy of looking at and what details we are attentive to. Looking is also influenced by the affordances of the environment surrounding us (Gibson, 1979), what is readily available, what is given prominence and visibility, and what is made invisible. In a visual culture saturated with images, there will be always some form of attention scarcity (Chapter 6). We only have a limited capacity to what we can attend to and what we can look at, and those producing images are striving to win that attention. The act of clicking on an image and the amount of time we look at an image while scrolling online are used to inform stakeholders about how they can best grab our attention.

Since our looking is intentional and the environment can only afford or inhibit certain ways of seeing but cannot dictate where we look, there is always a choice of looking away and of seeking to look at images that are not made readily visible, images that are made absent. One can seek out censored images and can (re)produce them in an act of defiance. One can be offended by what one sees and decide to censor or report an image so that it is not seen by others. Alternatively, one can decide to disengage with certain images, stop looking, and render them to the background of one's everyday life. Redundant images of advertisements, social media, or news could lead one to look in the other direction, turn off the screen, or unfollow certain news. Provoking images that are meant to attract our attention can also lead us to eventually look away if the image makes us uncomfortable or leaves us feeling helpless.

7.2 The Gaze and the 'Other'

Like all other social practices, looking involves power relations. We look at images from a certain social position and images position us in relation to their placement and what is portrayed in the image. Our experiences in the world are shaped by how we engage in this positioning that is inherent in the social practice of looking.

Image interpretation involves an act of argumentation and social positioning (B. Davies & Harré, 1990). The viewers do not just respond to what the image portrays but they position themselves from the arguments they imagine the image to be saying (Lonchuk & Rosa, 2011). Social positioning highlights the dynamic aspect of social encounters, where we position ourselves and are positioned in different contexts in relation to others. One could take up the position the image is suggesting, for example that of a buyer who desires the idea or the lifestyle that an advertisement image is selling. One could also contest and resist the positioning and look at the advertisement from the position of a critic rather than a buyer.

Social identities (social class, gender, ethnicity, nationality, etc.) can all inform which positions we are socialized into and can perform. Through socialization we learn how to see, what to look at, and how to interpret what we see around us. Sociologist Pierre Bourdieu's (1984) concept of *habitus* shows how growing up in a certain social class shapes our taste and informs a certain way of being in and seeing the world. In his study of museum visitors, he argues that to be acknowledged as 'proper' middle class, one has to know how to 'appreciate' art and how to perform that appreciation adequately in the setting (Bourdieu, 1984; Bourdieu et al., 1991). To take up the 'right' viewing position of a museum art piece, one needs to know and follow the code: *No touching, no talking, contemplate in quiet awe, walk slowly from one image to the next, don't skim, dress right, and no popcorn please.* Further studies into digital space show how our taste and way of looking today are not only influenced by our habitus but also shaped by digital media algorithms (Beer, 2013).

Looking into the social identities of the viewer informs how certain images manage to 'talk' to certain people, how they manage to 'reach' a certain viewer better than others. It also highlights how our taste and interpretation is influenced by who we are, what we find relatable, desirable, or distasteful and repelling. Certain images appeal to us because they represent us or they represent who we want to be. This could lead to an experience of resonance and belonging in what we see. This could also lead to a never-ending yearning after what we see and want but cannot have, be it a 'perfect' body, material possession, or lifestyle sold by an advertiser or a social media influencer.

We do not only look at what resembles us and what we want to be, but we are also attracted to looking at what is different from us. Images portraying some form of distinction of certain social identities or portraying social difference, attract a certain way of seeing, where we are not just looking at what is in the image but at the relation between what and who is in the image and ourselves (Berger, 1972). This is clear in the European far-right use of images of Muslim women wearing headscarves or face covers. Images of social difference rely on portraying the *others*, those who are – in any value-significant way – different from the dominant or powerful group. Images of the *other* often rely on sharply opposed, polarized, and binary extremes – good/bad, civilized/primitive, capable/dependent (Hall, 1997a). Those images are often not about the people themselves but about their 'otherness', marking their difference (Hall, 1997a).

Cultural theorist Stuart Hall (1997a) argues there are different linguistic, social, cultural, and psychoanalytical arguments for the fascination with the representation of otherness. Building on de Saussure's linguistics, he argues that difference matters because linguistically it is essential to meaning. Meaning is relational; we know of black not because of an essence in blackness but because it is contrasted with its opposite: white. It is the difference between white and black that signifies, that carries meaning. Those binaries are rarely neutral or power-free oppositions, as philosopher Jacques Derrida (1972) argues – one side of the binary is usually the dominant one through which the other binary is defined. Socially, we need difference because we can only construct meaning through a dialogue with the *other*. As Bakhtin (1981) argues, meaning is sustained in dialogue, it does not belong to one speaker, and there is no one final meaning, so there is always a struggle over meaning. From a societal perspective, binary oppositions are crucial for the classificatory system of any society. It brings order to classify and create symbolic boundaries between the different categories. It defines the normative versus the forbidden, the taboo, and the threat to the cultural order. From a psychoanalytical perspective, the other is fundamental to the constitution of the self and its construction as a subject.

This goes in line with social psychological and cognitive factors that drive our attention to the other. We identify ourselves through groups, our social identity is constructed around our knowledge that we belong in certain social groups with certain norms, and we set certain emotional and value significance on these group memberships (Tajfel & Turner, 1978). As we categorize ourselves in these groups, we do not only identify within an 'in-group', but we do so in opposition to an 'out-group', to which we compare ourselves and seek positive distinction from. Thus, our social identities influence our practices of looking at difference and our positioning in relation to the image and to others. Those social identities also influence who is granted the power of being in a viewing subject position – the subject that looks – and who is positioned as the object of the gaze – the other.

The concept of the gaze captures the power relation involved in looking. The concept has been used within visual culture and feminist studies to explore who is able to see whom and with what effects (Rose, 2016). A gaze is a kind of a look, a sustained intentional way of looking rather than a glance, where one turns one's gaze upon certain objects, people, or places (Sturken & Cartwright, 2018). Some would also define a gaze as a field, rather than an individual act of looking, a field that includes objects, technologies, built and natural environments, as well as other people 'who are either present and looking with us (or at us), or those who we imagine to have looked before or are looking simultaneously at the same image elsewhere, perhaps in a different place or next to us but on a different screen' (Sturken & Cartwright, 2018, p. 103).

Art critic John Berger (1972) in his book *Ways of Seeing* identified a clear distinction between how men and women were represented in his analysis of European classic paintings. He argued that the different representations invited different gazes. Men were positioned as the ones who act and look, while women were positioned as the ones to be looked at. Feminist and film theorist Laura Mulvey (1975) similarly showed the dominance of heterosexual male perspectives in the media and used the term male gaze to refer to this unbalanced power between the man observer and the woman being observed.

Much has changed in the male gaze-dominated visual culture those studies explored – and some aspects have also sustained. Today, the binary distinction between a man and a woman subject is challenged, and men are not necessarily the dominating power behind production of media or are the main consuming viewers of this media. This requires a revision of what kind of gaze dominates the production and viewership of images today. One could look, for example, at the different examples in which the male gaze is contested by counter-images and how men's bodies are portrayed and sexualized (Gill, 2011). In my observation, the images in today's consumer society are designed less for a specific male gaze perspective, and more for the gaze of whoever the potential consumer could be. Marketers are fast to adapt their images to represent different minorities and different social positions that can resonate with the growing diverse groups of consumers.

7.3 The Right to Look Back

Challenging the established ways of looking becomes then a site of resistance and reconstruction of meaning in society. Looking from the place of the other, as psychoanalyst and philosopher Frantz Fanon (1986) argues, fixes us by its violence, hostility, and even ambivalence of its desires. We can learn to look differently, to practise what social critic and feminist scholar bell hooks (2001) refers to as an oppositional gaze. This could be in choosing to look back critically instead of accepting the established way of looking and instead of accepting being the passive object of spectatorship. hooks shows how the gaze has been a site of resistance for colonized black people globally, developing a critical gaze that looks, documents, and opposes. One can relearn to look in a certain way to resist established power relations and to challenge the way image producers position us to look.

Practices of looking back can be in the process of interpretation, when one takes a reflective look to interpret an image and reflect on the social actors shaping a certain representation and the discourses, stereotypes, and social structures that normalize certain ways of seeing. Cultural historian and feminist Annette Kuhn (1988) explains how this could be experienced as a pleasurable process of resistance in analysis as one deconstructs meaning and reads against the grain. It is the pleasure of saying no to being a passive audience and to the structures of power that expect us to consume in an uncritical and highly circumscribed way.

Practices of looking back could be also in the use of image tools and technologies to look back at those in power. Image technologies can allow – to some extent – the reversing of the top-down surveillance – where we are continuously looked at and watched – to also 'look back' at those in power (Thompson, 2005). This is clear in the different instances where people use their phone camera to document the – otherwise hidden – practices of those in power and share them to be viewed publicly, exposing state corruption and violence. This practice could be seen as a form of visual activism and *countervisuality* (Mirzoeff, 2011, 2016), where people confront a certain invisibility and affirm their 'right to look' and their right to defy a visuality in which looking is deployed by the powerful as a means of repression.

7.4 Methods: Viewers' Engagement

There are several research questions one could ask about the viewer: their position, how they see, what attracts their attention, and the feelings, memories, or attitudes an image evokes for them. These research questions guide the choice of which methods can best answer the question.

In my previous research on the revolution street art in Egypt mentioned in Chapter 4, I supplemented my interviews with graffiti artists with interviews of pedestrians to see how the images were noticed and perceived in the street (Awad, 2017). The approach was similar to that described earlier of qualitative semi-structured interviews combined with either photo elicitation (Harper, 2002) or the go-along walking interview method (Kusenbach, 2003). The go-along is an ethnographic method that is used to capture the spatial practices and to get a situated embodied perspective, triggering space-specific memories. I used this qualitative approach to explore how the different revolution and government images were perceived by pedestrians and how did the pedestrians recall and make sense of the images' transformations. The results showed how even though the images triggered the same memories for participants, the specific reconstructions of those memories and the narratives they produced varied greatly based on the political position of the viewer rather than the position the image was promoting. The method was useful in unfolding those dynamics and hearing participants as they remembered, interpreted different parts of the images, and connected images to what was going on in their life and in society at large at the time. The results also showed how, in a continuously changing urban environment, participants did not notice several significant changes even when those changes had sentimental value for them (Awad, 2017).

For instance, the engagement of viewers in the interview with the Nefertiti image presented in Chapter 4 (Figure 4.1) mediated a dialogue about the position of the viewers regarding the protests and the role of women within protests more generally. For some, it represented the proud role of women in the Egyptian revolution. For others, it was a reminder of the vulnerable and violent position women protesters put themselves into.

The interviews unfolded the processes by which viewers positioned themselves from the arguments they perceived the image to be posing, and how they constructed arguments and counterarguments in their interpretation process. Qualitative interviews can also inform how people respond emotionally to certain images. In a study about visual representations of climate change, interviews and focus groups methods showed that fear-inducing images make people recognize the significance of the climate crisis but it also makes them feel disempowered to act in response to it (O'Neill & Nicholson-Cole, 2009).

Viewers' engagement with images could be also investigated quantitatively and experimentally. There is a long tradition in psychology of using experimental settings to understand how people perceive images. Those methods could compare how people perceive the same information with and without images. For example, Schmuck and Matthes (2017) used a survey experiment to test the effect of portrayals of immigrants as an economic and symbolic threat in the Austrian context in visuals versus text alone. Their study shows that it is especially in visuals that both threats had an influence on anti-immigration attitudes and stereotypes. These methods can also explore the affective response and engagement with different images online. In one study, Casas and Williams (2019) investigated the mobilizing role of online images in relation to social movements. They looked specifically at images posted on Twitter in relation to Black Lives Matter protests. They operationalized viewer engagement online through looking at attention and diffusion through different numbers of 'retweet' data on Twitter. Image contents were coded for the emotional mechanism they provoke (anger, enthusiasm, fear, sadness, and disgust) and for their social collective identity mechanism (containing protest symbols). Their results highlight especially the role of enthusiasm and fear images in predicting engagement. In another study, computational data analysis was used to investigate the affective economy of images of the Finnish far right on Facebook, showing how the images catalyse and mobilize through affects, especially fear, anger, and resentment (Hokka & Nelimarkka, 2019).

Quantitative methods are especially useful in studying digital big visual data and their online engagement. Those methods can show which images grab attention more than others, the engagement with and circulation of viral images, and how certain image contents promote certain ways of engagement with an image. There is a growing attention on developing digital and computational methods (e.g. image recognition software) to address specifically digital data including images, and on developing methodologies that align with the critical and interpretive approaches within humanities (Van Es et al., 2018). New media and digital culture scholar Richard Rogers (2024) argues that digital objects are best analysed using digital techniques that utilize the way in which data is organized online (e.g. using datestamps, hits, hyperlinks, or tags). Especially in terms of image circulation, digital methods can be used to investigate circulation within a platform, cross-platform circulation, and the convergence culture of online spaces, and to investigate the algorithms shaping what images appear in what kind of image searches (Rose, 2016).

Those tools afford many possibilities, but one should also consider their limitations and how far we can explore through them the complex psychological dynamic of how people interact with and use digital media. There is also a limitation in how much those tools can inform us about who the viewers are. In digital spaces viewers can be in many cases anonymous; we can get information about how many engage in certain ways, but we might lose the diversity of who are those numbers, what are their background, motives, and ways of seeing that are shaped by their social class, ethnicity, or gender, for example. There are also many ethical concerns with how digital data is analysed by researchers and by companies, and how consent and anonymization can be achieved with big visual data. The 'viewers' online are not only humans but also machines running our photographs through image-recognition software, our statuses through sentiment analysis programs, and our health data through risk indication assessments. This affects not only what companies know about us and how they use it to influence us, but also this affects how we learn to see ourselves through those technologies (Rettberg, 2014).

7.5 A Political Campaign Image: The Woman in the Veil

Recent research shows how the rising Western far-right movements utilize images of the 'other' in their online communication to mobilize followers (O. Klein & Muis, 2019; Yurdakul & Korteweg, 2021) and how they construct a visual boundary between the in-group 'we' identity in opposition to the invading non-European 'other' through provocative visual content (Doerr, 2021; Özvatan & Forchtner, 2019; Richardson & Wodak, 2009). Together with colleagues, I have researched this in relation to the Danish People's Party (Dansk Folkeparti, or DF) and its use of images to construct ideas of *Danishness* and *otherness* (Awad et al., under review; Awad et al., 2022; Nissen et al., 2021). In our previous studies, we looked at the party's visuals in its social media posts, newsletters, and street campaign posters. We utilized a variety of approaches which included theoretical schematic narrative (Nissen et al., 2021), content analysis and qualitative iconographic analysis (Awad et al. 2022), and mixed-method viewer online engagement analysis (Awad et al., under review). For the purposes of this chapter, I will focus on the popularity of one specific image that the DF uses frequently, that of the Muslim woman in the veil, and discuss possible reasons for why it attracts viewers and triggers high engagement online.

The DF was founded in 1995 in Denmark, and since its start the party has promoted strong nationalist and anti-immigration messages. The party presents a good case for investigating viewer engagement online because DF has been known for its elaborate and at times provoking visual political communication, and it was one of the first movers on social media platforms among the other Danish parties. The dataset for these studies was a *producer-specific dataset* (see Chapter 5), where it is limited to what one party produces in its visual communication. In the second and third study (Awad et al., under review; Awad et al., 2022), the dataset was also *space- and time-specific*, where the source of the data is only from the party's Facebook page and only covering posts for certain year ranges. Throughout the different studies, we explored the frequency of different visuals in the party's campaigning and tested for the correlation between the content of different images and the viewers' engagement online. There was the hypothesis from existing literature that images using 'othering' visual content are normally more 'sensational' and attract more engagement, so we tested if this was also the case with the party's images of immigrants in comparison to images using Danish national symbols or representing ethnic Danes and Danish politicians.

The methods used included coding all images in each dataset for their visual and textual content and the engagement they received on Facebook. Engagement is understood here as the number of viewers pressing a 'reaction', commenting on an image, or sharing it. These could be interpreted as indicators of attention, engagement, or resonance (Rieder et al., 2015). Given the purpose of this investigation and the number of images, we only looked for the first layer of image interpretation (see Chapter 5), focusing on the main subjects and objects represented in the images. The coding process utilized methods from image content analysis (Bell, 2012) in combination with thematic analysis to account for both pre-decided codes as well as emerging codes and to identify main patterns in data (Braun & Clarke, 2022; Gleeson, 2011). Codes included the people represented in the images, any national or cultural symbols, nature,

7.5 A Political Campaign Image: The Woman in the Veil

institutions, and out-group symbols. We also utilized a critical multimodal analysis to combine the visual content analysis, online engagement data, iconographic analysis, and contextual interpretations (Awad et al., 2022), as well as statistical models to test for correlations and qualitative discursive analysis to further understand viewers' engagement through commenting on images (Awad et al., under review).

One key finding across all three studies is that the party relies heavily on images of the 'other' (mainly through images of migrants, criminals, and Muslim symbols) to demarcate a clear boundary between *Danishness* and *otherness*. The frequency of such images is the second highest after images of the party's politicians. Visual depictions of generic people who are represented as *others* were always higher than depictions of generic people represented as *Danes* across the time span of the data. However, images of the *others* continuously increased over time and intensified when the party was losing popularity and its vote share (Awad et al., 2022). In terms of engagement, images of the *other* in combination with anti-immigrant textual content on those images attracted the highest engagement numbers (Awad et al., under review). Interestingly, among the *othering* images, it was one specific visual that attracted the highest engagement numbers across all categories, that is of the Muslim woman wearing face veil (niqab/burqa) (Awad et al., under review).

These results show that visual and textual content of the *other* – especially the Muslim woman wearing a face cover – drives high engagement in comparison to other content in the party's images. However, the results say little about the nature of this engagement and the attitudes and affects involved. Therefore, we further analysed qualitatively the first 500 comments of the top five face cover images (2,500 comments = 59,470 words) (Awad et al., under review). The analysis used the qualitative and discourse-based appraisal framework developed by Martin and White (Martin & White, 2005), after adapting it to better address affect from a psychological perspective (Benítez-Castro & Hidalgo-Tenorio, 2019) and to address the overt and covert emotions and opinions in online comments (Bednarek, 2009; Cavasso & Taboada, 2021).

The images were posted between 2018 and 2019. Even though all of the images portray women wearing face covers, it is only one that tackles the topic of face cover as the post celebrates the enforcement of a ban of face covering in Denmark, which DF has called for. The other images are used to advocate for more strict rules in relation to accepting Syrian refugees and use the subject of the woman as a stereotype of refugees, asylum seekers, and terrorist fighters.

The analysis showed – as expected – most of the comments expressed negative affect (85.5 per cent); however, the target of that affect varied in unexpected ways. Despite the images promoting anti-immigrant attitudes, immigrants were the most prevalent subject of positive affect (attraction and satisfaction) expressed in comments (51.8 per cent), with DF coming in second (28.1 per cent). In terms of negative affect (repulsion and dissatisfaction), DF was the most prevalent subject (36.9 per cent), with immigrants coming in second (27.4 per cent). These results nuance the idea that images promoting hate and anger attract online engagement from supporters of those ideas in echo-chamber-like online spaces. Overall, around 40 per cent of the comments were from people who do not agree with the opinions expressed by the images. It appears from the results that *othering* images and images promoting hate do mobilize engagement, and this engagement is often expressing negative polarity of affect; however, the target of that negativity is not necessarily in line with what is promoted by the image producer or image content.

Aside from the polarity and target of affect, a question that remains is what makes the woman in the face cover a strong attraction image for engagement. The environment of those images within the Danish context and their third layer of interpretation (Chapter 5) in relation to discourses on Muslims in Denmark could be a starting point for interpreting the attractiveness of those images. The images' meanings are embedded in the context of Danish public debate about a burqa ban that was presented by the centre-right government coalition in 2018 that resulted in a law banning garments that cover the face (niqab/burqa) in August 2018. This political – and media – focus on Muslim communities in Denmark has a longer past that started in response to the increasing numbers of non-Western immigrants in the 1960s who came as guest workers from countries such as Morocco, Turkey, ex-Yugoslavia, and Pakistan. Slowly, those immigrant groups were identified not so much as being Turks, Arabs, or Pakistani but as being Muslim groups who pose a 'problem' because their different cultural and religious practices pose a 'threat' to Danish culture and values (Yilmaz, 2016). Communication scholar Ferruh Yilmaz (2016) traces how the Muslim subject in Denmark was constructed around cultural notions of difference and became the distinguishing marker of the insider European versus the outsider Muslim in media and political discourses.

The question remains: why did the Muslim woman in face cover become *the* visual symbol of this cultural threat? It is certainly not because this is the typical way in which most of this minority group look. There are no clear statistics of the number of Muslims in Denmark, but according to a recent study there is an estimate that, in January 2020, there were around 256,000 Muslims in Denmark, which corresponds to around 4.4 per cent of the population (Kristensen, 2020). It is even harder to estimate the number of Muslim women wearing headscarves or face coverings, since this group is a rare and elusive religious subculture group, but according to one study an estimate of around 150 women wore face coverings in Denmark in 2013, which corresponds to 0.1–0.2 per cent of Muslim women in Denmark (Warburg et al., 2013). This number reveals a bit of the paradox in the amount of political, media, and viewer attention given to this symbol when its actual prevalence in the society is that little. When looking at the images of face coverings in the dataset longitudinally controlling for dates, the frequency of the images varies from 2017 to 2022. It is in 2020 and 2021 that the face cover visual symbol was used the most. This counters the argument that the images were mainly used to advocate for the face cover ban, which was implemented in 2018. The images are used the most two years after the passing of the law, where one could imagine that the number of women wearing the face cover might have even decreased from the estimate made in 2013 as a result of the law. The party continued to extensively rely on that one visual representation and generalize it to stand for a wide range of issues it opposed such as migrant integration, acceptance of refugees, criminality, and the European Union.

Previous literature on the far right provides a possible interpretation as to why the party uses this specific image. Many studies have shown how different far-right movements in Europe consistently use images of Muslim women in face and hair coverings representing them as an oppressed group of people who pose a threat to the freedom of 'Western' women and to liberal cultural values (Berg, 2018; Sayan-Cengiz & Tekin, 2022). Studies of digital media space have also shown that it is especially images provoking fear (Casas & Williams, 2019) and anger (Hokka & Nelimarkka, 2019) that mobilize online engagement, and that images of symbolic threat can provoke anti-immigrant reactions and stereotypes (Schmuck & Matthes, 2017).

This goes in line with a social psychological explanation for the popularity of such images. The face cover image combines the cultural and security threats into one concrete symbol. This symbol represents a cultural practice that is de-individualizing in a sense because one cannot see or relate to the face of the person. Social psychology literature on intergroup conflict, discrimination, and dehumanization shows that a first step of 'othering' and creating an 'out-group' is to see that out-group as undifferentiated and de-individualized. The reliance on the cultural difference represented in clothing makes that symbol also a 'safer' out-group signifier to justify the threat, rather than a signifier of skin colour, for example, that would be quickly labelled as racist and unacceptable. The distinctiveness of the face cover as a polarizing visual symbol (in comparison to other visual symbols such as a generic migrant or a Muslim woman with headscarf) draws more people who would see it as an out-group signifier, even if they do not necessarily see a migrant or a Muslim as part of a threatening out-group. The face cover and head scarf have come to symbolize the crucial cultural differences in Europe in the past years. For any community, othering strategies rely on constructing a 'crucial' difference 'that matters more than any similarity and makes all common features seem small and insignificant' (Bauman, 2000, p. 176). Those differences create the 'ideal other' (Said, 1978) that poses a cultural invasion and therefore justifies the need for protection of the community. The representation of difference through the woman's body could be also seen as a way of representing a pathological form of *otherness* (Hall, 1997a) that does not fit into an ethnocentric norm of what a European woman should look like and that provides 'evidence' of the irreversible difference between the cultures.

These interpretations could explain why the party uses this image and why it could be popular among party followers but does not explain the engagement from those opposing the party's views. One interpretation for this could be that the de-individualizing features of the subject of the image make her the site of dialogue and debate between different views. By the de-individualizing features of the woman in the image, she becomes the 'object' of discussion for the viewer who is positioned as the progressive social actor, who supports or refuses those cultural practices. This *othering* brings value significance to the in-group identity, drawing on Western liberal values and ideas about women's emancipation, as well as freedom of belief and expression. These images are addressing and expecting a Danish viewer, who takes a position against or for the *other* woman. Another explanation could be in the gender aspect of those images; the woman's body often quickly becomes the terrain of cultural, moral, and political debates (Hafez, 2014), and gendered stereotypical images of who is the 'oppressed' woman and who is the 'emancipated' woman invite the viewer to take different positions in relation to the arguments they perceive the image to be making.

It could be interesting to investigate how these images are viewed by Muslim women living in Denmark. This could be with an interest in the

7.5 A Political Campaign Image: The Woman in the Veil

stereotype threat (see Chapter 3) and the influence of othering images on those represented and how identity strength could act as a protective factor. In one informal conversation with a Syrian refugee who wears a head scarf (hijab), I asked her about her impression of a DF street billboard we had just passed. The poster portrayed one of the party's politicians with a speech bubble that read 'drop your scarf and join Denmark' (transl.). She said that those posters are talking about her, but not to her, even when they have such direct statements. She interpreted the image as a left- versus right-wing dialogue that uses her case as an object of debate, but the dialogue does not actually involve her as a subject. She said she tries to distance herself from being affected by those messages by reminding herself that this is about wider political battles, and she should not take it personally. She then adds: 'Even if I took the meaning personally and literally, do you think if I actually take off my headscarf as he asks me in order to "belong", would that type of politician accept me with open arms? With my skin colour, Arab background, and religion?'

CHAPTER 8

The Development of the Image

Figure 8.1 Alan Kurdi and Omran Daqneesh, illustrated by Khalid Albaih.
Source: Khalid Albaih.

In the aftermath of the Syrian revolution in 2011 and the civil war that followed, many civilians have lost their lives in Syria and on their way escaping Syria as refugees. On the right side of Figure 8.1 is an illustration of Alan Kurdi, who was a two-year-old Kurdish boy whose body was found in 2015 on the mediterranean shore in Turkey alongside his mother and brother as they were trying to reach Europe through Turkey. His photograph became iconic of the European refugee crisis and triggered many responses of empathy as well as blame for the danger parents put children into on those illegal routes. To the left is an illustration of Omran Daqneesh, who is a five-year-old boy who was pulled from under the ruins after an air strike in 2016 in Aleppo, Syria. His video, sitting in the back of an ambulance car, dazed and silent despite his injuries, became another iconic image of the Syrian war crisis. Images of both children were circulated globally and especially Alan's image was transformed and appropriated to many different forms reflecting different pro- and anti-refugee arguments and sentiments.

Artist Khalid Albaih illustrates these two iconic images in relation to one another to reflect the available choices for Syrian children if they stay and if they leave. In a way, his image is a response to the many controversies raised by Alan's photograph.

Albaih is a Romanian-born, Qatar-raised, Oslo-based artist and cultural producer from Sudan. I reached out to him to ask to use his illustration for the book and he kindly agreed.

An image can have a short life; it is produced, placed in a certain environment, seen by a few who interact with it by briefly viewing it, and eventually fades away. In other instances, an image can develop and take on a long rich transformative social life. Using the idea of development within an image's life cycle can help us trace images across time and across different cultural, economic, and political environments that shape its development. When and where are images born, how do they develop, and how do they decline, die, or go extinct? And, most importantly, *what do people do with images?* And why do certain images intrigue people so much so that they will not let them stay as they are? They would appropriate them, refute them, change them, even physically attempt to destroy them. The developmental approach to images also brings us to evolutionary metaphors. As Mitchell (2005) asks: Can we identify a cultural selection process that determines the development of an image? Are images like biological species in that some survive, mutate, and flourish while others die, go extinct, or remain marginal? If the answer is yes, then what makes an image succeed or fail in the cultural ecology of images? What makes an image 'the fittest to survive'?

The diverse social lives an image can take demonstrate how images tempt us to appropriate them to our own meanings. The circulation and transformation of the image is central to understanding the circulation and transformation of meaning and the psychological influence of those circulating images in shaping what we see and how much we see it. Every time an image is reproduced or reconstructed, its meaning is transformed. Similar to how psychologist Frederic Bartlett (1932) analysed the meaning transformation in serial reproduction of stories, the development of the image could also reflect how meaning is transformed during image transmission and diffusion; how image meaning is elaborated, simplified, partly omitted, or countered as it travels across people, time, and space (Awad, 2017). In *The Social Life of Things*, anthropologist Arjun Appadurai (1986) argues convincingly that we need to follow the objects as they travel and how they change as they travel, for it is in their materiality, uses, social practices, and trajectories that their meanings are inscribed. It is in those trajectories that we can understand human engagement with the objects and how humans give life to the objects, and how those objects in their mobility can methodologically illuminate their human and social context.

The development of an image is always dependent on its viewers and what they do with it. There are different possibilities for the development an image can take; next I will discuss two forms of image development. One form is circulation of the image without modification; here we look at images that are reproduced, diffused, shared, circulated, travelling from one medium and context to another. The meaning of the image is often transformed in the process, but the image body remains the same. Another form is transformation of the image in its development; here we look at images that were changed in the process of reproduction. A change is implemented in the image's form and content, it is reconstructed, modified, certain parts of it added or omitted, and subsequently also its meaning is transformed in the process.

8.1 Image Circulation

Even though new technologies have significantly facilitated the speed and geographical range of image mobility, the idea of image circulation and travel is not new. Images have always travelled in different ways. Paintings moved between different artists' workspaces, kings' palaces, churches, and art galleries. Newspaper and magazine images also move through their own distribution channels, which is sometimes followed by people cutting off images from them and hanging them in different places for different purposes. Family photographs, scientific images, and travel images are also always travelling to and from archives and transmitted from one generation to another and from one institution to another. As cultural critic Walter Benjamin (1935) shows, the introduction of print and photography technologies has greatly influenced the circulation and reach of images. Those technologies meant that the original authentic painting that was

8.1 Image Circulation

only seen by the few before the fifteenth century, was now mechanically reproduced and seen by many more viewers and in diverse places and contexts than where the image was originally produced and placed. Image circulation in digital media goes beyond the conception of images as representations of people, events, and places. Images become also a way to capture attention, generate data, and form networks; they capture a network of affects and associations in time and place (Carah, 2014). Thus, a focus on circulation of images on digital media could shed light on the management of participation and attention in value, identity, and cultural practices production online (Carah, 2014).

Whether we are talking about print or digital technologies, the argument is that the circulation of images always involves some form of meaning making. Circulation, as a useful analytical construct for cultural analysis, is more than the movement of people, ideas, or commodities, it is the cultural process created by interactions between interpretive communities in certain structures with their own politics of circulation (Beer, 2013). Even in the identical reproduction of an image in a new place, the repetition of the same image in the same context, or the travel of the same image across mediums, there is always an exchange and transformation of meaning. As Benjamin (1935) argues, in every replication, an image always takes on a new presence with every new viewer in time and space.

Most digital media platforms have a 'sharing' option for images and other content; this is one example of everyday image circulation that happens based on what people find interesting and worth sharing with others. Anthropological ethnographic studies have been particularly interested in the site of circulation, looking at the social practices surrounding images as visual objects and how they are shared and exchanged in different cultural contexts (Rose, 2016). Different practices of image sharing are characteristic of today's globalized visual culture. The use of 'evidence' or solidarity images in a protest or on social media has become a common practice to bring visibility to a cause. The image of Alan Kurdi in Figure 8.1 is an example of a photograph that went from Turkey to worldwide circulation within the first few hours of its sharing. Also, the sharing of images of Khaled Said in the context of the 2011 Egyptian revolution and sharing frames of the witness video of George Floyd in the context of the Black Lives Matter movement in the United States are examples of image sharing that brought visibility and evidence of police brutality in both contexts and mobilized action against the oppression.

The sharing of solidarity symbols on people's online profiles is another example, where the person positions themselves and their identity in relation to the cause. After the 2015 terror attacks in Paris, graphic artist Jean Jullien created an illustration merging the Eiffel Tower and peace symbol. The image went viral online and in protests and quickly became a solidarity symbol. In such examples, people spontaneously generate iconicity by the mere action of posting and sharing such images (Sturken & Cartwright, 2018). The circulation of protest symbols counters the idea that the image should be unique, sacred, and copyrighted to one author. Here, the power of the image is in being reproduced and appropriated by as many people as possible and in as many locations as possible to reach strong visibility and impact.

There are many factors that influence how far an image can get diffused in a certain environment such as copyright, censorship, and institutional and political control over image access. Another factor that is relevant to online environments is algorithms. Image circulation and flow through new technologies is not completely free or democratic, but it is subject to economic, legal, and political power struggles, as the routes of image transmission are entangled with the flow of data in different areas of knowledge, life, and politics (Sturken & Cartwright, 2018).

Sociologist David Beer (2013) illustrates how new media forms influence popular culture and the meanings that circulate within it. He argues that we now have new media infrastructure that affords the circulation and transformation of popular culture. Those infrastructures do not only facilitate circulation and mediate flow, they also manipulate and block circulation. He follows the 'social life of data' and how algorithms play a key role in shaping circulation and in shaping our culture, our preferences, and our taste. Algorithms are a set of rules in a computational procedure that produces solutions or outputs based on different input values. They can do different things including the creation of search results and tailoring content to different users. The powerful social implications of algorithms come from how they can select and reinforce one ordering at the expense of others, and in a way actively shape and constitute social life (Mackenzie, 2006). They can then naturalize certain orders and animate certain movements, affecting what can be said and done, and doing that while naturalizing who does what to whom as they subsume existing patterns of cognition and communication. This, as Mackenzie (2006) argues, makes algorithms an invisible structural force that contests agency in everyday life.

Digital technologies redefine what it means to view and share an image on digital media, and how even 'passive' viewing, clicking, or pausing on an image for few seconds before scrolling to the next has implications on what one sees next, what is promoted for others to see, and what can go

8.1 Image Circulation

viral. This would also redefine the idea of social action in relation to images, and how those 'mini' actions could bring meaning, value, visibility, or invisibility to certain images. This also has implications on advertising and the intentional shaping of attention and taste. Earlier work such as that of sociologist Pierre Bourdieu (1984) focused on social class with its associated economic, cultural, and social capital as key in shaping our taste. Beer (2013), however, argues that the social power of algorithms today lies in the fact that they do not just predict our tastes to target us with relevant content, they also have the capacity and potential to shape our taste by designing our cultural encounters and our cultural landscapes. The decentralized mediascape means that media is ordered and reordered to better 'find us' and actively shape and constitute our social life. Algorithms thus matter because they have power over the circulation of knowledge (Beer, 2013), and those powers are used for different commercial and political goals by those who design them.

Image circulation – whether triggered by individuals, institutions, algorithms, or all three – has a psychological influence on us. It regulates what we see, how much we see, and in how many spaces of our daily life do we encounter certain visuals. As mentioned with the example of the protest symbol, an image going viral could help visibility to a cause, mobilizing a collective identity, and subsequently political action. However, image repetition does not always have such influence. Sometimes the overexposure to one image makes it lose its meaning, it becomes banal and in the background of our environment, failing to call our attention anymore. The continuous sharing of images of suffering could also have a countereffect. It could lead to viewers distancing themselves and looking away, either because they feel helpless in stopping the suffering or because they normalize the suffering (Sontag, 2003). Another potential consequence of circulation is that an image becomes appropriated by many different actors who use it for alternative purposes such as commercial merchandise, where the image along the way loses its association with the cause and becomes depoliticized.

Therefore, image circulation by continuous repetition and reproduction of an image has a double edge. It will always have an influence, but the kind of influence will always vary. From one side, continuous repeated exposure to certain images brings familiarity to what is represented and has an influence on changing people's attitude towards what is represented; they become taken-for-granted meanings. This could be explained through the *mere exposure effect* (Zajonc, 1968), presented earlier in Chapter 3. After all, this is what many advertising strategies rely on – repetition, exposure, and subtle clues all around us. Many studies have shown how repeated exposure can help normalize certain ideas presented in images and shape public opinion (Comstock & Scharrer, 2005; Drakett et al., 2018; Ferguson et al., 2009; Gelpi et al., 2013; Marcus et al., 2000). This normalization could also influence that we stop looking or stop reacting to certain images, they fail to grab our attention or our moral responsibility anymore, they make an event seem fixed in time and less real. An interesting question is then how – and can we – moderate image circulation to sustain a desired influence? In her *On Photography* book philosopher and cultural critic Susan Sontag (1977) wondered if we could work on an ecology of images that regulates circulation and effect of images before people turn numb to them, but then later in her *Regarding the Pain of Others* (2003) book realizes that there is no 'committee of guardians' that can regulate horror or can maintain an image's ability to shock. I will argue in the final chapter of the book that it is in what people do with images that can lead to an afterlife to an image that has gone 'dead' or can banalize an image to a meaningless social life.

8.2 Image Transformation

As an image gets circulated, some actors instead of just reproducing the image as it is, decide to appropriate or change its meaning further by modifying it. They reconstruct the image, adding or omitting parts of it to strategically communicate a certain meaning. A typical example of an image where transformation is characteristic is online digital memes, where an image is appropriated to express many different emotions by adapting the text on the meme image then sharing it. Another example is viral images that get widely diffused in different spaces; most of the time viral images are circulated widely by reproduction and are also transformed and reproduced with adaptations. Transformation does not have to be an actor that intends to reproduce the image; many street art images are transformed by pedestrians who decide to cross out a part of the image or add something to it. Cultural jamming or guerrilla communication is a typical example of this latter transformation, where anti-consumerist activists transform the message in an advertising billboard to reveal its underlying problematic meaning.

Tracing an image's social life longitudinally and analysing how people transform certain parts of an image can help show what intrigues people in images, what resonates, and what offends and cannot be tolerated. In the reproductions of the Nefertiti with the gas mask poster in the context of

8.2 Image Transformation

Egypt (see Figure 4.1) the image was mostly left untouched, but it was the statement underneath that was cut off in many of the posters in the street; the statement, as explained earlier, is an appropriation of a religious statement that some might have found offensive. Similarly, with the 'refugees welcome' posters being transformed to 'terrorist welcome' posters (see Figure 5.3), when tracing them in the street it was especially the word 'terrorist' that was scratched out. The image of Alan Kurdi (Figure 8.1) used in this chapter is especially intriguing in its transformation. One would think that an image of a child victim can only afford certain interpretations and transformations; if people disagree on many things, children's deaths are often what can bring their sympathy and respect for the magnitude of death together. Unfortunately, that was not the case. As I will show in the last section of this chapter the image was transformed by changing the setting around Alan Kurdi's body, and the change of the setting and background afforded many different sympathetic and unsympathetic appropriations.

The visual dialogue, especially the tension in that dialogue, is most visible in the transformative stage of an image. It is where people creatively use and appropriate images to confirm or refute an argument that is posed by an earlier image. People provoke and call attention through mixing images and text together, as well as editing, adding, and omitting visual elements. We can understand image transformation as a form of creative appropriation. Appropriation here refers to cultural appropriation, where there is a process of borrowing and changing the meaning of a cultural product, slogan, or image (Sturken & Cartwright, 2018). Creativity here refers to the process of perceiving, exploiting, and generating novel affordances in a socially and materially situated practice (Glăveanu, 2012). The symbolic power of creative appropriation lies not in one single reproduction but in the cumulative effect of the different transformative practices over time, leading to a form of collective authorship (a term MacDowall, 2014 uses in relation to graffiti) or group creativity (a term Sawyer, 2006 uses in relation to collaborative improvisation in music and theatre).

Image transformation is closely tied to image destruction and censorship. The creative transformation can be used sometimes not only to appropriate an image but to also destroy an image and its earlier meaning. I will discuss this 'creative destruction' process in Chapter 9. Creative transformation can also be a response to censorship. When an image is censored and its circulation life is cut short, people can sometimes transform its symbol into another form to be able to reproduce it for its meaning to continue. An example of this is when the Palestinian flag image

Figure 8.2 The Palestinian flag and its transformation into a watermelon symbol.
Source: Author.

was transformed into a watermelon image. After the six-day war in 1967, Israel seized control of the West Bank and Gaza, and made the public display of the Palestinian flag a criminal offense. To circumvent the ban, Palestinian activists started using the image of watermelon, a fruit that when cut open has the same colours as the Palestinian flag (Figure 8.2). The ban was later lifted – though the confiscation of flags and arrests still prevail – but the watermelon image continued to circulate and became a protest symbol that stands for Palestinian solidarity.

Image transformation is also one way of looking at the development and change in meaning over time. One example of this kind of change is the rainbow flag (also known as the pride flag) as a symbol of lesbian, gay, bisexual, transgender, and queer (LGBTQ+) rights. The rainbow colours are meant to represent the diversity and spectrum of sexualities and genders. Over time the abbreviation LGBTQ+ was elaborated to include more diversities such as 'I' for intersex and 'A' for asexual, among others. The flag image has also transformed over time to reflect further diversities. The rainbow colours were first designed by artist Gilbert Baker and used in the San Francisco Gay Freedom Day Parade in 1978. In 2017, two colours (black and brown) were added to the flag by the Philadelphia Office of LGBT Affairs to draw attention to people of colour within the community. In 2018, designer Daniel Quasar developed the 'progress flag', adding more colours and a triangular shape to the flag to represent trans people and those living with HIV. In some versions developed later, a purple circle was added to represent intersex people, the Black Lives Matter symbol to represent the movement, and black and white stripes to represent heterosexual allies. The rainbow flag has continued to be a collaborative transformative symbol in the making across generations. The changes to its meaning not only come from appropriations and changes in colours

and shapes but also in its different uses in diverse contexts. Many have criticized how it has been commercialized and used in products and parades to emphasize an 'image' of diversity, when social structures of inequalities remain unchanged. Its use in broader colonial projects has been also criticized, where it is claimed as a 'liberation' intervention justifying crimes and wars against certain groups.

The transformation of images to adapt to different causes is a common feature of protest symbols, as seen in the examples of the watermelon or rainbow symbols. Even though activism usually aims for social change, protest symbols are often conventional, relying on repeating familiar symbols with some alteration (Jeziorowska, 2021). One reason for this is that for a symbol to be effective it relies on familiar and comprehensible symbols that are already available in a given culture and are easy and quick to reproduce. As Jeziorowska (2021) illustrates, this is clearly seen in the Situationist International artistic revolutionary avant-garde group and their work between 1957 and 1972. The group adopted the method of *detournement* (a French word meaning diversion, misappropriation, or hijacking), where they relied on reusing and recontextualizing saturated visual and verbal elements from everyday life to create new artwork. This again brings in the creative aspect in image transformation, where even when the new image is 'just' a reshuffling of the same visual elements in an older image, it can sometimes still be a very creative and effective process of creating a new image with new meanings that trigger dialogue with the previous meanings. It can pose a strong support, development, or condemnation of the previous images and their meanings.

8.3 The Viral Image: The Fittest to Survive

When we think of viral images today, digital social media platforms come to mind with images that overnight attain thousands, if not millions, of views, engagement, and sharing across different spaces. However, the word viral comes from medical terminology referring to processes relating to or caused by viruses. Common examples of a viral infection are influenza, HIV, HPV, or Covid-19. The life cycle of viruses – which include attachment, penetration, gene expression and replication, assembly, and release – could provide inspiration for thinking about the life cycle of viral images. There is the entry stage, where attachment occurs in the first encounter of the image in its host environment, then there is a process of penetrating a certain space and getting diffused in it. Then there is the replication stage, where circulation and transformation of the image occurs. Finally, there is the exit stage.

Is this a good metaphor for fast-spreading images? Similar to viruses, images need a suitable host environment to spread in. Also, after replication in one space and reaching saturation, images need to find new hosts – new environments – to spread further. However, I am not sure this metaphor can be taken further to an exit stage, where images 'leave' the host environment. It is more relevant to think of the 'exit' in terms of viral latency rather than viral shedding. In viral shedding, the virus leaves the cell, while in viral latency the virus hides within a cell. Similar to viral latency, images can sometimes hide or stay inactive for some time until there are external stimuli (new actor, new event, new context) that prompt its activation and restart its social life. There is something interesting about equating the social life of images with the life cycle of viruses and exploring what contagion would mean for images, but there is also something inherently negative about equating images to infections that sicken and kill us. Yet, one could argue that not all viruses are harmful; some viruses keep us alive and – like images – it is about what we do with them – we could harness viruses to treat illnesses and produce vaccines.

Image virality does not only apply to online spaces; images can go 'viral' by spreading in different material forms and in different geographical contexts. In her book *Image Politics in the Middle East*, Middle East scholar Lina Khatib (2013) refers to those images as 'floating images' – images that have transformative enduring power that they are able to travel through multiple physical and virtual spaces producing different meanings. It is important to study how those images spread, the psychological consequences of their spreading, and what makes them fit to mutate and survive travelling across contexts.

What characterizes an image that gets broad circulation? There are factors that one could argue can promote and facilitate circulation, while acknowledging that sometimes the process involves much more of unpredictability, luck, and good timing. One factor could include the environment, including the medium and the social and temporal context, that facilitated certain engagement with an image from viewers. The body of the image and what it contains of course also plays a central role. Another factor could be who the image producer is, their power and visibility (whether we are talking about a corporate, a government, or a social media influencer), and the platforms they have access to. As the analysis of communication scholar Nicholas Carah (2014) shows, the circulation of images on social media platforms is organized from one side by users through practices such as tags, likes, and shares that manually position images within a larger flow. From another side, they are also organized by algorithms that in an automated way determine how images circulate within a network based on certain sets of rules. Those algorithms are central to the production of value, assemblage of identities, and creation of social spaces as they manage the quantity and quality of what circulates on social media and thus regulate the circulation of meaning and attention (Carah, 2014).

It appears that images with this enduring power are often ones that develop through both circulation and transformation. They are initially spread widely due to something in them that triggers an affective response from their viewers. This affective response could be resonance, empathy, repulsion, or anger. During circulation and due to that affective response, people appropriate and transform the image to better resonate with their response to the arguments they perceived the image to be making. A characteristic that is common to the content of those images is that they combine familiarity with novelty. For the image to be relatable, it relies on familiar content that is easily identifiable in everyday culture. However, if it stops there then it is just another repetition of a familiar object/subject that does not call for attention. This familiarity has to be challenged with something new or unexpected. Finally, the content of images that spread across contexts have a certain level of flexibility and relatability that allows the content to be adapted during travel to fit and be appropriated to a variety of contexts beyond their original meaning or context.

The balance between incorporating the familiar and the unfamiliar in an image is key for its wide circulation. In her analysis of knowledge circulation and dialogues in a society, social psychologist Ivana Marková (2003) argues that every artistic and literary work represents in a way the existing social realities of the time, while simultaneously communicating something new that violates those realities. An affective image is one that provokes and creates some form of tension or challenge. If that challenge is too easy or too familiar, with no new element, it becomes no more than a cliché. If that challenge is too unfamiliar and incomprehensible, if the image producer distances themselves too much from social norms and familiar ways of seeing, then the viewer might disengage and not relate. The balance is in the ability to create a special kind of tension for the viewer, a tension that arrives from the collision between the familiar and the unfamiliar, the old and the new, the expected and the unexpected, and the continuous and the discontinuous (Marková, 2003). Powerful images trigger circulation by triggering perceptual, emotional, and representational tensions.

To take a few examples, the blue bra image (Figure 1.1) from the Egyptian revolution was broadly circulated within the context of Egypt, especially among activist spaces, and travelled across to other countries during the Arab uprisings. The image is of the familiar object of the bra, but the tension the image brings is in moving this familiarity from the private sphere to the conservative public sphere and transforming the meaning of the original incident the image refers to from one of shame and hiding to one of public confrontation. Another example is the image of the nuclear mushroom cloud (Figure 3.1). The image captures the power and unfamiliarity of a new destructive power in the shape of the familiar objects of mushrooms and clouds. The image powerfully distances the viewer from the horrific destiny of those affected by the bomb, by setting the attention on the aesthetic explosion in the form of a mushroom-shaped cloud.

Studying viral images can be informative of how their diffusion allows them to quickly become integral to people's way of seeing, thinking, feeling, and remembering. The iconic image of Albert Einstein with his wild hair sticking his tongue out has come to form the public imaginary and stereotype of the 'genius' person. The blue bra (Figure 1.1) or the Nefertiti with gas mask image (Figure 4.1) has come to construct the collective identity of the Egyptian activists. The nuclear mushroom cloud (Figure 3.1) has come to form the global collective memory of the end of the Second World War. The interest here is less in trying to predict which images can go viral and more in investigating the psychological influences those images have when they become part of everyday common-sense knowledge. For example, investigating when is their meaning normalized that they no longer trigger attention, when is their meaning taken over by new actors and causes, and when does their meaning get forgotten after they are no longer viral.

8.4 Methods: Tracing the Development of One Image

To investigate the circulation and transformation process of an image, a longitudinal *visual symbol-specific* dataset (see Chapter 5) would be the most relevant. This dataset could be relatively easy to retrieve if it is limited to one social media space online, where the images are tagged with certain key terms. However, it is more complex to follow the development of an image across physical spaces, news and print media, and different social

8.4 Methods: Tracing the Development of One Image

media platforms. In physical spaces, visual ethnographic practices (Pink, 2021) of image tracing and documentation could be useful for collecting data; also, using the snowball method where one image source leads to another, and talking with one image producer leads to knowledge of different life trajectories of an image. These methods have their limitations since they are not systematic and are mostly explorative. In online spaces, several digital ethnographic (Pink et al., 2015) and computational and digital methods (R. Rogers, 2024) have been developed to tackle circulation of content online. For investigating the circulation and transformation of specific images online, some researchers have used reverse search engines (Horsti, 2017), while others have utilized big data mining and information visualization in combination with multimodal discourse analysis (O'Halloran et al., 2019). Computational tools have been also developed to trace images across social media platforms (Pearce et al., 2020) and across different online communities (Hokka & Nelimarkka, 2019).

Analytically, a sequence of an image that has been circulated and transformed across different spaces can provide us with a qualitative lens into a visual dialogue, where each image reproduction is an instance in a sequential interaction (Awad, 2021; S. Hansen & Flynn, 2015). Interpreting this dialogue is informative of how meanings change as they get transformed and elaborated. Psychologist Frederic Bartlett (1932) has investigated the serial reproduction of symbols in an experimental setting, analysing how participants serially reproduced images that they were not familiar with, and how in using reconstructive remembering they transformed the images into something more familiar. However, the transformation of images in everyday visual culture is different from Bartlett's experiment: first, people transform images they are familiar and engaged with, and second, transformation is triggered by the motivation to appropriate and transform meaning, rather than due to forgetting. Nevertheless, there are several useful analytical ideas from Bartlett's experiments that can be used to analyse the development of the image. The study of serial reproduction of images and cultural symbols highlights the different kinds of meaning change that occur in cultural transmission and the agency of individuals and groups in this transmission (Wagoner, 2017). Similar to Bartlett's serial reproduction experiments, we can see in image development when the meaning is elaborated or simplified, when certain image contents are kept while others are omitted to change or refute meaning, and when the content is readapted to fit into a different local context or a different time. Some of these processes can be seen in the development of the image of Alan Kurdi, which I discuss in Section 8.5.

8.5 A News Photograph: Capturing Death

As mentioned in the introduction to this chapter, the image of Alan Kurdi circulated widely on a global scale and became part of many refugee debates. The image also developed in that circulation into many different adaptations and transformations. The transformation of this image brings an especially intriguing case given the sensitivity of the topic. Despite the context and different political views, the image is of a dead young child on the shore of a beach. From an empathetic perspective, one could argue that the image should not afford much transformation and reinterpretation beyond the tragic loss of a child. However, that was not always the case, as the photo developed into a visual tool that was serially reproduced and transformed to serve many different political arguments and nationalist discourses (Topinka, 2018). This case example raises questions about how children's bodies are understood as 'grievable lives' (Butler, 2004) and about the politics and ethics of sharing images of dead bodies and giving visibility to children in contexts of crisis (Berents, 2019).

The image was captured by Turkish photojournalist Nilüfer Demir and quickly became world news in September 2015. The photograph circulated across international news channels and travelled on to be part of parliamentary debates (especially in Canada, where it was reported that the boy's family were trying to obtain immigration visas) as well as academic discussions and publications (Adler-Nissen et al., 2020; Berents, 2019; D'Orazio, 2015; Maricut, 2017; Mielczarek, 2020; Olesen, 2018; Prøitz, 2018; Slovic et al., 2017; L. G. E. Smith et al., 2018; Vis & Goriunova, 2015). As the photograph was shared on social media, it was quickly circulated and transformed as viewers responded to it. After twelve hours of its circulation on social media, more than 20 million people have seen it on Twitter, and after forty-eight hours, the most frequently circulated image on Twitter changed from the original photograph to transformed versions by viewers (D'Orazio, 2015). The image triggered strong emotional responses that had an impact, though short-lived, on foreign policies and regulations with explicit reference to 'Kurdi' in the USA, Canada, EU, Germany (Adler-Nissen et al., 2020; Maricut, 2017), growth of public support for the refugee cause (L. G. E. Smith et al., 2018), and donations for the cause (Slovic et al., 2017).

The circulation of the image shows important factors in relation to different social actors producing and engaging with the image globally. The main social actor producing the image was the Turkish photojournalist Nilüfer Demir. For the first five hours after the photos were published

8.5 A News Photograph: Capturing Death

online, the Turkish Press was the only official news agency involved in sharing the image (D'Orazio, 2015). During that period users on social media platforms acted as decentralized catalysts for the spread of the image, especially through highly followed profiles of activists, politicians, aid workers, and journalists concerned with the region. In those first five hours, the image already reached more than half a million viewers across 100 countries. Following that, the image was taken up by mainstream media and more than 500 articles were published online by the international press by the end of the day (D'Orazio, 2015). After forty-eight hours of this circulation, viewers started appropriating the original image by transforming it into user-generated variations to pose different arguments and responses to what the image represents (D'Orazio, 2015). This journey shows the dynamic development of the image, which includes circulation, travel, and transformation across different social actors, geographical contexts, and media spaces.

There are two important aspects to analyse in this case. First, why was this photo especially powerful in mobilizing engagement in comparison with the many other images of the refugee humanitarian crisis? Second, how was image transformation used to construct new meanings, counter-arguments, and affective responses to the image?

In relation to the first question, it is important to note that this image was not the only one taken of the incident. The same photographer also captured an image of the child on the shore with an adult officer nearby, and another one where the officer is carrying the child and walking away with him with the shore in the background. The image that circulated and got transformed the most was the one of the child alone, lying on the beach, just where the water met the shore; the camera captures him from his back, his face in the direction of the sea, and the background of the image is the sea horizon landscape. As with most news photographs, the image that gets to represent an event among the many sequence of images is the one that strategically freezes and encapsulates an event in its most powerful moment (Zelizer, 2004). There are several aspects of image analysis that can explain how this specific image became a symbolic one of the crisis. The features we see of the child are very familiar and relatable. We do not see his face but we see a small child in a red shirt, blue shorts, and pair of shoes on a beach. By his position and seemingly unharmed body, it is easy to see the image as that of a sleeping child (Drainville, 2015). The familiarity of 'this could be any child' is confronted with the tragic unfamiliarity of death; the child is not playing on the beach or lying down, he is dead. This familiarity shows in an analysis of online responses to the image that personalized and 'un-othered' the death of Alan, where many viewers positioned their response to the image 'as a parent' (Burns, 2015). Other than the powerful tragic visual that the image shows, there is also powerful absences (see Chapter 5) in what this one image does not show. We do not see rescuers or adults or other bodies. The child is alone against the sea background, an immediate image absence, resembling a broader absence of global humanitarian intervention that would have saved the child from this destiny, and triggering a hyper-generalized affective response of accountability coupled with helplessness.

There have been many images, news, and statistics of the Syrian civil war and the refugee crisis, but this image captured the crisis through a humanized story of one child that we can see and empathize with. From a social representations theoretical perspective (Moscovici, 1984), this image 'objectified' the crisis into something concrete and anchored it into something familiar. Social psychological studies show that people tend to react more strongly to individual humanized faces of a crises rather than by knowing about the massive number of people affected (Scott et al., 2021). The image of Alan did not produce new information about the crisis; what it did, however, was to shift the crisis discourse from numbers and statistics to an identifiable human with a face, a body, and a life story. This 'identifiable victim effect' (Lee & Feeley, 2016) triggered strong – though short-lived – impacts on individual aid in the form of donations and refugee policy changes in several countries (Slovic et al., 2017). This is further emphasized by the victim being a child, who are more commonly stereotyped as 'deserving refugees' rather than, for example, middle-aged capable men. This child is also seen as relatable; his attire and shoes are identifiable, resembling many children around the world. Social psychological studies on social identity and altruism show that we are more likely to help those who look like us in some socially relevant or salient criterion (Levine et al., 2005).

The representation of the refugee crisis through Alan's photo came in contradiction to the usual media images portraying certain refugees in de-individualizing and dehumanizing ways that invoke a politics of fear rather than compassion, and associate the refugees with threats to sovereignty and security rather than with humanitarian challenges (Bleiker et al., 2013). Studies have shown how newspaper photographs of refugees vary in their rhetorical strategy based on who the refugees are; they can dehumanize by massifying, demonizing, separating, and passivating (Martikainen & Sakki, 2021) or humanize by maternalizing, fragilizing, agonizing, and activizing (Martikainen & Sakki, 2024).

Controversially, the image also provides a suffering we are willing to look at, a case of 'beautiful suffering', an image of a 'well-clothed' seeming sleeping infant that is not particularly graphic (Makar, 2016), an image that introduces us to 'the scandal of horror, not to the horror itself' (Barthes, 1979). The image struck a balance between similarity and difference that is typical of how humanitarian photography represents 'distant suffering' (Byford, 2018). As psychologist Jovan Byford (2018) argues, it is the distance after all that made Alan's image become visible to Western viewers. It is only 'distant suffering' that would be represented that explicitly and 'brought home', while close suffering is already visible and perceptible in other ways.

Furthermore, Alan's image had an interpretative openness and familiarity that allowed for ideological and geographical diversity in meaning making (Olesen, 2018). The image created a space for collective grieving across borders. In a qualitative study of the reception of the image by a group of young volunteers in Norway and Britain (Prøitz, 2018), participants expressed how the image constructed a collective shared story that goes past politics and past the scapegoating of refugees. This image for them converted the abstract, distant, and complex geopolitical and economic complexity of the refugee crisis into something concrete, proximate, simple, and with a strong affective significance. The image presented bluntly and simply what is at stake that cannot be interpreted in too many different ways, in their view: *a child has died.*

The transformations of the image in online and urban spaces show, however, that the familiarity of the image and its composition opened up for diverse appropriations and reinterpretations that went beyond the grieving the loss. Through a qualitative visual interpretation approach of the many transformed images of Alan Kurdi, I identify below four common visual transformation strategies that served different argumentative and affective goals.

8.5.1 Recontextualization

In this first visual strategy, a further meaning is communicated through replacing the environment surrounding the death of Alan Kurdi. In one example, the death is mourned by Turkish artist Omer Tosun through placing Alan's body into a familiar safe environment, a child's bedroom (Figure 8.3a). In another example, the photograph is painted as a mural in Sorocaba, Brazil in 2015, reproducing the whole death image in a new urban environment and a new geographical location to draw attention and

184 The Development of the Image

Figure 8.3 An illustrative collage of different transformations of Alan Kurdi's photograph from different online platforms.

visibility to the cause. This was also done in Frankfurt where artists Oguz Sen and Justus Becker painted the mural as a criticism of the EU's migrant policy and placed it in another water setting, the banks of the River Main near the European central bank (Figure 8.3g). The mural was later transformed by defacement graffiti with the text 'borders save lives' (Figure 8.3h). The artists later transformed the mural by repainting it, this time painting one of Alan Kurdi's photographs when he was alive, laughing, and surrounded by teddy bears (Figure 8.3i). Another recontextualization strategy was done in images by graphically replacing the death scene in the middle of different parliaments, United Nations Security Councils, and Arab League meeting settings (e.g. Figure 8.3b). The recontextualization here brings an association between the death and the political entities that are positioned as holding moral responsibility. It also brings out the contradiction between the high visibility and engagement the image is receiving on digital media and the apparent indifference of those entities towards it.

8.5.2 Re-embodiment and Re-enactment

The re-embodiment and re-enactment strategies can be seen in images that replaced the body of Alan with other bodies. In one version, Alan's body is replaced in a graphic design image by an adult man in a business suit carrying a bag with an EU logo (Figure 8.3c). This was another strategy to bring moral responsibility onto relevant political bodies, and possibly in a way emphasizing that the death of Alan is a sign of the failure of those inactive entities. Another use of this strategy came from performative protest acts; by keeping the same body posture and the beach setting, the protestors re-enacted the death of Alan to bring awareness in different places and call for action. This strategy does not only bring strong affective visibility where they physically perform the re-enactment, it also triggers further image circulation as photos are taken of those protests and shared online. This strategy was done by protestors on a beach in Rabat, Morocco in September 2015 (Figure 8.3d) and by Chinese artist and activist Ai Weiwei on the Greek island of Lesbos in 2016. Other than the shock factor of such re-enactment that some found controversial, the larger adult body, especially of a famous artist such as Ai Weiwei, heightens the pathos of Alan's small otherwise invisible body (Mendes, 2023). This could be interpreted as a form of engaging with *countervisuality* (Mirzoeff, 2011), where the artist actively refuses how the refugee crisis is made invisible by authorities (e.g. through confinement in camps and outsourcing visa applications and detention centres), and instead confronts this invisibility with the 'right to look' at the refugee suffering through the re-enactment (Mendes, 2023).

8.5.3 Juxtaposition

Juxtaposing images are ones that rely on making an argument through contrasting or comparing one image to another. The image at the beginning of this chapter (Figure 8.1; also Figure 8.3e) uses juxtaposing to show the unfortunate destiny of Syrian children whether they stay or leave and highlights the lack of safe options. Juxtaposing strategies were also seen in transformations that used Alan's image to promote completely different political agendas. In December 2015, Alan's photograph was juxtaposed against another photograph showing a child dressed in army camouflage accompanying Egyptian president El-Sisi at a major state celebration (Figure 8.3f). Next to Alan's image the text in Arabic reads: 'a child who has lost his army', while next to the other child the text reads: 'a child who has his army'. This naïve propaganda juxtaposing image, which circulated within Egyptian social media circles and was claimed to be used on a state-owned billboard, dehumanizes Alan's image and uses it as a fear mechanism. The image feeds into the broader narrative of the military-backed Egyptian government that justifies its authoritarian regime with the claim that it guarantees stability in Egypt, showing how – thanks to the army – Egypt is in a better state in comparison to Syria, Libya, and other countries from the region that are suffering instability (Makar, 2016). Another dehumanizing juxtaposition comes from a cartoon image by the French satirical magazine *Charlie Hebdo* in January 2016. The cartoon is titled 'migrants', and it shows Alan's image and next to it the text in French reads: 'what would have happened to little Aylan if he grew up?'; underneath this there is a drawing of two lustful pig-like men chasing two terrified women and the text reads: 'a groper of women in Germany'. The cartoon refers to sexual assault incidents that occurred in Cologne, Germany and were allegedly attributed to refugees. This image, along with other images where Alan was compared to alleged terrorists, worked to undermine the central affective meaning of the image through juxtaposing Alan with adult refugees who are posed as a threat to safety and security (Thelwall, 2015). *Charlie Hebdo*'s image was criticized for bad taste, moral disgust, callousness, and racism (Mortensen, 2017). The image was refuted by further appropriations of the cartoon; in one of them it shows Alan growing up to be a doctor.

8.5.4 Contesting the Spectacle of Death

A fourth strategy I identified in the image's many transformations is one that rejects the spectacle of death altogether. As much as images of death have a powerful and shocking influence on viewers, they can also quickly become objects of voyeurism, and the tragic human loss images as they circulate and transform online can be turned into spectacles (Ibrahim, 2018). This is especially evident in the juxtaposing examples described from *Charlie Hebdo* and the El-Sisi image, where the image is depersonalized, it is no longer about the tragic loss of Alan, it is more of a spectacle image that can be used to induce fear and shock. As the photograph of Alan circulated, many news agencies, viewers, and Alan's relatives did not see it appropriate to share the image of his dead body. For some, it was the critique of how refugee images are viewed as objects generating spectacle rather than sympathy. The sharing here is seen as a further form of revictimizing and reviolating those who suffer. It is a position that some viewers took up intersubjectively, thinking that this is not how they or their children would like to be represented. It also tackles the collective memory aspect of images (Chapter 3), that we want images to not only remind us of Alan but to remind us of him as a lively happy child who could have had an alternative future. This theme of images can be seen in social actors who decided not to share the images of Alan after death and instead shared images of him alive to call attention to the tragic loss of his life. This is also seen in the remaking of the mural of Alan by artists Oguz Sen and Justus Becker, where in the later version they draw him alive, laughing, and among teddy bears (Figure 8.3i). This theme could also be seen as a response to the community or official censorship (Chapter 9) of sensitive images. The dynamics around not circulating the photograph were governed by the decisions of media editors (official censorship), viewers' (community censorship), as well as algorithms that are designed to automatically remove sensitive and graphic material. This specific photograph of Alan did not seem to trigger much gatekeeping from algorithms; even though the image is incredibly sensitive and upsetting, it is not graphic in the sense that it would be automatically detected as showing death (Wardle, 2015). It did, however, trigger much societal debate about the ethics of sharing death photographs.

The different strategies I have presented show the variation by which images are used as a form of appropriation and argumentation in contested societal dialogues. Appropriations provide a lens to the critical-reflexive dimension of the production and reception of visual icons, as they construct, confirm, and contest discourses surrounding their topic (Mortensen, 2017). The act of copying, imitating, and satirizing are signs of the iconicity of an image (Hariman & Lucaites, 2007). The appropriations of Alan's image illustrate how image viewing is a dialogical social act of interpretation, argumentation, and social positioning (Chapter 7). Viewers cognitively and affectively reconstructed the meanings in the image in ways that re-emphasized the tragedy, brought attention to it in new contexts, or dehumanized the loss. The viewers also positioned themselves in relation to the image and transformed the image to position those responsible for the tragedy as accountable. In these processes the meaning of the image was also elaborated from the loss of a child to the broader war and refugee humanitarian crisis, and further to broader meanings of humanity and grieving. The serial reproduction of the image across different spaces and in the same spaces (Figure 8.3g, h, i) show how each of those images could be interpreted as an instance in a continuous dialogue that is embedded in the societal politics of meaning circulation and exchange.

The circulation and transformation of the image also raises questions about the power of the image to facilitate social change. Alan's image triggered questions about political responsibility, moral spectatorship, the public's compassion fatigue, and the media's bias in favouring certain images over others (Mortensen, 2017). The sharing of the image was in a way a social and political action, a form of emotional politics (Ahmed, 2004), by which the public opinion was negotiated and personal attitudes formed in relation to different political actors and policies (Hariman & Lucaites, 2007). The appropriations, as a form of iconoclasm, were a form of intervention in two senses: an intervention within the icon itself, and an intervention in the discursive field of which the appropriation becomes a part of, challenging the values and meanings associated with the icon (L. Hansen, 2015). However, studies on the impact of Alan's photo show that its influence on change in public opinion, policies, or donations was short-lived. This raises further questions about the fading or desensitizing (i.e. the reduction of cognitive and emotional response to a stimuli as a result of continuous exposure) effect of shock images and the ethics and value of sharing such images.

I had my own doubts about using this image as an example in this chapter. There is something problematic about the use and overuse of it in media, digital, urban, and academic spaces. In her book *Regarding the Pain of Others*, Susan Sontag (2003) argues that images of death can produce rage and frustration, but they also produce apathy as the images become normalized. She argues further, that even if images evoke sympathy, this could be even more problematic if we stop at sympathy and do no further action to alleviate the suffering of others:

> But if we consider what emotions would be desirable, it seems too simple to elect sympathy. The imaginary proximity to the suffering inflicted on others that is granted by images suggests a link between the faraway sufferers seen close-up on the television screen and the privileged viewer that is simply untrue, that is yet one more mystification of our real relations to power. So far as we feel sympathy, we feel we are not accomplices to what caused the suffering. Our sympathy proclaims our innocence as well as our impotence. To that extent, it can be (for all our good intentions) an impertinent – if not an inappropriate – response. To set aside the sympathy we extend to others beset by war and murderous politics for a reflection on how our privileges are located on the same map as their suffering, and may – in ways we might prefer not to imagine – be linked to their suffering. (pp. 102–103)

Sontag's argument becomes especially relevant in the case of Alan, when it is the rich minority of the world gazing at and consuming the spectacle of the suffering of the global south, some of whom are seeking refuge and safety in the land of the spectator. There is a fine line between projecting raw reality, to trigger empathy and action, and making a spectacle of a tragedy. Looking at the images of a dead child is an accountable activity. This accountability is complex when that child is culturally and geographically distant from those who gaze upon the image (Byford, 2018). Humanitarian imagery has historically played a role in fostering racial and class differences, presenting those in need as 'passive but pathetic objects capable only of offering themselves up to a benevolent, transient gaze' of those on whose compassion they supposedly depend (Tagg, 1988, p. 12). This has brought a problematic spectatorial sympathy with a sense of entitlement in looking at the suffering of distant others, with the assumption that this looking is for the benefit of those suffering (Byford, 2018).

The circulation of the image of Alan had the collateral consequence that as the image became a tragic symbol of the refugee crisis, it also became depersonalized, no longer about Alan, but Alan as a representative of the thousands of lost refugee lives (Burns, 2015). The transformation of the image further complicates the picture. Does turning the image from a photograph to a drawing in a way make the scene more tolerable, less real? Can we distinguish between 'ethical' transformations that serve a humanitarian purpose and 'unethical' transformations that use and abuse an image of death for other goals, such as certain political propagandas? Images of death occupy the spectrum between art and profanity, between the sacred and grotesque, triggering ethical and moral questions about representing the unpresentable (Ibrahim, 2018). Digital media does not make this complexity any easier; the internet is a medium where the dead are kept alive through circulation and transformations into martyrs, pity symbols, or memetic avatars; the dead are in a state of restlessness on this media (Ibrahim, 2018). The decisions of production, reproduction, transformation, looking, and not looking all raise questions in relation to the *need to see, the purpose of seeing*, and the *right to not see or be seen*.

CHAPTER 9

The Death and Afterlife of the Image

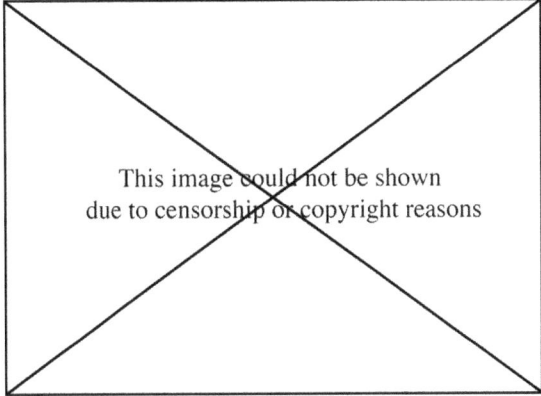

Figure 9.1   An image of absence, to represent the many absent images we cannot use for illustrative purposes due to copyright regulations.

In May 2017, cartoonist Matt Furie officially 'killed' his most famous cartoon character, that of Pepe the Frog. The character was first born in 2006 in San Francisco and introduced in the 'Boy's Club' comic series. In that same series, Furie drew an image of Pepe's funeral, announcing his death. This came in response to how Pepe's image had been appropriated by alt-right movements and used as a meme promoting hate as well as a white supremacist mascot during the 2016 US elections, which resulted in the Anti-Defamation League adding it to its hate symbols database.

Furie later announced through a fundraising campaign on kickstarter.com that there is hope for the resurrection of Pepe: 'He began his life as a blissfully stoned frog in my comic book Boy's Club where he enjoyed a simple life of snacks, soda and pulling his pants all the way down to go pee. Boy's Club debuted in 2006, Pepe became a meme around 2010, then stuck around the internet long enough to become an institutionally recognized hate mascot. Needless to say it's a nightmare so I killed him off. But now I'd like to bring him back ... We understand there's no way to fully control the internet or how people decide to use Pepe the Frog. Trying to control that would be a completely unreasonable goal. That said, the aim of this project is to positively resurrect Pepe through the creation of a brand new comic in the spirit of the original Boy's Club.'

I tried reaching Furie for permission to use Pepe the Frog's image in this book, but my efforts were unsuccessful. I therefore used instead an image of absence (Figure 9.1), to represent the many absent images we cannot use for illustrative purposes due to copyright regulations.

After an image lives, travels, and transforms, does it ever die? And if so, does it have an afterlife? Images' lives are often circular, they fade out or die at times, to then return in the form of a rebirth with new meanings in a new context. If images followed a religious system, it would be one that involves reincarnation, where the image is immortal. It might die in one sense, but then it can transmigrate and start a new life. The nature of the death and rebirth of images relates to the dialogical nature of image production discussed earlier, where in a broader sense every production is a rebirth that relies on previous lives of other images. Every birth is an instance in an ongoing dialogue that relies in its meaning on previous lives and anticipates in its production future lives through its viewers and their response.

The focus on the death of images triggers many questions: When do we announce an image as dead? Is it when its initial meaning is dead (such as in the case of Pepe the Frog losing its original character and becoming recognized publicly for its new hate symbolism), or is it when the image ceases to exist in public space (due to disappearance or censorship, for example)? Is it possible to censor or destroy an image in a way that it ceases to exist in any form? My focus in this chapter will be on the different motives and ways through which social actors destroy images, and the consequences of these actions on different forms of image 'death'. This stage of an image's social life highlights the temptation and luring power of images sometimes; when an image presents us with something that we cannot bear to see or be confronted by such that we seek to kill it. Analysing image destruction can show the different dynamics of what is tolerated in the public space, what is deemed appropriate, representable, and visible, and what is deemed offensive and needs to be made invisible.

What makes an image so dangerous that one would want to kill it or, better put: 'What is it about people that makes them so susceptible to being offended by images? And why is the response to the offensive images so often a reciprocal act of violence, an "offending of the image" by destroying, vandalizing, or banning it from view?' (Mitchell, 2005, p. 125). The affordance of an image to offend or go against the norms is always context-specific and can change in the same context over time as the image circulates, becomes part of public debate, and becomes normalized. Some images offend because they degrade something valuable or desecrate something sacred (e.g. the ban of images that ridicule religious symbols in some societies), others offend because they glorify something hateful or despised (e.g. the ban of the Nazi symbol in some societies). Some images violate moral taboos and social norms, while some are politically offensive, they insult national symbols or present unwelcome reminders of an ignoble past. Some offend because of the manner of representation, for example a caricature of a dictator offends authority not because of who is represented but how they are represented. Other images offend because they make something material and visible that should be immaterial and invisible. For example, the controversy over the caricature drawings of Islam's prophet Muhammed were problematic for some Muslims for both those reasons, visually representing what should not be represented according to Islam, and the way he was represented in the caricatures. Like persons, images can be found 'guilty by association' with the wrong kinds of people, values, or materials (Mitchell, 2005).

The social action of destroying images can become a spectacle in its own right producing new images. When images and statues of Saddam Hussein, Hosni Mubarak, or Muammar Gaddafi were destroyed after their fall, the acts of destruction became symbolic images of the end of an era where those images were glorified and untouched. Not to mention the more recent 'statue wars', where people tear down statues of men that are seen as tainted from today's moral standards and understandings of the past. The destruction of images of a previous religious or political system has been a common practice historically to mark change and establish dominance of a new system (i.e. iconoclasm). Sometimes the image is the target of destruction, some other times it is also the image producer who becomes the target of imprisonment, threats, or even killing. In many instances, those acts of destruction or censorship result in only succeeding to pump more life, circulation, and power into those despised images.

I will focus next on actions oriented towards the image itself. I present three main intentional acts that target the death of an image: official censorship, community censorship, and creative destruction. Then I will discuss regulations that limit the social life of images such as archiving and copyright practices. These regulations are not usually ones that target the 'death' of the image; on the contrary, they are often targeted at protecting images from certain uses. However, I include them in this chapter because they limit and gatekeep image circulation in the public space, and therefore 'cut off' certain trajectories of an image's social life. Since I focus on the intentional act of image destruction, I will not cover unintentional death of images; those images from ancient civilizations that never survived for us to see, or those images that never got to be visible or circulate in public space and stayed confined within limited private spaces.

9.1 Official and Community Censorship

When we think of the death of an image through censorship it is easy to associate censorship with authoritarian and religious regimes that ban certain images from sight, burn them, and possibly imprison those who produce or possess them. In 2017, images of the teddy bear Winnie the Pooh were censored in China after they were used in internet memes that compared the character to Chinese president Xi Jinping. In the same year, Russia banned images of President Putin presented as a 'gay clown' in internet memes. In 2015, a law student was jailed in Egypt for three years for creating and posting a doctored image of President El-Sisi with Mickey Mouse ears.

Paradoxically, there is a good chance many people only got to know about those images because of the censorship. The real joke becomes not of a resemblance to Winnie the Pooh or having Mickey Mouse ears, but of the fact that these images irritated authority enough to be perceived as a 'threat' that needed to be banned. Those bans come as no surprise. In monopolized visual cultures there is clear control over who is represented, how they are represented, and who gets to represent. This control is always context- and environment-specific; even in the most authoritarian censorships, certain images can be tolerated that would not be allowed in the most democratic cultures, such as hate symbols or racist images against foreign or minority groups that authorities do not care to protect or are themselves against.

The listed examples are too simple to summarize what image censorship as a social action is about. The social position of an image censor is broader and more complex than a direct ban on a specific image. Censorship is a process of continuous filtering and gatekeeping to manage what people see, and how that seeing is intertwined with ways of thinking, feeling, and remembering, and consequential to certain potentials for action in a society. The social position of a censor can be taken up by a person, a

9.1 Official and Community Censorship

group, an institution, or a government. It is whenever an action is taken to cut the social life of an image short by limiting or totally banning its circulation. This could be via a law that bans images that are seen as contradicting with societal values, or via a copyright law that limits who can circulate an image where. This could be via an algorithm that is designed to detect sensitive, illegal, or hateful images. It could also be by a person individually reporting an image online to ban what they deem inappropriate.

This stage of the social life of the image is the one where the politics of visibility become the clearest. What is visible and how this visibility has implications on power relations is especially evident when we look at times of social and political change in societies, when there are intentional efforts to replace an old regime or a way of thinking with a new one. The 1789 French Revolution (Landes, 1992), the 1917 Russian Revolution (Campbell & Moghaddam, 2018), and the 1978 Iranian Revolution (Jaspal et al., 2015) are a few examples of how those who come to power destroy and overlay symbols and images of the old system with new ones in an attempt to alter the collective identity and the collective memory of the 'people'. The censorship and destruction of images of the old 'kings' and their replacement with the images of the 'new times' becomes a way to establish the legitimacy of the new images and symbols, and thus the power of the new system (Awad & Wagoner, 2020). Religious and political motives are also often behind the destruction of religious images, icons, and monuments (i.e. iconoclasm), where for example early Israelites destroyed the visuals of the Canaanite religion, the Christians destroyed those of Roman paganism, and the Muslims destroyed Christian and pagan images and monuments. These acts could be understood as oriented towards an 'art of forgetting' – created as a counterpoint to the art of remembering – where individuals and groups cannot deliberately forget many things, but they can artfully forget them by overlaying new images on top of the old. This would be akin to forgetting someone problematic by finding a new person with the same name.

Other than attempts at 'killing' certain images and representations of the past, another strategy – often used by those in power – is to keep certain images from getting off the ground in the first place. Especially in contexts of war and conflict, there is much deliberation and gatekeeping about what people can have access to see. Governments initiating war attempt to limit certain images that highlight the heavy cost of the war. During the Gulf War, restrictions were made on media coverage of the fallen soldiers' return to the United States and photographers were banned from taking images of the ceremonies at Dover Air Force base where the coffins of the fallen soldiers overseas returned. Similarly, photographic evidence of the damage and consequences of the atomic bombs in Japan were highly monitored in the United States, as the sharing of such images would be regarded as a most unpatriotic endeavour for the American collective memory (Sontag, 2003). Susan Sontag (2003) shows how the relationship between photography, ideology, censorship, and the authorities is clear in the history of war photography. Starting in 1855, when the British government sent Roger Fenton to capture 'positive' images of the Crimean War, images of the dead and the ill were kept outside of the series, which only included staged behind-the-frontlines photographs. Years later, one of the most iconic images of the Second World War from an American perspective, that of the raising of the American flag on Iwo Jima, turned out to be a reconstruction. It was not until the Vietnam War that the practice of staged war photographs sharply declined, especially after the emergence of independent war photographers. Censoring became instead about the military limiting the access of photographers to certain areas, such as in the case of the British campaign in the Falklands in 1982 (Sontag, 2003).

This intentional invisibility is important for the censors to keep certain realities, emotions, and consequent oppositions as far away from the viewers as possible. This form of censorship is challenged by further developments in who has the access to documentation and circulation of images of wars. Many of the wars happening today, such as between Russia and Ukraine or Israel and Hamas, are live streamed and broadcasted on digital media through ordinary civilians (i.e. citizen journalism). This changes the earlier power dynamics where the military was the one in control of the representation and broadcast of the war. This development in digital media meets new forms of censorship, such as ones designed by social media platforms through algorithms, or in governments banning certain social media websites.

9.1.1 Community Censorship

Other than official, centralized, and authority-initiated censoring of images, individuals and communities also play a role in gatekeeping and negotiating the politics of visibility. I refer to this decentralized and bottom-up censorship as community censorship. Community censorship is when individuals or groups contest the circulation of an image and attempt to censor it. It is different from official censorship because it often tackles images that are within the legal or the authority's framework of sharing, but they challenge certain community values for certain groups. Community censoring is not binding and has more room for societal negotiation and less consequences for going against this censorship. Some groups are successful, however, in gaining legal recognition and having the images they work against their circulation become officially censored.

Community censorship can be triggered by a contestation over how people want to remember a certain collective event or a certain group of people. One example is from the images of the 9/11 terrorist attack on the World Trade Center in New York in 2001. Some of the most circulated images were those with the buildings on fire and those of the rescuers. There were a certain set of images, however, whose circulation was contested and deemed inappropriate to represent the event and honour those who lost their lives. These were the images of the 'about-to-die' moments of desperate office workers jumping from the building before its collapse (Zelizer, 2004). Shortly after those images were released some of the victims' families, viewers, and journalists asked for them not to be circulated. Some news editors responded to this and stopped their circulation. Another example is of the images of US journalist James Foley being killed by the terrorist group ISIS in 2014. Many people called for the images or videos of his execution not to be shared on social media, as they would be serving the terrorist group's objectives. A social media hashtag (#ISISMediaBlackout) emerged to mobilize for a community censorship of the circulation of those visuals. In both examples, the photos were deemed inappropriate for the remembrance and grievance of the victims. The images captured the moment their lives were violently taken by the terrorist attacks, rather than capturing their life and what they meant for others around them.

There are different ways in which individuals or groups intervene to stop a certain image. In the urban space this could take a very material action form of physically destroying or spray painting over images that provoke people. After the 2011 Egyptian revolution and the toppling of the Mubarak regime, there were many images of people in the street cutting off the otherwise glorified untouched images of Mubarak in the urban space; similar images were of children removing his image from their classrooms in public schools (Awad, 2017). Community censorship was often seen in response to graffiti images as well, where pedestrians would cross out or paint over parts of a graffito that they deemed inappropriate for different cultural, religious, or political reasons. In digital spaces, community censorship could take the form of reporting images online for social media platforms to censor them, and this reporting could feed into algorithms detecting and censoring images automatically and labelling them as 'not following the community standards'.

The deliberation about which images are necessary to see and which images should be censored represents a continuous meaning negotiation on the individual and collective level. Many images never get to have a social life in the public space because they have already been censored by their producer. We engage in self-censorship in relation to images we decide to never share because they do not depict us or people we belong to in a favourable light. Self-censorship among photojournalists is often behind the double standards in depicting friendly and enemy causalities (Sontag, 2003). Self-censorship is always embedded in any process of image production, where the image producer is in a continuous deliberation about what to edit, what to choose, and what to omit in an image as one is drawing it, capturing it, or sharing it. That same deliberation and negotiation over what to produce, circulate, or censor motivate actions against censorship. The act of sharing a censored image, documenting causalities that are made invisible, or looking for absent images are all acts of resistance to censorship. The act of censorship in many instances triggers counteractions of preservation and circulation. Some images only gain a powerful viral life when they are censored. The reason we have access today to images that were meant to 'die' by some actors, is because there was a committed minority that reserved those images and saved them from extinction – they kept their social lives in hibernation until they could be resurrected in a new time or a new space.

9.2 Symbolic Destruction

In censorship, actions are directed towards a certain image to stop its circulation or limit it. Another form of acting against an image is to not target its material destruction at all, but instead to produce another image, a counter-image, that would symbolically destroy the meaning of the first image. This latter form of destruction is sometimes more powerful and effective than trying to completely kill an image or force it into disappearance and extinction. The desire to get rid of an image could be realized through a new image that critiques it (Groys, 2008). Creative destruction, as Mitchell (2005) refers to it, transforms an already existing image through the production of a counter-image, one that defaces, disfigures, mutilates, or humiliates the targeted image and what it stands for (Mitchell, 2005). Consider, for example, the girl statue placed in front of the bull of Wall Street. Here, the target is not to make the image disappear, but rather to render its appearance in a new way, to appropriate its meaning and intention, and make people see it in a new way that is offensive to the intention of the initial producer.

When alt-right social media users appropriated Pepe the Frog images on Reddit, 4chan, and other social media platforms, they did not intervene with Matt Furie's images of the frog, as in they did not try to limit their circulation or censor them; instead they created their own images of the frog, in new settings and with new hate symbols, such as Pepe holding a swastika or wearing a Ku Klux Klan hood. Those images managed to circulate widely enough that they became known and debated faces of Pepe the Frog, and as such countered and violated the original peaceful meaning intended by Furie.

Counter-images drive their meaning from the original image. They re-represent the content of the image in a new light or manipulate part of the design of the image to counter its meaning in an often ironic intervention. Irony here relies on a form of 'double-voicedness' (Marková, 2003), where an actor uses another actor's words or images to express one's own meanings and intentions that are hostile to the other's voice. Counter-images' main meaning and power draw upon the image they are countering. Without the prior knowledge of the original image, the counter-image is often in itself less meaningful. Using Bakhtin's dialogic theory (1986), counter-images could be understood as utterances that refute a previous utterance and presuppose the viewers' knowledge of that previous utterance. The street poster discussed in Chapter 5 (Figure 5.3) is a clear example of this, where the image of a fleeing family with the text 'welcome refugees' was transformed to a weaponized family with the text 'welcome terrorist'. Without the knowledge of the original poster, the counter-image does not make much sense of why it is 'welcoming' terrorists.

Counter-images could be created by physically and creatively manipulating the original image, omitting part of it or adding a part to it that alters its meaning and turns it into an opposite voice. One such practice is that known as 'culture jamming', which is a practice that became known around the end of the twentieth century targeting advertising images. In cultural jamming, viewers, artists, or activist groups (such as Rodriguez de Gerada or San Francisco's Billboard Liberation Front) hijack and parody advertising billboards by adding something to them or layering them with another image that often aims at revealing advertisers' manipulation and inviting viewers to critically reassess the advertisers' messages. Cultural jamming is an act against how advertisers buy their way into taking up public spaces and an act to reclaim viewers' right to answer back images they never asked to see (N. Klein, 1999). Another intervention in symbolic destruction is that of groups who aim to reappropriate and destroy hate symbols. For example, the de-radicalization group EXIT-Germany produces 'trick' t-shirts that have the iconography of far-right symbols and distribute them at far-right concerts; once the t-shirt is washed the hate symbols are washed off, and one can see a message and a telephone number encouraging people to seek help if they want to leave far-right extremism (Miller-Idriss, 2018).

Yet another way of symbolic destruction can take the form of excessive production and saturation of an image by a different producer in a different context that contradicts the initial one. One clear example of this is the commodification and commercialization of protest symbols, where they are mass produced by commercial entities into different forms and products in a way that renders the protest symbol meaningless and banalizes its meaning as it is used as an everyday commodity void of its contextual meaning as a protest or a solidarity symbol. The face of Che Guevara, the Palestinian keffiyeh, and the feminist symbol of a raised fist and a Venus symbol are clear examples of this. Radical subcultures and their images are often the target of appropriation through commodification, where the subculture is dismissed as meaningless as its symbols are turned into mainstream commodities (Hebdige, 1979). This is paradoxical in a way, because for an image or protest symbol to circulate widely and become recognized, it needs to be freely accessible and free for others to reproduce, yet it risks being abundantly used and misused in different directions. Alternatively, an image can be copyrighted and its reproductions highly regulated, but this comes with its own challenges.

9.3 Copyright and Archiving

Since in this chapter I discuss the actions that lead to keeping the life of an image still, or to its complete or symbolic death, it is important to consider regulations around the circulation and gatekeeping of images and how they affect their public social life. Copyright regulations, ethical standards, and archiving practices do not end an image's social life – though they can – but they limit its life and accessibility to certain spaces, certain uses, and certain social actors.

Decisions regarding how to store public and historical images in a culture, which ones to display, and which ones get forgotten in archives present one way in which the collective memory of a community is regulated. There is thus political, social, and cultural power in choosing what gets stored, how, where, and who gets access. In *Archive Fever*, Jacques Derrida (Derrida, 1996) explores similarities between the physical archive and the human mind in its motives for remembering and forgetting. Using a Freudian psychoanalytic lens to understanding archives, he argues that archives are driven by our desires to recover moments of inception. Since our death drive tends to erase our past, we rely on archives as an external memory in our environment when we are triggered by a self-defeating desire to return to the 'origin'; this is what Derrida refers to as 'archive fever'. A psychoanalytic lens to reading archives can help us explore what has been hidden and made absent – or repressed – to not hold us back and what has been declared private versus public and belonging to a community's collective memory. Practices surrounding archiving always involve a negotiation between our own marks – what we wish to record and remember – and the marks, traces, and absences of those long gone. Archiving practices today also take place in digital culture, where there is control over what is stored, for how long, how it is accessed, and who gets to manage that; all these open up questions about cultural hierarchies and call for a broadening of the concept of archiving to understand emergent types of archiving and how they mediate circulation and knowledge in everyday life (Beer, 2013).

When Marxist and cultural critic Walter Benjamin (1935) wrote about the age of mechanical reproduction at the beginning of the twentieth century, he predicted that the technological advancement of print and mass production would provide accessibility of art and images in different contexts and places that goes beyond the few that were previously able to see original authentic paintings. He predicted that access to reproduction can potentially free the image and allow its circulation and use for politics. Benjamin's vision did not predict the current regulations and legal debates about image ownership rights and the many new ways of gatekeeping that limit the accessibility and reproduction of many images. From a legal perspective, images are forms of intellectual property that are governed by ethical and legal codes regulating who can copy an image and what constitutes a legitimate use of a copy versus what constitutes an infraction of ownership rights (Sturken & Cartwright, 2018).

Other than copyright laws, there are different ethical standards that gatekeep images from going to public space. Those ethical standards can be institutionalized – for example, a university's ethical committee or a newspaper's editor deciding what image use is appropriate and does not cause harm to those identified in the image or to the general public. The ethical standards can also be the image reproducers' own moral assessment of what is legitimate reproduction of an image. Using images in research raises different ethical questions. For example, when is it appropriate that researchers use publicly available images for analytical and academic purposes? How can participants in research remain anonymized if images show their faces or the places they live in? How can participation consent highlight clearly how and where the images will be used? There are also macro ethical considerations in relation to the consequences of the images we share: Do they revictimize a community? Do they reproduce discrimination? If they document human suffering and show its impact, what are the risks embedded in this showing? Research practices with digital images have implications regarding the circulation and reproduction of those images. As researchers search and collect image data, they could be also boosting the traffic of those images through clicks and downloads. As researchers publish academic work in different forms, they also engage in reproducing and circulating further the images they research. In researching discriminatory or fascist images, this could pose an ethical challenge as the research work could potentially amplify the discourses of those images (Askanius, 2021).

The ethical considerations are broad and involve different rights as well as social responsibilities of different social actors. The copyright law is more concerned with the rights of the image owner; this could be the individual image creator or an entity such as a news agency or a media production company. Copyright includes the right to copy, distribute, produce, display, create, and transform a previous image, so in a way copyright tackles the different stages of an image's social life. Copyright was established to protect the rights of an image owner, and this is of course important in order to protect against stealing others' creations and profiting off other people's work. However, there are major implications of copyright for access to images and the basic understanding of dialogical creativity, where creating is a process of recombining, reproducing, borrowing, and reinterpreting previous ideas. Copyright regulations can sometimes be problematic because of the sole focus on the rights of the owner, and less on the social responsibility in relation to knowledge sharing, collaborative creativity, and accessibility.

There are exceptions introduced through fair use or fair dealing laws, where one is allowed to copy without permission of the copyright holder, on the condition that the copying is done for a limited and 'transformative' purpose, such as to comment, educate, criticize, or parody a copyrighted work. It is always an issue of debate as to what falls under fair use and whether the reproduction adds something new and transformative or just imitates the original (Sturken & Cartwright, 2018). Law scholar Amy Adler (2016) argues that the conception of fair use could ultimately be destructive in the context of art styles that are based on borrowing and appropriating. When an image is questioned on whether it is 'transformative', it is judged based on searching for certain 'new meaning' of the reproduction, which is problematic when some artistic productions aim to reject the concept of 'newness', to destabilize any meaning, and to provide multiple new ways of seeing (Adler, 2016). Some of the critics of such restrictions have worked towards establishing databases of images and other resources that are open for others to use such as Creative Commons organization. Adding a creative commons licence to an image does not mean that the image creator loses their right to the image but that they allow its reuse and sharing under clear guidelines.

The attempt to restrict and regulate the ownership and circulation of images goes against the meanings behind certain image genres, such as digital memes and graffiti. Digital image memes would not be able to develop without copyright infringement (Patel, 2013). In recent years, companies have started to chase after bloggers and internet users who use their photographs in a meme. See, for example, the story of the socially awkward penguin meme (C. Dewey, 2015). The question often raised is whether a version of the photograph adapted into a meme is a copyright infringement or whether the meme is a transformed commentary on the original image. There is a good chance that digital meme users would be able to defend their case as 'fair use', but this requires having the funds to take up the case in the courts, which is one of the reason companies go after independent and non-profit individuals, where the more convenient option becomes paying the back licensing fees and taking the image down. In the case of memes or in the broader case of transforming already existing images for different contemporary uses, copyright regulations are putting much of the cultural artefacts and heritage of the past legally off-limits for adaptation and commentary and pushing them out of the public domain (Lessig, 2003).

Graffiti is another image genre that goes against copyright and in many cases is done as an intervention protesting ownership over public spaces and is considered a criminal activity in many contexts. Yet, in recent years it has become increasingly recognized as an artistic undertaking and commercial opportunity, which made it subject to copyright law. Looking at how copyright is negotiated in relation to graffiti and street art opens up a range of issues in relation to the contestation over how copyright law is applied and its formal and moral boundaries (Bonadio, 2019). When I published research articles tackling street art, I sometimes used my own photographs of graffiti on different public walls, but I was still often asked by publishers to get the permission of the graffiti painter because I am reproducing their work from the street to the article. This is challenging on different fronts: one of graffiti's main characteristics is that it is an anonymous and public intervention, and many times one cannot trace the painter except if they tagged their painting and their tag or signature is famous enough to be found online (this was the case for Figure 6.1), but in many other cases it is not possible to trace and it contradicts the idea of graffiti.

Many of the images I would have liked to use in this book I was not able to due to copyright. The images in this chapter were left blank on purpose, to show what it would be like to not be able to show what we discuss and the limitations censorship and copyright pose. In other chapters, there are images I did not use for different reasons: they cost too much; I could not find the producer or owner to request permission; or I found the producer, but they no longer owned the rights to their own images and referred me to image archives or news agencies that charged for reproduction. For example, in Chapter 2 I wanted to use the iconic image of Albert Einstein with his wild hair and sticking his tongue out as an example of a common representation of the 'genius mind'. I do not think Einstein or the person who took the photograph would have minded my use of the image for illustration; however, as it turned out, in Einstein's will he pledged his literary property upon his death to his secretary and stepdaughter, and upon their death to the Hebrew University of Jerusalem, the institution he co-founded in 1918. Einstein did not mention in his will the rights to use his name or image in books or products; there was no such thing as publicity rights at the time. When the Hebrew University took over Einstein's estate in 1982, publicity rights had become an aggressive field of battle as they control who could use Einstein's name or image and at what cost. Einstein has been listed in Forbes' list of the ten highest-earning historic 'dead celebrity' figures given his post-death earnings for the Hebrew University (Parkin, 2022). Would this have been Einstein's own method in regulating the circulation of his name, image, and ideas?

The choices of which images lived on in the book were thus governed in part by my own self-censorship of what is relevant and important to show, and with copyrights that determined what I can reproduce rather than

9.3 Copyright and Archiving

what could have provided the best example. My method in response to image copyright has been in checking within a range of images I find relevant to use if I could find any of them that are available freely for reproduction under a Creative Commons open licence. For other images where the producer was alive and accessible, I contacted them for permissions. Many of those I contacted, who also still had the ownership to their images, agreed, kindly knowing that it is for the purpose of illustration in an academic book and not for commercial purposes. There were certain sets of images that I found relevant to illustrate the social life of an image; however, I did not have access to every image in a sequence; in that case I decided to put the different images in a collage to show the images in comparison to one another (e.g. see Figure 8.3), drawing on the fair use law. I decided to also use detailed descriptions under each image to mention explicitly how I reproduced it and if I acquired permissions and from whom. I think it is not only a legal responsibility but also an ethical one to document and discuss when images are censored out of our productions because we were not able to obtain permissions to reproduce, could not afford the cost, or our permission requests were rejected. There are many image producers, such as authoritarian governments, where one might want to avoid having to ask for permissions to use their images. It is not expected that they would agree for their images to be used for a purpose that is clearly critical and where asking for permission would pose a risk of them attempting to censor the whole work or going after the producer. Does that mean we do not produce those images and self-censor in response to their censorship, or produce without permission and trust that the fair use would protect us, or stay away from criticizing 'dangerous' images at all and fulfil the goal of such image producers of having an authoritarian monologue that cannot be answered back or refuted?

These questions address the consequences of copyright law and the choices one needs to make in response to them. The consequences of copyright law affect image producers as well as image viewers and their ability to interact and respond to images. It is important to protect the rights of producers, but it is also important to protect accessibility and the ability for creative appropriations. Copyright regulations have major repercussions on the freedom to create and imagine and on the development of ideas in a culture (Lessig, 2004). The copyright dilemmas do not get any easier with further technological developments such as AI-generated images, where the image producer is non-human, or with digital certificates of authority such as non-fungible tokens, where new forms of ownerships are created for digital images. The main ethical dimension that I think is important to maintain in those dilemmas is that image use is an ethical act that involves rights as well as responsibilities. With every right to use and get access to an image, there is a responsibility in how one uses it. Every use, reproduction, or transformation of an image needs to be an ethically dialogical one that acknowledges and builds on, rather than denies or steals, earlier productions.

9.4 Methods: Researching Absences

The death stage of an image's social life is not as accessible to research as other stages. How can one research an image that is no longer accessible, one that was made absent from public spaces? In other words, how can absence be researched?

Within every single image and within the visual culture of any given space there are always absences. Every time there is a choice of what to show, there is a choice of what not to show. In research, it is important to recognize the powerful presence of absences in our environment:

> '*Here, there was* a bakery'; '*That* is where old Mrs. Dupuis *lived*'. We are struck by the fact that sites that have been lived in are filled with the presence of absences. What appears designates what is no more: '*Look*: here there *was* …', but can no longer be seen … Every site is haunted by countless ghosts that lurk there in silence, to be 'evoked' or not. One *inhabits* only haunted sites. (de Certeau, 1984, pp. 143–144)

In the image interpretation section in Chapter 5, I discussed how absence is part of the interpretation of any image: what is immediately absent from the content of an image and what is – in the broader sense – made absent from a visual culture and why? For every image of the atomic bomb (Figure 3.1), what images of the aftermath of the bomb are not shown? For every image of Muslim minorities in Danish far-right communication (Figure 7.4) what other representations are not shown, and which spaces show the minorities' own self-representation? In the context of the Egyptian revolution, for every image of President El-Sisi in the urban space today, how many images of the revolution (Figures 1.1 and 4.1) have been censored?

When I researched the area of Tahrir Square, the epicentre of the 2011 revolution, five years after the beginning of the protests, there was a strong presence of absence. The new government was active in its counter-revolution measures, making sure to 'clean' the space out of the traces of the revolution and replace them with images of the new regime to affirm the dominance and authoritarian monologic voice over public space. Researching the visual production of the revolution became then an endeavour of tracing the 'past lives' and the 'afterlives' of the images that were made absent in the urban space. There were two routes that guided my research: image documentation and afterlives on social media, and participants' own storytelling and memories (Awad, 2017, 2021). Met by a restrictive urban space overtaken by censorship and arrest, the images travelled to online spaces, which are freer – though not completely safe from security risks and online censorship. Participants' stories provided an important emotional aspect in relation to how people experienced the censorship and the overtaking of the visual culture by the new regime. Participants who were supportive of the revolution expressed that the renovation of the square by the new government with all the fresh new paint and the new billboards and monuments was, in their experience, an act of 'covering up' rather than 'cleaning up'. It was an act of suppressing the collective memory of the revolution and an act that alienated them from those spaces (Awad, 2017).

Tahrir Square today is a powerful 'empty' space that is filled with the presence of absences. The renovated square with its clean secured roads is a space that is only allowed to be used passively. It is a space that is transformed into a new symbol of defeat, of a betrayed revolution, and of grief. However, the revolutionary image of the square did not die; it became a dominant global image that travelled to other geographical contexts and sites, inviting others to occupy places for difference causes, such as Zuccotti Park with the Occupy Wall Street movement in the United States (Mitchell, 2012).

In 2022, protestors across China occupied squares and streets, holding a blank A4 sheet of paper. The protests became known as the *white paper* or the *A4* revolution and were in objection to the strict zero-covid policy and more broadly against censorship and the lack of freedom of expression. Choosing a blank page (Figure 9.2) as a protest poster could not have sent a better message against censorship. Researching absences is about tracing all those voices and messages that ought to be on these blank pieces of paper but were censored. Those voices could be traced in their travel life to subcultures where they found an outlet or in the voices of those holding the papers and occupying the squares.

Figure 9.2   Protest poster against censorship and prolonged Covid-19 regulations in China, 2022.

9.5   A Digital Meme Image: The Death of a Frog

The image of Pepe the Frog provides an example that tackles image appropriation, creative destruction, the image producer's attempts at regaining ownership and killing their own image, and image censorship.

After cartoonist Matt Furie created the character of Pepe the Frog in 2006, the image took on a life of its own on social media. The laid-back 'feel good' frog became the subject of many memes and humorous images. As the image circulated further, the character changed into a frog that expresses racist, antisemitic, and Islamophobic sentiments, claims white supremacy, and wears hate symbols such as that of the KKK and the Nazi swastika. This development was specific to certain online platforms such as 4chan and 8chan, which are anonymous image-based online forums. These platforms have quickly grown following several right-wing extremist attacks in 2019 and have become a common platform for 'politically incorrect' discussions and for fostering a certain far-right subculture (Baele et al., 2021).

By 2016, the Pepe the Frog image was considered by the Anti-Defamation League to be a hate symbol as a result of how it had been appropriated by the alt-right and white supremacist movements. The image was not constrained to online subcultures but travelled in between platforms such as Twitter (renamed X) and Reddit and, with the help of algorithms, it travelled to mainstream sites and political discourses. During the 2016 US election, the image was denounced in a speech by presidential candidate Hillary Clinton (Daniels, 2018) and a meme of Pepe as Donald Trump was retweeted by the Donald Trump campaign. In 2020, the *Feels Good Man* documentary was created by Arthur Jones and Giorgio Angelini to trace the history and multiple interpretations of Pepe the Frog. In an interview by Artnet, Jones and Angelini narrate how the cartoon became a blank canvas affording all kinds of expressions. It went from a 'feel good, man' frog, to a 'feel sad' frog, to a 'feel angry' frog. This development was in a context where American political discourses were becoming more and more angry and irrational, with republican figures such as Donald Trump utilizing polarizing content and misinformation on digital media. Furie, the image producer, tried in several ways to 'save Pepe'. First, he tried to launch a campaign online inviting other artists to reproduce images of Pepe that resemble his peaceful character. Later, he found a law firm that was willing to take up the case as pro bono given its popularity, and the copyright attorneys helped him pursue far-right figures who used and profited from Pepe as a promotion image and was able to make some of them stop using it as their logo. Neither attempt, however, was able to revert the new alt-right meaning and the symbolic destruction of the 'feel good' frog, hence Furie's later attempt with announcing the death of *Pepe*.

The case of Pepe the Frog is especially interesting in considering what makes a symbol for a movement or a group, and how symbols emerge, circulate, and get embedded with different layers of meaning until they come to be the emblem of certain ideas. Symbols (as discussed in Chapter 2) embody multiple meanings; they have a face value as well as an underlying sentimental value that gives them their affective power and stability (Bartlett, 1924). Powerful symbols that come to represent a movement, a cause, or a group are often ones that are able to vividly condense broad meanings into a concrete objectified form that can mobilize a group behind it, ones that bring familiarity and an anchoring point for a collective identity, and ones that can travel across contexts and times to carry on the meaning and mobilize broader collectives. These arguments could be clearly seen in symbols such as the hammer and sickle image of communism or the Nefertiti in a gas mask image of the Egyptian revolution (Figure 4.1), but the prominence of Pepe as a unifying symbol for the alt-right challenges these arguments. A green frog to represent white supremacy or Nazi ideology seems random.

In her analysis of different far-right symbols, including Pepe the Frog, Miller-Idriss (2018) shows how sometimes images that have no one intended political meaning are appropriated as ideological symbols in ways that are hard to predict. Semiotic and structural linguist de Saussure argued that unlike signs that have an arbitrary relation to meanings, symbols have a non-arbitrary motivated relationship to meaning (de Saussure, 2021). However, Miller-Idriss (2018) shows that this relationship is disrupted in the case of far-right symbols especially on digital media where online memes have shifted the linear relationship between the symbol and its meaning, and the relationship has become much more of a random association.

Maybe symbols never had a clear arbitrary relationship to meaning. Symbols get layered with meanings and affective power through what people do with them, how they use them especially in significant collective moments such as a protest, and how they transform the symbol's social life through time and across different spaces. The effectiveness of many symbols builds on cultural norms and conventions, but many other symbols initiate that relationship. An apparently random colour or animal when used in a certain way in a protest or a cultural ritual can establish its visibility and association to a movement, then could live on to carry that meaning and become an affective mobilizer for later developments of that movement. Pepe as a symbol of the alt-right is random in a sense, but the tracing of its social life and the understanding of the digital spaces in which it 'grew' can provide some explanations as to its fame.

Pepe represents ugliness in a way; it is an ugly careless frog that is in stark contrast to the dominant social media platform cultures promoting beauty and extravagant lifestyles through consumerism and social influencers. Pepe is the outsider, the left-out, the odd one out; characteristics that resonate with certain digital media subcultures, where alternative views flourish (e.g. the misogynist views of incel groups or racist views of white supremist groups). In fact, the image producer, Matt Furie, describes his artistic style as one that engages with ugliness in the world; it combines happy little frogs, awkward family portraits of fast-food mascots, horror movie monsters, and family portraits people hang over their mantels, where the whole family is dressed in white and are barefoot on the beach, which he finds kind of creepy (Thielman, 2020). His art, he argues, insists on 'the normality of those deemed weird by the world' and giving hope and understanding to kids who are frustrated by the world. Maybe that is exactly what brought the resonance of the frog to certain online communities.

There is also another factor that has to do with the accessibility of the image form. Pepe the Frog is simple and relatively easily redrawn; that simplicity is also generative of many different adaptations of the frog. The basic illustration of Pepe represents it as somehow innocent and carefree, while at the same time having an edge of creepiness in its looks and what it can do in the image transformations. In a visual content analysis of digital meme images produced by the Nordic Resistance Movement (NRM) – one of the biggest and most active extreme-right neo-Nazi groups in Scandinavia – Askanius (2021) shows that those groups have been increasingly using accessible humorous and ambiguous images in their online communication inspired by online communities such as 4chan, 8chan, Reddit, and Imgur. The group, she argues, uses popular culture iconography such as that of Pepe the Frog to craft white supremacy, homophobia, anti-feminism, and antisemitic ideas onto popular digestible material. One of its members reflected openly on the underlying strategies behind these choices: 'some might be wondering why NRM should dedicate time to such folly. The answer is that humor and satire, or silliness if you will, is a very powerful weapon. Not least because humor breaks the first mental barrier in "ordinary people" when it comes to "forbidden topics". If a person laughs at "the Holocaust", the first barrier is gone' (Askanius, 2021, p. 153).

Pepe might remain a symbol for those ideals, its producer might manage to announce its death or resurrect a new social life for it with a new meaning, or Pepe might subside from public attention given its censorship as a hate symbol and disappear then come up again in a new time or space. In 2019 Pepe's image was used by protestors in Hong Kong as a symbol of resistance against the government. The reappropriation of Pepe as a hate symbol seems to not have caught on in Hong Kong; instead, the frog took on the yellow construction helmet that was symbolic of the pro-democracy movement and the frog's meaning became associated with the movement. The frog shows us that images do not seem to go extinct; they have no final death or final meaning and their lives are circular and adaptive to what people do with them.

CHAPTER 10

Concluding Thoughts
The Mattering of the Image

Figure 10.1   Belgrade, Serbia, May 2024.
Source: Author's photograph.

Images matter. Unlike the claim about the ceramics in the photograph in Figure 10.1, images have a psychological, social, and political function. They are not just signs and tools for communication; they are artefacts through which we act on the world. A psychological inquiry into the image is one that is concerned with three key questions: Who/what is (not) seen in everyday visual culture? How they are seen? How do people think, feel, and act in response to what they see?

I started this book questioning how images matter today and how our relationship to the image has changed over time. I grew up with a set number of print photographs in two photo albums that visually captured my childhood. I placed the photo albums on a shelf in my room and

Concluding Thoughts: The Mattering of the Image

would go through them from time to time and show them to friends visiting me. My son has over 10,000 photographs capturing his first fifteen years of life. They are mostly digital images with very few printed ones. Sometimes I wonder if he will ever get the time or interest to go through them all. This change probably has an influence on the significance and affective value of those images for each of us and on how we both reconstruct our pasts through them. If an image can speak louder than a thousand words, can it still do the same when it is one among a million other images? Those changes are not only influencing our individual and collective memories, they are also influencing our lived experiences. Sometimes image taking and sharing can take precedence over being in the here and now of a certain experience, whether it is a tourist attraction visit, a concert, a social gathering, a workout, or even just eating a meal. A further change is in what we see. For a long time, we have been surrounded by mass media, news, advertisement, and political campaign images that we are collectively exposed to. Now, we also have images targeting us individually, tailored to our interests and even shaping them through digital media algorithms. Two people in the same space and same context could be getting a very different flow of images in their daily life. Does that make us look – or not look – at those images differently?

Psychological research so far can tell us something about how images influence how we see, think, feel, and remember (Chapter 3). Seeing is an embodied and socially situated act that involves choices and biases in relation to where we aim our gaze, what we pay attention to, and what we look away from. Our social position, our environment, and the images surrounding us have an influence on how we learn to see in certain ways. Images are also integral to thinking; images – in comparison to language – engage our brains differently and trigger open systems of thinking that rely on flexibility and openness to multiple cognitive and affective interpretations. Images we are continuously exposed to can normalize certain ideas about the world and shape our attitudes and behaviours. Images can also feed into certain arguments or narratives through how they position people represented in them and how they position the viewer. They can construct different dichotomies of social positions, for example us–them, normal–abnormal, and heroes–villains. This influences how we cognitively and affectively understand the world and people around us. Research shows that we are more likely to feel empathy and relate to an unfamiliar group of people when we see personalized images of them than when they are depicted as anonymized and de-individualized groups of people. We are also influenced by how – and if at all – our own identity group is represented in images around us. Being surrounded by negative stereotypical images of our groups could impact our self-perception, feelings of belonging, and our behaviour. Images also shape how we reconstruct our personal and collective memories, influencing who is remembered, how they are remembered, and who is forgotten.

This psychological influence of images is more complex, however, than a direct stimuli–effect relation. Who we are, where we are, the kind of society we live in, and how we respond to different images all play a mediating role in how images can influence us. We do not passively receive images; we actively interpret, produce, share, transform, and even censor them around us. Despite the many psychological studies and experiments studying the direct effect of images on us (e.g. exposure to certain advertisements and consequent buying behaviour, or exposure to certain stereotype images and their influence on academic performance), less work addresses the variety of ways in which we actively respond to and with images. This latter focus can take us a step further from asking if images matter, to investigating when and how and to what extent they can matter in different contexts. For this focus, I proposed the analytical framework of the *social life of images* (Chapters 4–9), which traces what people do with images through following the social life trajectory of different images, where they are produced and composed, situated in an environment, actively viewed, circulated and transformed, and censored.

This framework builds on a pragmatic pluralist sociocultural psychological approach to images, where images are cultural artefacts that individuals and groups use to act on their environment (Chapter 2). From this perspective, there is a reciprocal influence relationship between individuals and their environment. From the one side, our surrounding environment affords certain ways of seeing, thinking, feeling, remembering, and acting while constraining others. From the other side, we exercise agency in reshaping and reinterpreting our environment in a way that mediates our own experiences and in a way that allow us to also act on the experience of others. Images play a key role in this reciprocal relationship, as we use them in a dialogical and political process to produce, exchange, and transform knowledge in everyday life, influencing who and what is seen and how they are seen.

10.1 Realities That Matter

Images as cultural tools do have a material existence in the world with certain affordances. This material existence could be in a poster image that we can feel its paper material physically in our hands or in a digital image that we see through a screen and is stored on servers in physical data centres around the world and transmitted through the infrastructure of the internet. However, the reality that I would like to discuss here is the one that the image – as a cultural sign – represents or constructs. Images can help us get a glimpse of certain realities. Photography, for example, serves that purpose for visual documentation and news dissemination of different happenings around the world. Images can also construct a visual representation of an abstract or visibly inaccessible reality. A body scan image or an illustration of a viral infection process can help us understand certain realities about our biological nature. Images can also create fictional representations that can help us imagine alternative realities, for example through artistic productions in the form of paintings or caricature images. Images are also known to be used intentionally to manipulate and distort realities and create delusions that are presented as reality.

In considering how images matter and their contentious relationship with reality, there are three points that I want to make clear. *First*, no matter how 'accurate' we try to use images to 'picture reality as it is', images always remain a perspective on reality, a voice on how things are seen from one situated position in one point in time and space. They can provide a trace or a glimpse of a physical objective reality, but they are always a representation that involves a reconstruction process. In their production and viewership, we engage in a subjective reconstruction process of making sense of the world.

Second, even when images do not reflect reality, when they create fictions or distort reality, they have real consequences on people's minds and actions. Even if we are aware that we are immersed every day in a stream of banal images, consumer desires, fake news, and imaginary relations to celebrities, social influencers, and fictional characters, those environments do have real consequences on how we see the world, how we relate to others, and how we see ourselves. They also have consequences on the cultures we live in and what is valued in them, and the possible futures of our societies. Historical images produced by colonial powers of the 'others' to 'prove' their inferiority and justify the need for governing them – whether those images captured their brain size or their cultural rituals – still have enduring psychological and social consequences in relation to inequalities and oppressive social structures – this influence endures despite postcolonial critique (for a further discussion of this, see Chapter 3).

Third, those different layers of reality that images reflect, construct, and reproduce are important to investigate and distinguish between them to properly understand the influence of images. From a pragmatic pluralist perspective that goes beyond the realism–constructionism divide, those different realities with their varying degrees of objective or subjective existence tap into exactly how and to what extent images matter. Through images – as tools for social action – individuals intervene in those layers of realities differently. Combining a variety of ontological and epistemological approaches in studying images can help us understand the possibilities and limitations of those interventions. In what follows, I will elaborate on this third point and explain why I advocate for a pluralistic approach that distinguishes between those realities, investigates them each in their own right, and does not equate them in a relativistic manner.

In 1967, Marxist philosopher Guy Debord – who was a key figure of the situationist art movement – argued that late capitalist society is a society of the *spectacle*, that is created apart from reality, where representation takes over our real authentic lived experiences. When the real world is transformed to mere images, mere images become real beings, he argued. The spectacle is more than just images or screens; it is a new social relation between people that is mediated by an accumulation of images that alienate people from a genuinely lived life and normalize capitalist individualized ways of living and modern production structures (Debord, 1967/2009). For Debord, the spectacle that is created by spectacular industries (television, films, and publishing) is a world view that has materialized as unquestioned 'reality' that requires passive acceptance from a consuming subject. It reduces reality to appearance and commodities. Spectators – who live fragmented isolated lives in capitalist societies – are linked solely by their one-way relationship to the very centre that keeps them isolated from each other. 'The spectacle thus reunites the separated, but it reunites them only *in their separateness*' (p. 32). Around two decades after Debord's *Society of the Spectacle*, he published a commentary on the book arguing that the spectacle's active force has only grown in power and became more 'real' (Debord, 1988/1998). In his first book, he maintained a distinction between the reality constructed by the spectacle and other forms of reality, while in his second book, he talked of an *integrated spectacle* (p. 8), where the spectacle has spread itself to the point where it now permeates all reality.

This disappearance of reality is even more pronounced in another seminal work on the topic by philosopher and sociologist Jean Baudrillard (Baudrillard, 1981/1994). Baudrillard saw the spectacle as only a stage in the evolution of a much more complex and pervasive system of simulation. He argued that in postmodern capitalism we live in a society of the *simulacra*, in which we can no longer distinguish what is real from what is not. In his view, the image has moved from reflecting or masking reality, to masking the absence of a profound reality, to having no relation to any reality whatsoever. For Baudrillard, this has paradoxically made the image seem ever more 'real', where the image generates our sense of reality in a way that it precedes the real world. This make us live in a state of *hyperreality*, where reality is no longer represented in any recognizable way, and where our experience is mediated by signs that replace reality. He speaks of a decisive turning point in postmodernity, where signs became no longer referring to something, and therefore false can no longer be distinguished from truth, or real from artificial. Unlike Debord, Baudrillard argues that the development of the *simulacra* cannot be reduced to a certain economic development. It does not just keep people distracted from a reality, it creates its own oppressive reality by reducing everything and everyone to a consumable image, that becomes more real than the actual lived experience.

The ideas of Debord and Baudrillard could be relevant today especially in the realm of social media, reality shows, fan culture, digital consumer cultures, and social influencers. In these spaces one could be immersed in certain visual cultures where how things appear become perceived as *the* reality, or at least the reality that matters. In those spaces, there is an imagined reality, a spectacle, which presents itself as superior to the mundane lived experience of everyday life. One can observe in those spaces the superiority of the image or representations over lived realities. There is a glorification of the banal, giving distorted ideas about choice and significance, and keeping the person in a state of continuous immersion in the content they are viewing. This immersion can keep one in a constant consumer state that is maintained by one's own unhappiness and unsatisfaction. Those ideas resonate with Debord and Baudrillard's analysis; however, as I will discuss, there are several challenges with applying their ideas to visual culture and the society at large.

Debord (1967/2009) argued that the spectacle – in his time mainly addressing mass media – is a monologue that invites no engagement, only passive acceptance that keeps people distracted from reality and from genuine interpersonal community experience. Baudrillard (1981/1994) argued further that this creates a hyperreality that replaces objective reality. Those two arguments are problematic in different ways. First, the affordances of media today provide more than one-way top-down communication to a passive receiving audience. Second, the claim that a hyperreality has come to replace reality – effacing the line between real and not real and between true and false – erases the possibility of human agency, reflection, and resistance.

The first problem has to do with only focusing on the power of images in our environment to submerge us in whatever 'reality' they send our way and ignoring how individuals dialogically interpret and engage with those images differently. We can certainly get immersed in the abundance of images around us every day and come to see the world through the continuous flow of images that come our way in news and social media; we can look no further than the glimpse – however accurate or distorted it is – that the images give us, we can build a life immersed in this 'reality' and look no further. However, that does not mean that there is no possibility for distancing ourselves from this spectacle, reflectively thinking about it, and actively opposing it and building genuine communities through those same media tools. The internet has been a site of distraction and immersion, but it has also been a site of building solidaric communities across the world and the site of disseminating images that challenge and expose dominant spectacles. This is not limited to the 'internet age'; people protest about dominant mass media narratives that justify inequalities and wars. People also continuously 'disrupt' the spectacle in the public space by acts like graffiti painting and cultural jamming practices that hijack and parody advertisement billboards, exposing their manipulation.

Both Debord and Baudrillard reduced the people to their social position as spectators and emphasized the power of the few in power to manipulate the masses. Debord (1967/2009) argued that the 'spectacle is the opposite of dialogue' (p. 28). It is the society's ambassador to itself, delivering its 'never ending monologue of self-praise' (p. 29) in a court where no one else is allowed to speak. He also argued in his later book that there is no place left where people can discuss their realities because they cannot free themselves from the crushing presences of the media discourses surrounding them (Debord, 1988/1998). This has led in his view to the disappearance of the possibility of individuals to make independent judgement and to have the ability to verify facts and read beyond the image; for reading, he argues, demands making judgements at every line. 'The spectator is simply supposed to know nothing, and deserve nothing. Those who are always watching to see what happens next will never act: such must be the spectator's condition … Spectacular discourse leaves no room for any reply; while logic was only socially constructed through dialogue' (Debord, 1988/1998, pp. 22–29). Similarly, Baudrillard (1981/1994) argued that we have lost the critical distance needed to distinguish what is and what is not real, because we are immersed in visual representations that all present themselves to us as real.

10.1 Realities That Matter

Throughout the book, I have challenged this idea of passive spectatorship. Even when sitting in front of a screen 'just' looking, we are engaged in a socially situated act of viewing that involves choices and multiple interpretations. Those same technologies that the authors argue are powerful control mechanisms to keep individuals passively watching and consuming, have been used to act and resist. The same technologies that are used for propaganda and surveillance have been also used to 'look back' at authorities and engage in an oppositional gaze that challenges established ways of looking and power relations (see Chapter 7: the right to look back). Other than our agency as viewers, in the current visual culture we are not only viewers of images, we are also co-producers – though in significantly lesser ways than those in power – who act on the circulation and transformation of knowledge through the visual culture.

The second critique I address builds on the agency aspect. If there is a possibility for critical assessment and intervention in visual culture, then this presupposes our ability to distance ourselves from this submergence in a spectacle or hyperreality and to be able to distinguish representations from reality. This point of critique is especially addressed to Baudrillard's work rather than Debord's. Unlike Baudrillard's postmodernist ideas that are grounded in the semiotic aspect of visual culture, Debord's ideas were grounded in a Marxist lens that highlighted the economic and class structures dominating the production and maintenance of a spectacle that serves the interests of a capitalist system. Thus, Debord maintained – at least in his first book – a distinction between the perceptual reality and the underlying material structural realities. Baudrillard, on the other hand, claimed that the boundary between reality and its representation has completely dissolved.

Baudrillard's claim and the consequences of it become clear in his later provocative work titled *The Gulf War Did Not Take Place* (Baudrillard, 1991/1995). In this collection of essays, written before, during, and after the Gulf War, Baudrillard does not deny the reality of the events as the title may suggest, rather he argues that this war provides a clear example of a hyperreality in which the USA created a Hollywood-like script of what was happening – or possibly not happening – on the ground. This was not the first war to be photographed and shared on TV screens, but it was the first to be broadcasted live. The US military planning carefully created an image of a 'clean' war, with many photographs of weaponry and 'smart' bombs, and very few photographs of human causalities, creating 'instant history' and an accepted story of the war as one of high-tech weapons fighting for the liberation of Kuwait and fighting against an ecological disaster. As Paul Patton explains in the introduction to Baudrillard translated book, Baudrillard's response to the war events pursues a symbolic challenge to how those events were portrayed. It seeks to subvert this portrayal by pursuing its implicit logic to extremes: 'so you want us to believe that this was a clean, minimalist war, with little collateral damage and few Allied casualties. Why stop there: war? what war?' (Baudrillard, 1991/1995, p. 7).

There is a strong point being made here about the power of propaganda and the power of those who have the means to visual production and dissemination in fabricating certain 'realities' that have very real consequences. However, when Baudrillard takes the argument further saying that those hyperrealities become more real than reality, they can dissolve the boundary between real and not real, and they create the 'accepted story' of the war, I wonder here which audience is he referring to. The story – the hyperreality – is accepted by whom? For those living in Iraq and Kuwait and for the majority of the world where CNN is not their main source of information – let alone having access to it or trust in US media – the war was far from the 'virtual war' the US media represented, it was a real material loss of lives with subsequent effects that persisted well after the war. The material consequences of the war were described in a United Nations report as 'near apocalyptic', bringing Iraq back to a 'pre-industrial age' (UN, 1991). These realities persist whether they are covered by US media or not. Baudrillard's (1981/1994) claim that every situation has to be turned into a spectacle to be real and Debord's (1988/1998) claim that 'when the spectacle stops talking about something for three days, it is as if it did not exist' (p. 20) pose a very problematic and relativistic view on reality. As Susan Sontag (2003) argues, 'for a war to be a spectacle, we universalize the viewing habits of a small, privileged population living in the right part of the world where news is entertainment' (p. 18).

A more contemporary example of the problematic emphasis on the representation of the war rather than the realities of the war is clear in President Donald Trump's comment on Israel's attack on Gaza in 2023–2025. Trump expressed his concern over Israel losing its 'PR war' because of the visuals coming out of the war (Colvin, 2024). His critique was less targeted at the destruction and suffering of the war, and more at Israel's bad choices in releasing tapes of those destructions. His comments resonate with Baudrillard's (1991/1995) argument: it is the imagery that constructs the hyperreality, and this hyperreality becomes the one that matters – for some – and the one through which the cost of the war could be measured. Yet again, which viewing position is emphasized here? Certainly not that of those experiencing the war and its material 'real' consequences.

This is where my argument of the importance of distinguishing between different realities, those created by representations and those materially experienced, comes into play. Those different realities should not be equated in a relativistic manner that they are all as 'real' as they present themselves to be. There is a distinction between the war as experienced on the ground, the war as portrayed by images, and the war as fabricated by images. Baudrillard denies this distinction and denies the possibility to critically see the difference between these; he equates them in a relativistic manner, claiming that images and information are subject to no principle of truth or reality – since there is no real objective world, it is only in the realm of simulation that the world is created, and in this world it is the values and interests of the dominant groups that become real. Subsequently, this denies the possibility of resistance to those dominant groups, denies the possibility of using images as ethical, political, and dialogical tools to reflect reality, and denies the affordances of images as objects of contemplation to deepen our sense of reality or to imagine alternative realities and engage in social change.

Equating representations with reality not only dismisses actions against the spectacle, it also misguides any possible action. When the spectacle is seen as the hyperreality that matters more than reality, opposing it becomes an opposition aimed at the representations themselves rather than the underlying realities and structures of inequality that support them. Naomi Klein (1999), in her book *No Logo*, eloquently portrays different examples of such a misguided struggle over representations. Her book addresses specifically the consumer cultures and identities created by multinational corporations for the purpose of profit. When the world of representations becomes the one that seems to matter, then activism is directed at which identities are portrayed and how they are portrayed in advertisements and visual culture more broadly. Corporations quickly and easily respond to this activism by adjusting their representations, adding more diversity and minority groups' visuals to their advertisements, without making any substantial changes on the structural level that address the inequalities. Branding quickly takes over struggles over representations, springing them into a mall, rather than a revolution. As she describes it, the victories of identity politics amounted to a rearrangement of the furniture while the house burned down (Klein, 1999). Social and political movements that focus solely on representations, and equate representations with reality, risk a generation of activists that are trained in the politics of the image, not action.

How then can action against the dominance of the spectacle be achieved? Expectedly, Baudrillard (1981/1994) provided a deterministic picture of the simulacra, where we cannot escape it, or go back from it to an objective reality, since that disappeared. Debord (1967/2009), on the other hand, advocated for the need for a collective force, a revolution, a historical action, that can destroy the spectacle. He argued that effective political action and critical hermeneutics can unmask the underlying reality that the spectacle's illusions conceal. Debord was himself part of the situationist movement that called for the construction of 'situations' that can disrupt the passivity of the spectator and the dominant cultural order and foster authentic social interactions through various means such as art and psychogeography.

Possibilities for agency and action in opposition to dominant visual cultures can be observed in everyday practices of reflexive viewership and interventions in the different stages of images' social lives and circulation. These different practices transform the visual culture into a dialogue that can be negotiated and contested, rather than a dominant monologue that is received by a passive audience. The affordance of images as social and political tools for such social engagement makes them bound by certain ethical and moral considerations in what kind of reality they can construct or contest. Images can be used to reflect certain realities, to open up for different perspectives and dialogue on certain realities, or to help imagine alternative realities and possibilities. Images can be also used to purposefully manipulate realities, to dehumanize and reproduce oppressive ideas, and to dominate public spaces suppressing other voices. The social life of images framework presented in this book provides a critical and reflective visual analysis approach that traces images' social lives, identifies the social actors surrounding the image, and analyses the consequences of different images in everyday life. Such an approach can help us understand how images are used to understand and know the world, as well as to avoid and deny world realities. With this visual analysis model, we can critically distinguish between a liberating and an incarcerating use of images, between images that facilitate dialogue and engagement and those that close off our relation to others, those that democratize cultures and those that dominate and manipulate cultures. A critical analysis of visual culture should be able to distinguish between those different uses of images and their psychological and social consequences. This approach comes with its own challenges, of course. Assessing images morally assumes an elite position of the analyst doing those judgements and assumes that those assessments are absolute. This should not be the case; engaging in a critical reflective analysis is a dialogical process of meaning making and negotiation. It is aimed at finding the different ways in which an image as situated in the specific environment can afford different meanings and possibilities for actions. It is aimed at finding out how some images can be liberating for some while incarnating for others and unfolding these complexities for reflection.

10.2 Protesting Realities

Images can be used at times to protest certain realities; they can expose a hidden injustice through an evidence photograph or an illustrative graph, or contest invisibility by insisting on showing certain people or ideas. Much literature has been written on the power of the images of the horrific deaths of Tarek Bouazizi and Khaled Said as catalysts for the Tunisian and Egyptian revolutions in 2010 and 2011 (e.g. Awad & Wagoner, 2018). Or the power of the image of Phan Thi Kim Phúc – the napalm girl – in reflecting the horrors of the Vietnam War. Or the influence of the photographic documentation of the torture of Iraqi prisoners in Abu Ghraib by American soldiers in 2004 on US public opinion (Butler, 2010; L. Hansen, 2015). Or how the visual activism of the Black Lives Matter movement raised public awareness about US police violence and discrimination that has long been practised and hidden (Mirzoeff, 2016). These image examples have all become global injustice symbols that bring attention to events involving perceived moral and political transgression and trigger societal dialogues about collective perceptions of right and wrong (Olesen, 2015).

Many other iconic historic images can be mentioned here to make the point: images play a key role in how things are seen, and subsequently how people think, feel, and act in response to what they see. The political power of these photos comes from their capacity to frame reality through giving visibility to certain aspects of an event (Butler, 2010). The examples I have listed could be understood as a form of visual activism that affirms the right to look and the right to defy a visuality in which looking is deployed by the powerful as a means of repression (Mirzoeff, 2016). Images, especially photos, provide a way of relating and telling about the world cognitively, emotionally, aesthetically, morally, and politically (Berger & Mohr, 2016). Photography has especially played a key role in representing human suffering and violence. Other than challenging an oppressive authority, photos pose an invitation for the viewers to pay attention, reflect, and question the rationalizations offered by established powers for mass sufferings (Sontag, 2003). Furthermore, they alter and enlarge our notion of what is worth looking at and what we have the right to see (Sontag, 1977).

This power is definitely evident in the influence of some images, like the global injustice symbols I have mentioned, but is it that such images showing oppression or suffering always *do* something? Do they always serve the right to look, document, and remember those affected? Do they always have the capacity to mobilize action against the exposed realities and trigger social change? The case of the photograph of the child Alan Kurdi (Figure 8.3), who lost his life on the beach shores in Turkey, as he was fleeing with his family from the war in Syria, reveals a more complex picture about the power of the image. As discussed in Chapter 8, research showed a strong – but short-lived – influence of the image on public opinion and public policies. The widespread circulation of the image did not only gather empathy and support but also ridicule and dehumanization.

As I am writing this, it has been more than 600 days of ongoing Israeli forces' attack on Gaza in Palestine, in response to Hamas' attack on Southern Israel on 7 October 2023. Both attacks have been extensively covered by photographs and live videos. Each side uses images of their own victims, while questioning the reality of the other side's images. The images of continuous bombardment, death, and infrastructure destruction in Gaza appear to have had an impact on global public attention and protest. However, no portrayal of human suffering seems to be enough to stop war and trigger peace between Israel and Palestine. How then do images matter in this context? Do they serve an ethical obligation of documentation even when they cannot stop the suffering being documented? In one of the many videos coming out from Gaza in the past months, a woman asks the person filming to stop; she says 'stop taking pictures of our victims, no one is doing anything to save us, the world does not care, and will not stop it, so at least let us be and do not take images of our dead children'. Is it for her that if images do not do anything, if they do not matter, then they become an insult over injury, a further dehumanization of her loved lost ones? Another scepticism of turning suffering into a spectacle comes from Palestinian journalist Hind Khoudary, as she says in a video: 'we are being brutally killed and the world is watching ... the global gaze is upon us, treating our situation as if it were a trending topic on TikTok'.

This questions the value of images in those instances. Visual documentation can be an act to acknowledge a suffering; however, that does not always do justice to those suffering, as it does not necessarily protest the suffering. This dilemma was clear when photographer Kevin Carter captured his iconic photograph known as 'The vulture and the little girl', which first appeared in *The New York Times* in March 1993. The image captured powerfully the horrific famine situation in Southern Sudan at the time. The photograph shows a vulture stalking a starving child who had collapsed on the ground. The controversy surrounding the image was concerned with the role of Carter to document what is happening versus intervening and helping the child. Carter did scare away the vulture and the child did survive, but four months after Carter was awarded the Pulitzer Prize for this photograph, he committed suicide. There is possibly an unbearable weight to seeing, acknowledging, and documenting realities that one cannot change. The controversy focused on the image, the representation of the reality, and therefore blamed the photographer for the destiny of the child, rather than the governments that actively contributed to the famine.

How then do images matter in these contexts, and for whom? When do they serve an ethical purpose and when do they divert our attention from those causing the suffering? When do they support victims and when do they further stigmatize groups? When do they contest oppressive realities and when do they ignite more hate? When do they help us think about the world in a different way and when do they fix complex realities into one simplified snapshot that is void of historical and political context? Or am I posing the wrong questions altogether, overestimating what images can do in such contexts and undermining the structures of power underlying those realities that require more than a struggle over representation to influence a change?

These questions tap into the complexity of analysing the potential powers of images. The same image can oppress and liberate, can cause empathy from one group and hate from another, can become a powerful mobilizing symbol in one context and have no power or influence whatsoever in another context. There are no definite answers and there are no guaranteed 'powers' of the image. I am thus often critical of statements overestimating the power of images (e.g. 'the image that toppled a regime') or assuming some universal constant power (e.g. images 'speak louder than words' or 'are worth a thousand words'). Instead, a meaningful visual analysis addresses what factors and in which conditions an image can matter or 'do' something.

One factor has to do with who the image producer is and how their choices and their access to visibility platforms impact what is seen and how much this is seen. Those with power over visibility platforms determine which crisis and sufferings are worthy of our attention and caring. For authority, if a memory is deemed too dangerous for social stability, if it risks arousing the 'wrong' emotions against authority, those images are often censored. The images that get to circulate are the ones that blame the 'right' subjects and the ones that make us visit the atrocities from the past that the authority thinks we are obliged to visit (Sontag, 2003). In response to dominant representations, different social actors also produce counter-images, that challenge which cruelties and whose deaths should be seen. The potential of those counter-images to challenge the dominant ways of seeing and acting, will rely in part on their ability to compete over visibility spaces and occupy certain environments, whether it is urban space through protest, local or global media, or museums and archives. Some images get to be shared on social media broadly and taken up by major global news outlets; some others stay bound within their local communities, failing to reach nationwide let alone global visibility.

A second factor has to do with what/who is represented and how they are represented. The social and political process of turning a person or an event into a visual object to be consumed by viewers will also always have implications on the affordances of an image. In every image, there is a process of social representation (Moscovici, 1984) where abstract and sometimes unfamiliar ideas and people are objectified and anchored into a concrete visual form. This process is rarely value-free; in every representation there is some form of attribution and positioning: who caused what, who to blame, and who to sympathize with? To understand the emotional and political power an image can afford, we need to analyse the body of the image, interpreting its content, symbolism, what it shows, and what it conceals. Various representational practices and aesthetic cultural conventions can influence which images are recognizable as icons of suffering (Byford, 2018). In news photography, photojournalists and editors engage in different practices with implicit and explicit standards to choose how a war can be reduced to a photograph, and how that photograph in a highly competitive media market can stand out, can be vivid, dramatic, and thus memorable (Zelizer, 2004).

The way the subjects of the suffering are portrayed has psychological consequences on how people respond to the image. When the victims are represented in a personalized way, in a way that acknowledges their individual lives rather than as sheer numbers of people, there is a higher chance the image can facilitate empathy and intersubjectivity from viewers. There is a hard balance, however, in portraying the suffering and helplessness of a certain group of people, without reducing them to powerless objects of spectatorship with no agency, which would further reproduce other forms of suffering and stigma. Victim images can position their subject as someone to be seen, not as someone who also sees and acts (Sontag, 2003). Another hard balance is to portray one atrocity as shocking and unique enough to trigger action, yet as common and shared enough to trigger solidarity. Susan Sontag (2003) argues that from the perspective of those represented, victims want their suffering to be represented, seen, and recognized, but the representation must be unique. To set their suffering alongside that of others is to compare which hell is worse and to demote their suffering to a mere historical instance.

A third factor deals with the viewer position and the power dynamics inherent in the act of witnessing. The way the subjects in an image are positioned also positions who the viewers are expected to be. For every viewer, there are lives that are more grievable (Butler, 2010) than others. For a militant viewer, identity is everything; not every human suffering is the same. To the general viewer, identity also means something; we are more likely to empathize with those whom we share a social identity with and our empathy is also influenced by socialization processes affecting which object and subjects are worthy of our care in our *finite pool of worries*. Even images that trigger empathy from a humanitarian perspective, like child victims, can have varied responses from viewers based on social positions. For example, the image of Alan Kurdi (Chapter 8), though it triggered global solidarity and empathy across wide groups of people, for some viewers the identity of the child as a Kurdish refugee determined the response and delimited empathy. The practices of spectatorship have political and ideological dimensions that are reflected in how we make sense of images of suffering, how we feel about them, and which victims we get to gaze at, get moved by, and care about (Byford, 2018). For those to whom violence is inevitable, for those on the side of the violator, images of suffering supply no evidence or value to denounce violence (Sontag, 2003). For those who denounce the violence, the image could trigger only empathy, or could also trigger action, action towards peace, or maybe even action towards revenge. In a few instances, images can also trigger reflective thinking, perspective taking, and attitude change of the ones supporting, opposing, or indifferent.

A fourth factor therefore deals with the cognitive, affective, and behavioural responses to an image. The search for the impact of a certain image presumes a certain desired effect an image is expected to achieve, but what is that effect? For an agency producing an advertising image, the target is clear: the image needs to trigger positive attitude or affect towards a product that then translates into a purchasing behaviour. When it comes to images of suffering and protest images, what is the desired response?

An initial desired response could be that the image calls for our attention, that it can make us look and direct our gaze onto something as worthy of attention. Images of suffering can do this by their shock effect; they show vividly the unspeakable. This response is not sustainable, however; shock can quickly be replaced by numbness and avoidance as the viewer becomes familiar with the atrocity and learns to look away. An event known through images can become more real than it could have been had one never seen the photographs, but after repeated exposure, it can also become less real and distant (Sontag, 1977). As the image becomes widely circulated, abundant, and saturated it can even have a further countereffect of normalizing the atrocity. Shock photos introduce us to the scandal of horror rather than horror itself; they become more about the shock itself rather than the underlying reality the images are supposed to depict, and after repeated exposure we can become desensitized to that shock effect (Barthes, 1979). Through mediated vision we can see the world while at the same time be safeguarded against the impact and consequences of what we are seeing; we can be drawn too much into images of war that we become morally knocked out and neutralized (Robins, 1996). Can we moderate then images of shock to retain their ability to call for people's attention? In Sontag's book *On Photography* (1977), she wondered if we could work an ecology of images that keeps fresh the image's ability to shock. In her later book *Regarding the Pain of Others* (2003), she acknowledges that there is no possibility for a 'committee of guardians' to ration horror or regulate the circulation of images that matter. The idea is even more far-fetched now with the development of digital media, but even if it was ever attainable, it would bring us back to the power dynamics of image production and censorship: who decides which images get to circulate, and which victims are worthy of attention.

If attention wears off, then a desired response could be to move us beyond just looking, to engage us emotionally so we can feel with what we are seeing. This emotional engagement is complex. The same image that could trigger feelings of sympathy and compassion for one viewer, could trigger repulsion, anger, and hate for another. But even when images manage to trigger sympathy, if that is the only response they trigger, that could paradoxically further limit how a viewer can engage with and act in

10.2 Protesting Realities

response to what the image portrays. As Sontag (2003) argues, images give us the sense of an imaginary proximity to the victim, but this proximity is not true. It is our privileged viewing position that allows us to feel sympathy. When we feel sympathy, we feel that we are not accomplices to what caused the suffering. 'Our sympathy proclaims our innocence as well as our impotence' (p. 102). It could prevent us from a reflection 'on how our privileges are located on the same map as their suffering and may – in ways we might prefer not to imagine – be linked to their suffering' (p. 103).

If sympathy establishes that distance, then a desired emotion could be to feel empathy, to respond not from a position of viewership but to attempt to see the reality portrayed through the eyes of the victim. This requires a viewer that is not only capable and wanting to empathize but one that is willing to accept responsibly and act upon what they see. Powerful images could then be argued to be the ones that can trigger a reflective empathetic response while at the same time mobilizing action towards changing what one sees. If an image triggers emotions of empathy, but the viewer feels helpless in response to those emotions, then those emotions can easily turn into frustration. Even more, the viewer can learn to look away, not because of the oversaturation with the images or because of indifference, but because they are afraid of feeling helpless, to not being able to stop what they can now not unsee.

Do images of suffering then only matter for those who can do something about them? I repeat here Sontag's (2003) question of whether it should be only those who can *do* something that are the ones who have the right to look. I think this idea brings us back to the focus on a tangible effect of an image in a causal reductionist manner, where an image only matters if one can find a direct effect between viewing and acting in a certain desired way. While this might work with advertising images, in everyday politics the relationship between seeing and acting is more complex and the definition of acting in itself needs revisiting.

There is always some form of social action in the act of viewing, thinking, feeling, and remembering in response to an image. Looking at how images can matter in relation to those psychological processes speaks of how images can do something in the everyday politics of visibility, knowledge, and meaning making. Those processes can subsequently and over time influence and facilitate new ways of seeing and acting, that can further influence broader social, political, and structural changes. Expecting images to *do* a direct effect on a structural level, to stop a war or to bring about equality, is not only misleading and naive, it also misdirects social action. It drives the focus of social action towards representational struggles, rather than much needed political action addressing social structures of inequalities and violence.

A critical analysis can unfold the variety of social actions people engage with in response to images and the agency by which individuals can choose to engage and reflect on images that matter, despite their abundance. Social action can be in the agency to find the space to be reflective and attentive in a modern society whose chief model of public space is the mega-store (Sontag, 2003). We can reflect on who put which image where and why, what does the image show and what does it conceal, and who caused what the image shows? The meaning is never finalized or fixed (Bakhtin, 1986), it is always open for different interpretations. We can also learn to look differently and reject certain simplistic interpretations of images that rely on essentializing, reducing, naturalizing, and creating binary oppositions (Hall, 1997a).

We can also respond affectively to certain images, while not losing our agency to act in response to what we feel. When we see an image, we project ourselves into the work; we possibly take a place of trying to understand and empathize with the meaning communicated. However, if our response stops at the experience of empathy, we are disempowered, because our ability to act in the world relies on what Mikhail Bakhtin called the moment of separation, when we can empathize, then take a distance of separation, to return and reflect on our own unique position from the image (Haynes, 1995). For images to have social or political efficacy, the viewer must exercise agency in relation to their position from the image, and that position is a navigation between living-into and separation from what is in the image (Haynes, 1995).

Another social action in response to images is in acts of individual and collective remembering. Images as memory objects can trigger different reconstructions of the past. Photographs of the suffering and martyrdom of a people are more than reminders of death, or failure, or victimization. They can be reminders of what humans are capable of, of their capacity to resilience and survival, and also their capacity to inflict pain on others. Images of past events can trigger a reflective reconstruction of the past but can also trigger a static or simplified version of an event, where to remember a world happening is to remember a snapshot detached from its context. Agency in response to images can be in engaging in reflective thinking about the narrative behind the snapshot, and in engaging in remembering as an ethical act that does not only help us remember the past, but it also orients future possibilities. An image alone cannot repair our ignorance about history: what actually happened beyond the image, who caused the suffering, what happened to the victims afterwards? Images cannot be more than an invitation to pay attention, and think about whether it was inevitable? Was it excusable? Is it continuing to happen in different forms? A static way of recalling an event through a snapshot can hold us in a moment, unable to move forward, or to reconcile. Engaging in constructive remembering can help us imagine a better world beyond what happened.

What makes an image matter is how we engage with it and how we shape its social life in a way that helps us and others see, think, feel, and remember in a multitude of ways, opening up dialogues rather than inducing silence. Those acts can make certain images still matter in a visual culture where we learned to look away. Looking and reflecting on current and past realities through images can also help us imagine and shape alternative future realities.

10.3 Imagining Alternative Realities

Images do not only represent realities that we live and see or ones that are far away and unfamiliar, but through images we create what we want to see and imagine. We create images to embody the abstract and invisible ideas we would like to see with our own eyes in the world (Lauwereyns, 2012).

Imagination is a psychological process of temporary 'uncoupling' from the socially shared world that can be at times dull, filled with anxieties about the future, or too overwhelming to bear (Zittoun & Gillespie, 2016). We 'uncouple' from the here and now to explore the past, the future, and alternative spheres of experience, to then 'recouple' with the ongoing shared reality with new understandings and actions that can help us to go beyond the real or the actual – what is – and engage with alternative possibilities – what could be (Zittoun et al., 2022). Image production and viewership can nourish processes of imagination that mobilize collective imagination and action towards alternative futures.

Throughout the book, I have had less focus on art, in the traditional sense, and focused more on images as accessible tools for social and political action in the hands of the many rather than bound within art institutions. However, it is important to recognize the different movements within art that attempted to mobilize the image for social transformation. For example, in the 1960s The Situationist International, Artists Placement Group, and Art Workers' Coalition all tried to mobilize avant-garde art as a political tool to address social issues and bring about social transformation (Bolt Rasmussen, 2009). They all tried to move away from the institutional structures of art toward a broader cultural and political practice using new and relatively accessible means of expression such as photography and postcards. They challenged the prevailing modernist art institutions that valued unique works of art and worked to create art that is beyond the control of the creator to enable the participation of the viewer.

Posters, digital memes, photographs, and graffiti have all been used by social and political non-violent resistance movements to protest realities of injustice and orient towards alternative more just futures. Those movements often produce images that counter dominant ways of seeing and thinking, and those images struggle for visibility among powerful social actors that dominate visual production and circulation. For those movements to influence social change, they need to achieve an extraordinarily strong cohesion, coordination, and collaboration globally to have a chance at moving the world towards an actualized democracy (Moghaddam, 2024).

Social and political movements can utilize image technological advancements to widen the capacity of what we can see and imagine, and consequently act upon. However, the affordances possible by images today do not in themselves promise more democratic or equal societies. Image technologies have provided more tools for self-representation and expression but have also created more ways of surveillance and dominance. Image accessibility online has facilitated global solidarities and movements against inequalities but has also facilitated the growth of terrorist and hate movements. Those same technologies have also created more ways to distance ourselves and disengage from significant world happenings, while immersing in endless spectacles of social media feeds that at times could be reproducing inequalities and discrimination through their algorithms. Practices of archiving and copyright regulations have preserved and protected the lives of some images but have also meant a powerful dominance over our freedom to create and imagine. More recent technologies of artificial intelligence have facilitated further accessibility to image production but can also have negative consequences on the imaginative and meaning-making processes involved in image creation. Will those technologies provide more ways of seeing and imagining the world or will they diminish further the power of the image to move us and rupture further our ability to distinguish between the imaginary and the real?

Social transformation towards imagined futures is interlinked with the future of the image and its mattering. The change towards more democratic and equal societies involves democratizing access to representation and visibility for different groups, and this will require a turn towards wider accessibility to visibility platforms (e.g. global news outlets), more transparency into practices of image circulation and archiving (e.g. algorithms), and more collaborative platforms for image production (e.g. Creative Commons). Whatever the future of the image is, it will require a continuous revisiting of our position as social and political actors and what it means to see and act in future image societies.

10.4 A *Just* Image

Can images do us justice? Have they managed to do so in the past or do they have the capacity to do so in the future?

We want images to do us justice, whether it is individually for our personal memories or grieving, or collectively for our group identities and history. In our pursuit to be seen and recognized, we do not seek accuracy or images that just mirror what we can already see, we seek a 'just image' (Barthes, 1981) that would speak on our behalf, that would reflect what it is like to be in our position and to feel the way we feel.

If images were capable of *doing* something themselves, we could deem certain images as 'just', as the ones that matter, and the ones that have the power to do something. Image mattering is, instead, embedded in what we do with images and in our capacity to engage and recognize what matters in images. Through the social life of images framework, we can trace how people negotiate and struggle over meaning and how they reproduce, contest, and transform meanings.

Images that matter are ones that we are able to engage with despite the abundance, ones that we can act in response to despite the repetition of the suffering it portrays, ones that we can be critical towards despite their mastery in distortion or manipulation, ones that we are able through them to engage in new ways of seeing ourselves, others, and the world. A *just* image does not have to give the full picture or the final say – no image does. A *just* image is one that we can open a dialogue through, one that we can facilitate a narrative beyond its representation, and one that we cognitively and affectively can share a reality through. A *just* image is one that we can co-construct through it a world that resonates with us and others.

Through images we can create cognitive and affective engagement. We cannot make revolutionary structural social transformations through images, but we can create many instances of rupturing encounters that challenge the status quo and invite us to entertain alternative ideas. We can represent existing social realities, while simultaneously communicating something new that triggers critical thinking about those realities. We can revert the normal, the used-to, the dominant, and represent them as paradoxical. We can redefine the boundaries of what is see-able and think-able. Through images we can make the unfamiliar familiar or, even more, we can connect the unfamiliar to the familiar. We can engage with images in ways that help us connect to others and see our own social position as subjects in history. We can engage with images in ways that resist mere consumption.

Appendix

Interview Questions Guide: Protest image producers
Introducing the interview
- Informed consent and permission to record
- Information about interviewer and research topic

The image producer background
- Could you tell me more about yourself and your background in relation to creating images?
  - Education, work, age, city...
  - Image production skills and any art training
- What kind of images have you produced? (e.g. photography, drawings, caricatures, memes...)
- Could you tell me a little about how and when did you start doing street art/caricatures and what were your motivations?
  - Intentions, feelings, and context associated with the beginning

Creation process
- What is your creative process from idea formation to implementation?
  - Specific inspirations or triggers
- Is there a specific purpose that drives your creation process?
  - (including work purposes for those producing images as part of their work)
- What topics do you tackle in your images?
  - Have your style/topics changed throughout the years?
  - Any external influences on topic choices?
- What is your favourite image that you have created, and why?
- How much is image production part of your daily life?
  - How much does it affect your daily life?
- If you were to classify your images and work, what would be your genre (graffiti, street art, political caricature, paintings, memes, protest images...)?
- How are your images different from images one could see in a museum?
- How are they different from what could be labelled as non-political images?
- What are your thoughts about distinctions between art/non-art, graffiti/vandalism?
- Do you always sign your images? Do you have any anonymous images or ones with a pseudonym? (and why?)

Materiality, placement, and context
- What tools and materials do you use?
- Where were your images first placed (online, print, etc.)?
  - Secondary places where you reproduced your images?
  - Secondary places where other people reproduced your images?
  - Do those different spaces affect how the image is produced and viewed?
- Your images are produced in a specific time and space that has its own cultural, social, and political context. Could you take me through how you see that context and how it has influenced you?
  - Can you imagine how your images would be different if you were creating them in a different time or different geographical place with different context?
- City space (for urban image producers):
  - What is your relationship with the urban space in your city? What areas do you feel part of and belonging to and which areas do you feel excluded from?
  - Do you feel a sense of ownership of certain city spaces?
  - Has your intervention in the space changed this relationship and feelings?
  - Do you think your images change city culture?
  - How did the internet and social media affect urban images?

Dialogue and viewers
Now I would like to talk with you about the role and voices of 'others' in a broad sense as you create your images.
Pre-production:
- Any specific images or artists that inspired you and you think have influenced some of your work?
  - Can you recall your first encounter with that image/artist? How was it?
- Do you consider yourself part of a certain group/movement/collective in terms of your images?
  If yes,
  - How does belonging to this subculture influence your image creation?
  - Do you consult with people from this group? Co-create together?
  - How are disagreements managed within the group? Any ideas rejected based on established boundaries of what should and shouldn't be produced?

During the creation process:
- Who are the viewers you have in mind while creating? In other words, who are the 'public' you're speaking to?
- What are the different voices you dialogue with in your thought process?

After production:
- What are the different ways through which you experience how viewers receive your images? (e.g. direct feedback, online comments)
- For street artists: did you experience the public's reaction first-hand while drawing in the street? Would you share examples of such situations?
- Some would say once the image is produced and starts circulating in the world, it becomes less relevant who the creator is and what they meant, and more relevant what people make out of the image in different times and spaces. So almost

announcing the death of the author with the birth of the image. What do you think of that?

Circulation, transformation, and censorship
- Once your image is produced to the public in one format, take me through how it circulates, and the different media/spaces you find it travelling to.
- Have you experienced others appropriating your images? (As in taking them and sharing them under their name, changing something in their message, or using them for commercial purposes)
  - What kind of appropriations do you see fair and engaging with you in a dialogue versus other appropriations that you find 'violating' your image?
  - How would you distinguish between a creative appropriation or reproduction of your image versus stealing your images?
- Self-censorship: Are there any instances where you tried to pull back an image after it was in the public? Why and what happened then?
  - Were any images were rejected or censored before production? By whom and why?
- Were there any attempts by others to censor your images after being made public?
- How about the government's response to your images?
  - How do you think the people in authority perceive your images?
  - Do you think they see them as a threat? Why?
  - How safe and free do you feel about producing your images?
  - In case of danger, how do you assess the worthiness of what you do?

Photo elicitation and the body of the image
I have picked some of your images as well as some other relevant images that I would like us to go over and discuss. I am looking mainly for your own meanings and interpretation of those images.
Producers' own images:
- Can you take me through your image here, from the idea to the implementation?
  - What are the different components/signs in the image and what do they refer to?
  - What meanings did you mean to convey by it? And to whom?
  - How was it received? What are the different understandings (misunderstandings) of it that you have experienced from viewers?

Others' images:
- Do you remember seeing this image before?
  - If yes, where?
- Who do you think made this image, and who was it made for (viewers)?
- Where do you think this image was used/placed?
- What is the story behind this image? Does it refer to a specific incident or debate? Do you associate the image with any specific person, group, topic?
- What feelings does this image trigger for you (if any) and why?

Future-oriented reflections
This is the final part of the interview. I would like us to take a step back and look at your work and similar works within the broader political scene.
- What do you wish to achieve through images?

- What do you think images are actually capable of achieving in society?
    - Can they trigger change? If yes, what kind of change?
    - Can images influence how we think, feel, or act? How?
- What ideas do you fight against? (e.g. culture, social structures, government)
    - Can you individually make a change in those ideas? (agency)
    - What do you need to make a change?
    - What change would you hope for if there were no constraints at all?
    - Would you continue to do what you do, if you don't see signs of that change?
- What is resistance/political art, in your view? And how effective is it in fighting against oppression and social injustice?
    - Some would argue that you can only achieve symbolic effects through art; for real life changes one needs work, protest, and 'fighting' on the ground. What do you think of that?
    - Do you think ideas can transform culture and society? How?

And finally:
- Do you see value in researching images of protest and resistance from a psychological perspective? What do you think are important angles that I should look at in my research?
- These were all my questions. Do you have any questions for me?

References

Abaza, M. (2014). Post January revolution Cairo: Urban wars and the reshaping of public space. *Theory, Culture & Society*, *31*(7–8), 163–183. https://doi.org/10.1177/0263276414549264

Abdelmagid, Y. (2013). The emergence of the Mona Lisa battalions: Graffiti art networks in post-2011 Egypt. *Review of Middle East Studies*, *47*(2), 172–182. https://doi.org/10.1017/S2151348100058079

Adler, A. (2016). Fair use and the future of art. *New York University Law Review (1950)*, *91*(3), 559–626. https://search.informit.org/documentSummary;res=agispt;dn=20191014018403

Adler-Nissen, R., Andersen, K. E., & Hansen, L. (2020). Images, emotions, and international politics: The death of Alan Kurdi. *Review of International Studies*, *46*(1), 75–95. https://doi.org/10.1017/S0260210519000317

Ahmed, S. (2004). *The cultural politics of emotion* (2nd ed.). Edinburgh University Press. https://doi.org/10.4324/9780203700372

Appadurai, A. (1986). *The social life of things: Commodities in cultural perspective*. Cambridge University Press.

——— (1996). *Modernity at large: Cultural dimensions of globalization*. University of Minnesota Press.

Appel, M. (2012). Anti-immigrant propaganda by radical right parties and the intellectual performance of adolescents. *Political Psychology*, *33*(4), 483–493. https://doi.org/10.1111/j.1467-9221.2012.00902.x

Armbrust, W. (2019). *Martyrs and tricksters: An ethnography of the Egyptian revolution* (1st ed.). Princeton University Press. https://doi.org/10.1515/9780691197517

Askanius, T. (2021). On frogs, monkeys, and execution memes: Exploring the humor-hate nexus at the intersection of neo-Nazi and alt-right movements in Sweden. *Television & New Media*, *22*(2), 147–165. https://doi.org/10.1177/1527476420982234

Associated Press in Cairo. (2010, 17 September). Egyptian paper defends doctored photo of Hosni Mubarak. *The Guardian*. www.theguardian.com/world/2010/sep/17/al-ahram-newspaper-doctored-photo-hosni-mubarak

Avramidis, K., & Tsilimpounidi, M. (2017). *Graffiti and street art: Reading, writing and representing the city* (1st ed.). Routledge. https://doi.org/10.4324/9781315585765

Awad, S. H. (2017). Documenting a contested memory: Symbols in the changing city space of Cairo. *Culture & Psychology*, *23*(2), 234–254. https://doi.org/10.1177/1354067X17695760

(2020a). Political caricatures in colonial Egypt: Visual representations of the people and the nation. In A. Gorman & S. Irving (Eds.), *Cultural entanglement in the pre-independence Arab world* (pp. 163–193). I. B. Tauris & Company, Limited.

(2020b). The social life of images. *Visual Studies*, *35*(1), 28–39. https://doi.org/10.1080/1472586X.2020.1726206

(2021). Urban dialogues: The lives and after-lives of political street art images. *City*, *25*(3–4), 510–525. https://doi.org/10.1080/13604813.2021.1943233

(2022). Street art. In V. P. Glăveanu (Ed.), *The Palgrave encyclopedia of the possible* (pp. 1579–1587). Palgrave.

Awad, S. H., Doerr, N., & Nissen, A. (2022). Far-right boundary construction towards the "other": Visual communication of Danish People's Party on social media. *The British Journal of Sociology*, *73*(5), 985–1005. https://doi.org/10.1111/1468-4446.12975

Awad, S. H., Frydendahl, M. U., Hansen, M., & Nielsen, L. M. B. (under review). Online engagement towards far-right visuals.

Awad, S. H., & Wagoner, B. (2014). Agency and creativity in the midst of social change. In C. W. Gruber, M. G. Clark, S. H. Klempe, & J. Valsiner (Eds.), *Constraints of agency: Explorations of theory in everyday life* (pp. 229–243). Springer International Publishing. https://doi.org/10.1007/978-3-319-10130-9_14

(2017). *Street art of resistance* (1st ed.). Springer International Publishing. https://doi.org/10.1007/978-3-319-63330-5

(2018). Image politics of the Arab uprisings. In B. Wagoner, F. M. Moghaddam, & J. Valsiner (Eds.), *The psychology of radical social change: From rage to revolution* (pp. 189–217). Cambridge University Press.

(2020). Protest symbols. *Current Opinion in Psychology*, *35*, 98–102. https://doi.org/10.1016/j.copsyc.2020.03.007

Awad, S. H., Wagoner, B., & Glăveanu, V. (2017). The street art of resistance. In N. Chaudhary, P. Hviid, G. Marsico, & J. W. Villadsen (Eds.), *Resistance in everyday life* (pp. 161–180). Springer Singapore. https://doi.org/10.1007/978-981-10-3581-4_13

Awcock, H. (2021). Stickin' it to the man: The geographies of protest stickers. *Area*, *53*(3), 522–530. https://doi.org/10.1111/area.12720

Azevedo, R. T., De Beukelaer, S., Jones, I. L., Safra, L., & Tsakiris, M. (2021). When the lens is too wide: The political consequences of the visual dehumanization of refugees. *Humanities & Social Sciences Communications*, *8*(1), 1–16. https://doi.org/10.1057/s41599-021-00786-x

Bäcklund, J., Oxvig, H., Renner, M., & Søberg, M. (2019). *What images do*. Aarhus University Press.

Baele, S. J., Brace, L., & Coan, T. G. (2021). Variations on a theme? Comparing 4chan, 8kun, and other chans' far-right "/pol" boards. *Perspectives on Terrorism*, *15*(1), 65–80. www.jstor.org/stable/26984798

Bakhtin, M. (1984a). *Problems of Dostoevsky's poetics* (C. Emerson, Trans.). University of Minnesota Press.
 (1984b). *Rabelais and his world* (H. Iswolsky, Trans.). Indiana University Press.
Bakhtin, M. M. (1981). *The dialogic imagination: Four essays by M. M. Bakhtin* (M. Holquist, Ed.; C. Emerson, M. Holquist, Trans.). University of Texas Press.
 (1986). *Speech genres and other late essays* (V. W. McGee, Trans.). University of Texas Press.
Barad, K. (2017a). No small matter: Mushroom clouds, ecologies of nothingness, and strange topologies of spacetimemattering. In A. L. Tsing, N. Bubandt, E. Gan, & H. A. Swanson (Eds.), *Arts of living on a damaged planet* (pp. 103–120). University of Minnesota Press.
 (2017b). Troubling time/s and ecologies of nothingness: Re-turning, re-membering, and facing the incalculable. *New Formations*, *92*(1), 56–86. https://doi.org/10.3898/NEWF:92.05.2017
Baron, B. (1993). The construction of national honour in Egypt. *Gender & History*, *5*(2), 244–255. https://doi.org/10.1111/j.1468-0424.1993.tb00175.x
 (2005). *Egypt as a woman* (1st ed.). University of California Press.
Barthes, R. (1973). *Mythologies* (A. Lavers, Trans.). Paladin.
 (1978). *Image, music, text* (S. Heath, Trans.; 1st paperback ed.). Hill & Wang.
 (1979). Shock-photos. In R. Howard (Ed.), *The Eiffel tower and other mythologies* (pp. 71–74). Hill & Wang.
 (1981). *Camera lucida: Reflections on photography* (R. Howard, Trans.). Hill & Wang.
Bartlett, F. C. (1924). Symbolism in folklore. *Proceedings of the VIIth International Congress of Psychology*, 278–289.
 (1932). *Remembering: A study in experimental and social psychology*. Cambridge University Press.
 (1958). *Thinking: An experimental and social study* (1st print ed.). George Allen & Unwin Ltd.
Baudrillard, J. (1994). *Simulacra and simulation* (S. F. Flaser, Trans.). University of Michigan Press. (Originally published 1981)
 (1995). *The Gulf war did not take place* (P. Patton, Trans.). Indiana University Press. (Originally published 1991)
Bauman, Z. (1998). *Globalization: The human consequences*. Columbia University Press.
 (2000). *Liquid modernity* (Reprinted ed.). Polity Press.
Bayat, A. (2013). *Life as politics: How ordinary people change the Middle East* (2nd ed.). Stanford University Press.
Bednarek, M. (2009). Language patterns and attitude. *Functions of Language*, *16*(2), 165–192. https://doi.org/10.1075/fol.16.2.01bed
Beer, D. (2013). *Popular culture and new media: The politics of circulation*. Palgrave Macmillan. https://doi.org/10.1057/9781137270061
Bell, P. (2012). Content analysis of visual images. In J. Hughes (Ed.), *SAGE visual methods: Interpretation and classification* (pp. 31–57). Sage.

Beloff, H. (1988). The eye and the me: Self-portraits of eminent photographers. *Philosophical Psychology*, *1*(3), 295–311. https://doi.org/10.1080/09515088808572946

Benítez-Castro, M. Á., & Hidalgo-Tenorio, E. (2019). Rethinking Martin & White's affect taxonomy: A psychologically-inspired approach to the linguistic expression of emotion. In J. L. Mackenzie & L. Alba-Juez (Eds.), *Emotion in discourse* (pp. 301–322). John Benjamins Publishing Company.

Benjamin, W. (1935). *The work of art in the age of mechanical reproduction*. Penguin.

Berents, H. (2019). Apprehending the "telegenic dead": Considering images of dead children in global politics. *International Political Sociology*, *13*(2), 145–160. https://doi.org/10.1093/ips/oly036

Berg, L. (2018). Between anti-feminism and ethnicized sexism: Far-right gender politics in Germany. In M. Fielitz & N. Thurston (Eds.), *Post-digital cultures of the far right: Online actions and offline consequences in Europe and the US* (pp. 79–92). Transcript Verlag. https://doi.org/10.14361/9783839446706-006

Berger, J. (1972). *Ways of seeing*. Penguin Books Ltd.

Berger, J., & Mohr, J. (2016). *Another way of telling: A possible theory of photography* (1st ed.). Bloomsbury Publishing Plc.

Billig, M. (1995). *Banal nationalism*. Sage. https://doi.org/10.4135/9781446221648

(2013). *Learn to write badly: How to succeed in the social sciences* (1st publ. ed.). Cambridge University Press.

Blanché, U. (2015). Street art and related terms: Discussion and working definitions. *Street Art and Urban Creativity Journal*, *1*(1), 32–39. https://doi.org/10.25765/sauc.v1i1.14

Bleiker, R., Campbell, D., Hutchison, E., & Nicholson, X. (2013). The visual dehumanisation of refugees. *Australian Journal of Political Science*, *48*(4), 398–416. https://doi.org/10.1080/10361146.2013.840769

Bleiker, R., & Hutchison, E. (2008). Fear no more: Emotions and world politics. *Review of International Studies*, *34*(S1), 115–135. https://doi.org/10.1017/S0260210508007821

Bolt Rasmussen, M. (2009). The politics of interventionist art: The situationist international, artist placement group, and art workers' coalition. *Rethinking Marxism*, *21*(1), 34–49. https://doi.org/10.1080/08935690802542374

Bonadio, E. (2019). *The Cambridge handbook of copyright in street art and graffiti*. Cambridge University Press.

Bourdieu, P. (1984). *Distinction: A social critique of the judgement of taste* (R. Nice, Trans.). Routledge and Kegan Paul.

Bourdieu, P., Darbel, A., Schnapper, D., Beattie, C., & Merriman, N. (1991). *The love of art: European art museums and their public*. Polity Press.

Braun, V., & Clarke, V. (2022). Conceptual and design thinking for thematic analysis. *Qualitative Psychology*, *9*(1), 3–26. https://doi.org/10.1037/qup0000196

Bridger, A. J. (2010). Walking as a 'radicalized' critical psychological method? A review of academic, artistic and activist contributions to the study of social environments. *Social and Personality Psychology Compass*, *4*(2), 131–139. https://doi.org/10.1111/j.1751-9004.2009.00243.x

Brinkmann, S. (2006). Mental life in the space of reasons. *Journal for the Theory of Social Behaviour*, *36*(1), 1–16. https://doi.org/10.1111/j.1468-5914.2006.00293.x

(2012). *Qualitative inquiry in everyday life* (1st publ. ed.). Sage. https://doi.org/10.4135/9781473913905

Brinkmann, S., & Kvale, S. (2018). *Doing interviews* (2nd ed.). Sage. https://doi.org/10.4135/9781529716665

Bruner, J. (1991). The narrative construction of reality. *Critical Inquiry*, *18*(1), 1–21. https://doi.org/10.1086/448619

Bruner, J. S. (1990). *Acts of meaning*. Harvard University Press.

Burns, A. (2015). Discussion and action: Political and personal responses to the Aylan Kurdi images. In F. Vis & O. Goriunova (Eds.), *The iconic image on social media: A rapid research response to the death of Aylan Kurdi* (pp. 38–39). Visual Social Media Lab.

Butler, J. (2004). *Precarious life: The powers of mourning and violence*. Verso.

(2010). *Frames of war: When is life grievable?* (1st publ. ed.). Verso.

Byford, J. (2018). The emotional and political power of images of suffering: Discursive psychology and the study of visual rhetoric. In S. Gibson (Ed.), *Discourse, peace, and conflict: Discursive psychology perspectives* (pp. 285–302). Springer International Publishing. https://doi.org/10.1007/978-3-319-99094-1_16

Campbell, S., & Moghaddam, F. M. (2018). Social engineering and its discontents: The case of the Russian revolution. In B. Wagoner, F. Moghaddam, & J. Valsiner (Eds.), *The psychology of radical social change* (pp. 103–121). Cambridge University Press. https://doi.org/10.1017/9781108377461.007

Carah, N. (2014). Curators of databases: Circulating images, managing attention and making value on social media. *Media International Australia*, *150*(1), 137–142. https://doi.org/10.1177/1329878X1415000125

Casas, A., & Williams, N. W. (2019). Images that matter: Online protests and the mobilizing role of pictures. *Political Research Quarterly*, *72*(2), 360–375. https://doi.org/10.1177/1065912918786805

Castells, M. (2015). *Networks of outrage and hope: Social movements in the internet age* (2nd ed.). Polity.

Cavasso, L., & Taboada, M. (2021). A corpus analysis of online news comments using the appraisal framework. *Journal of Corpora and Discourse Studies*, *4*, 1–38. https://doi.org/10.18573/jcads.61

Christensen, I. L. (2021). At gøre det usynlige synligt: Geigertælleren, radio-aktivitet og angst i den offentlige debat i Danmark 1945–1963 [Making the invisible visible: The Geiger counter, radioactivity and anxiety in the public debate in Denmark 1945–1963]. *Tings Tale*, *3*, 49–63.

Cole, M. (1988). Cross-cultural research in the sociohistorical tradition. *Human Development*, *31*(3), 137–152. https://doi.org/10.1159/000275803

(1996). *Cultural psychology: A once and future discipline*. The Belknap Press of Harvard University Press.

Collier, J., & Collier, M. (1986). *Visual anthropology: Photography as a research method (revised and expanded edition)*. University of New Mexico Press.

Colvin, J. (2024, 4 April). *Trump says Israel has to get Gaza war over 'fast' and warns it is 'losing the PR war'*. AP Online. https://tinyurl.com/5yyexaus

Comstock, G. A., & Scharrer, E. (2005). *The psychology of media and politics*. Elsevier Academic Press. https://doi.org/10.1016/B978-0-12-183552-1.X5013-2

Cornish, F., & Gillespie, A. (2009). A pragmatist approach to the problem of knowledge in health psychology. *Journal of Health Psychology*, *14*(6), 800–809. https://doi.org/10.1177/1359105309338974

Dafaure, M. (2020). The "Great Meme War:" The alt-right and its multifarious enemies. *Angles (Société des Anglicistes de l'Enseignement Supérieur)*, *10*(10). https://doi.org/10.4000/angles.369

Daniels, J. (2018). The algorithmic rise of the "alt-right". *Contexts*, *17*(1), 60–65. https://doi.org/10.1177/1536504218766547

Davies, B., & Harré, R. (1990). Positioning: The discursive production of selves. *Journal for the Theory of Social Behaviour*, *20*(1), 43–63. https://search.proquest.com/docview/57475846

Davies, P. G., Spencer, S. J., Quinn, D. M., & Gerhardstein, R. (2002). Consuming images: How television commercials that elicit stereotype threat can restrain women academically and professionally. *Personality & Social Psychology Bulletin*, *28*(12), 1615–1628. https://doi.org/10.1177/014616702237644

Dawkins, R. (1989). *The selfish gene* (New ed.). Oxford University Press.

de Certeau, M. (1984). *The practices of everyday life* (S. Rendall, Trans.). University of California Press.

de Saint Laurent, C., Glăveanu, V. P., & Literat, I. (2022). Mimetic representations of the COVID-19 pandemic: An analysis of objectification, anchoring, and identification processes in coronavirusmemes. *Psychology of Popular Media*, *11*(4), 340–354. https://doi.org/10.1037/ppm0000370

de Saussure, F. (1916). *Course in general linguistics*. Open Court.

(2021). Arbitrary social values and the linguistic sign. In C. Lemert (Ed.), *Social theory: The multi-cultural, global, and classic readings* (7th ed., pp. 161–170). Routledge.

Debord, G. (1998). *Guy Debord comments on the society of the spectacle* (M. Imrie, Trans.). Verso. (Originally published 1988)

(2009). *Society of spectacle* (M. Jerkins, Trans.). Soul Bay Press. (Originally published 1967)

DeCook, J. R. (2018). Memes and symbolic violence: #proudboys and the use of memes for propaganda and the construction of collective identity. *Journal of*

Educational Media: The Journal of the Educational Television Association, *43*(4), 485–504. https://doi.org/10.1080/17439884.2018.1544149

Derrida, J. (1972). *Positions*. Nouvelles Editions Latines.

(1996). *Archive fever* (E. Prenowitz, Trans.; paperback ed.). University of Chicago Press.

Dewey, C. (2015, 10 September). How copyright is killing your favorite memes. *The Washington Post*.

Dewey, J. (1896). The reflex arc concept in psychology. *Psychological Review*, *3*, 357–370.

(1934). *Art as experience*. Minton, Balch.

Dilley, R. S. (1986). Tourist brochures and tourist images. *The Canadian Geographer*, *30*(1), 59–65. https://doi.org/10.1111/j.1541-0064.1986.tb01026.x

Doerr, N. (2017). Bridging language barriers, bonding against immigrants: A visual case study of transnational network publics created by far-right activists in Europe. *Discourse & Society*, *28*(1), 3–23. https://doi.org/10.1177/0957926516676689

(2021). The visual politics of the Alternative for Germany (AfD): Anti-Islam, ethno-nationalism, and gendered images. *Social Sciences*, *10*(1), 20. https://doi.org/10.3390/socsci10010020

D'Orazio, F. (2015). Journey of an image: From a beach in Bodrum to twenty million screens across the world. In F. Vis & O. Goriunova (Eds.), *The iconic image on social media: A rapid research response to the death of Aylan Kurdi* (pp. 11–18). Visual Social Media Lab.

Drainville, R. (2015). On the iconology of Aylan Kurdi, alone. In F. Vis & O. Goriunova (Eds.), *The iconic image on social media: A rapid research response to the death of Aylan Kurdi* (pp. 47–49). Visual Social Media Lab.

Drakett, J., Rickett, B., Day, K., & Milnes, K. (2018). Old jokes, new media: Online sexism and constructions of gender in internet memes. *Feminism and Psychology*, *28*(1), 109–127. https://doi.org/10.1177/0959353517727560

Duque, M., Pink, S., Sumartojo, S., & Vaughan, L. (2019). Homeliness in health care: The role of everyday designing. *Home Cultures*, *16*(3), 213–232. https://doi.org/10.1080/17406315.2020.1757381

Edwards, D., & Middleton, D. (1988). Conversational remembering and family relationships: How children learn to remember. *Journal of Social and Personal Relationships*, *5*(1), 3–25. https://doi.org/10.1177/0265407588051001

Evans, J., & Hall, S. (2007). *Visual culture: A reader*. Sage.

Falk, F. (2010). Invasion, infection, invisibility: An iconology of illegalized immigration. In C. Bischoff, F. Falk, & S. Kafehsy (Eds.), *Images of illegalized immigration: Towards a critical iconology of politics* (pp. 83–100). Transaction.

Fanon, F. (1986). *Black skin, white masks* (C. L. Markmann, Trans.). Pluto Press.

Fentress, J., & Wickham, C. (1992). *Social memory*. Blackwell.

Ferguson, M. J., Carter, T. J., & Hassin, R. R. (2009). On the automaticity of nationalist ideology: The case of the USA. In J. T. Jost, A. C. Kay, & H.

Thorisdottir (Eds.), *Social and psychological bases of ideology and system justification* (pp. 53–83). Oxford University Press. https://doi.org/10.1093/acprof:oso/9780195320916.003.003

Flick, U. (2018). *An introduction to qualitative research.* Sage.

Forrester, M. (2000). *Psychology of the image.* Routledge. https://doi.org/10.4324/9780203446928

Foster, H. (1988). *Vision and visuality.* Bay Press.

Foucault, M. (1974). *The archaeology of knowledge.* Tavistock Publications.

   (1977). *Discipline and punish: The birth of the prison* (A. Sheridan, Trans.). Penguin.

   (1979). Authorship: What is an author? *Screen, 20*(1), 13–34. https://doi.org/10.1093/screen/20.1.13

Fraser, N. (1985). What's critical about critical theory? The case of Habermas and gender. *New German Critique, 35*(35), 97–131. https://doi.org/10.2307/488202

   (1990). Rethinking the public sphere: A contribution to the critique of actually existing democracy. *Social Text, 25/26*, 56–80. https://doi.org/10.2307/466240

Freud, S. (1922). *Group psychology and the analysis of the ego* (J. Strachey, Trans.). The International Psych-analytical Press.

Geise, S., & Vigsø, O. (2017). Methodological approaches to the analysis of visual political communication through election posters. In C. Holtz-Bacha & B. Johansson (Eds.), *Election posters around the globe: Political campaigning in the public space* (pp. 33–52). Springer.

Gelpi, C., Roselle, L., & Barnett, B. (2013). Polarizing patriots: Divergent responses to patriotic imagery in news coverage of terrorism. *American Behavioral Scientist, 57*(1), 8–45. https://doi.org/10.1177/0002764212463358

Gergen, K. J. (1973). Social psychology as history. *Journal of Personality and Social Psychology, 26*(2), 309–320. https://doi.org/10.1037/h0034436

Giardetti, J. R., & Oller, J. W. J. (1995). Testing a theory of photographic meaning. *Semiotica, 106*(1–2), 99–152. https://doi.org/10.1515/semi.1995.106.1-2.99

Gibson, J. J. (1979). *The ecological approach to visual perception.* Houghton Mifflin.

Gill, R. (2011). Bend it like Beckham: The challenges of reading gender and visual culture. In P. Reavey (Ed.), *Visual methods in psychology* (pp. 66–79). Routledge. https://doi.org/10.4324/9780203829042-13

Gillespie, A. (2007). Collapsing Self/Other positions: Identification through differentiation. *British Journal of Social Psychology, 46*(3), 579–595. https://doi.org/10.1348/014466606X155439

   (2009). The intersubjective nature of symbols. In B. Wagoner (Ed.), *Symbolic transformation* (pp. 43–57). Routledge. https://doi.org/10.4324/9780203856550-10

Gillespie, A., Glăveanu, V. P., & de Saint-Laurent, C. (2024). *Pragmatism and methodology: Doing research that matters with mixed methods.* Cambridge University Press.

Gillespie, A., & Zittoun, T. (2010). Using resources: Conceptualizing the mediation and reflective use of tools and signs. *Culture & Psychology*, *16*(1), 37–62. https://doi.org/10.1177/1354067X09344888

Glăveanu, V. P. (2012). What can be done with an egg? Creativity, material objects, and the theory of affordances. *The Journal of Creative Behavior*, *46*(3), 192–208. https://doi.org/10.1002/jocb.13

Glăveanu, V. (2014). *Distributed creativity: Thinking outside the box of the creative individual*. Springer International Publishing. https://doi.org/10.1007/978-3-319-05434-6

Glăveanu, V., de Saint-Laurent, C., & Literat, I. (2018). Making sense of refugees online: Perspective taking, political imagination, and internet memes. *American Behavioral Scientist*, *62*(4), 440–457. https://doi.org/10.1177/0002764218765060

Gleeson, K. (2011). Polytextual thematic analysis for visual data: Pinning down the analytic. In P. Reavey (Ed.), *Visual methods in psychology* (pp. 346–361). Routledge. https://doi.org/10.4324/9780203829042-34

Goldhaber, M. H. (1997). The attention economy and the Net. *First Monday*, *2*(4) https://doi.org/10.5210/fm.v2i4.519

Gómez Cruz, E. (2016). Trajectories: Digital/visual data on the move. *Visual Studies*, *31*(4), 335–343. https://doi.org/10.1080/1472586X.2016.1243019

Good, J. J., Woodzicka, J. A., & Wingfield, L. C. (2010). The effects of gender stereotypic and counter-stereotypic textbook images on science performance. *The Journal of Social Psychology*, *150*(2), 132–147. https://doi.org/10.1080/00224540903366552

Gramsci, A. (1971). *Selections from the prison notebooks*. International Publishers.

Gregory, R. L. (1997). *Mirrors in mind*. Freeman.

Groys, B. (2008). *Art power*. MIT Press.

Habermas, J. (1974). The public sphere: An encyclopedia article. *New German Critique*, *3*, 49–55.

Hafez, S. (2014). Bodies that protest: The girl in the blue bra, sexuality, and state violence in revolutionary Egypt. *Signs: Journal of Women in Culture and Society*, *40*(1), 20–28. https://doi.org/10.1086/676977

Halbwachs, M. (1980). Space and the collective memory. In *The collective memory* (F. J. Ditter Jr. & V. Y. Ditter, Trans., pp. 128–156). Harper & Row. (Original work published 1950)

(1992). *On collective memory*. University of Chicago Press.

Hall, S. (1997a). The spectacle of the 'other'. In S. Hall (Ed.), *Representation: Cultural representations and signifying practices* (pp. 223–290). Sage.

(1997b). The work of representation. In S. Hall (Ed.), *Representation: Cultural representations and signifying practices* (pp. 13–74). Sage.

(2001). Encoding/decoding. In M. Durham & D. Kellner (Eds.), *Media and cultural studies* (pp. 166–176). Blackwell Publishers.

(2019). The determinations of news photographs (1973). In C. Greer (Ed.), *Crime and media* (pp. 123–134). Routledge.

Hansen, L. (2015). How images make world politics: International icons and the case of Abu Ghraib. *Review of International Studies*, *41*(2), 263–288. https://doi.org/10.1017/S0260210514000199

Hansen, S., & Flynn, D. A. (2015). Longitudinal photo-documentation: Recording living walls. *Street Art & Urban Creativity Journal*, *1*(1), 26–31.

Haraway, D. (1988). Situated knowledges: The science question in feminism and the privilege of partial perspective. *Feminist Studies*, *14*(3), 575–599. https://doi.org/10.2307/3178066

Hariman, R., & Lucaites, J. (2007). *No caption needed: Iconic photographs, public culture, and liberal democracy*. University of Chicago Press.

Harper, D. (2002). Talking about pictures: A case for photo elicitation. *Visual Studies*, *17*(1), 13–26. https://doi.org/10.1080/14725860220137345

Harré, R. (2004). Staking our claim for qualitative psychology as science. *Qualitative Research in Psychology*, *1*(1), 3–14. https://doi.org/10.1191/1478088704qp002oa

Harré, R., Moghaddam, F. M., Cairnie, T. P., Rothbart, D., & Sabat, S. R. (2009). Recent advances in positioning theory. *Theory & Psychology*, *19*(1), 5–31. https://doi.org/10.1177/0959354308101417

Haskins, E. V., & Zappen, J. P. (2010). Totalitarian visual "monologue": Reading Soviet posters with Bakhtin. *Rhetoric Society Quarterly*, *40*(4), 326–359. https://doi.org/10.1080/02773945.2010.499860

Hayes, G. (2003). Walking the streets. Psychology and the flaneur. *Annual Review of Critical Psychology*, *1*(3), 50–66.

Haynes, D. J. (1995). *Bakhtin and the visual arts*. Cambridge University Press.

Hebdige, D. (1979). *Subculture: The meaning of style* (1st ed.). Routledge. https://doi.org/10.4324/9780203139943

Henkel, L. A. (2014). Point-and-shoot memories: The influence of taking photos on memory for a museum tour. *Psychological Science*, *25*(2), 396–402. https://doi.org/10.1177/0956797613504438

Hill, C. A. (2004). The psychology of rhetorical images. In C. A. Hill & M. Helmers (Eds.), *Defining visual rhetorics* (pp. 25–40). Lawrence Erlbaum Associates.

Himmelweit, H. T., & Gaskell, G. (1990). *Societal psychology*. Sage.

Hokka, J., & Nelimarkka, M. (2019). Affective economy of national-populist images: Investigating national and transnational online networks through visual big data. *New Media & Society*, *22*(5), 770–792. https://doi.org/10.1177/1461444819868686

hooks, b. (1995). *Art on my mind: Visual politics*. The New Press.

(2001). The oppositional gaze: Black female spectators. In J. Thomas (Ed.), *Reading images* (pp. 123–137). Palgrave.

Horkheimer, M., & Adorno, T. W. (2002). *Dialectic of enlightenment: Philosophical fragments* (G.S. Noeer, Ed.; E. Jephcott, Trans.). Stanford University Press.

Horsti, K. (2017). Digital Islamophobia: The Swedish woman as a figure of pure and dangerous whiteness. *New Media & Society*, *19*(9), 1440–1457. https://doi.org/10.1177/1461444816642169

Hutchins, E. (1995). *Cognition in the wild*. MIT Press. https://doi.org/10.7551/mitpress/1881.001.0001

Ibrahim, Y. (2018). The unsacred and the spectacularized: Alan Kurdi and the migrant body. *Social Media + Society, 4*(4). https://doi.org/10.1177/2056305118803884

Iloh, C. (2021). Do it for the culture: The case for memes in qualitative research. *International Journal of Qualitative Methods, 20*. https://doi.org/10.1177/16094069211025896

Irving, A. (2010). Dangerous substances and visible evidence: Tears, blood, alcohol, pills. *Visual Studies, 25*(1), 24–35. https://doi.org/10.1080/14725861003606753

Jahoda, G. (1999). *Images of savages: Ancient roots of modern prejudice in Western culture*. Routledge. https://doi.org/10.4324/9781315787909

James, W. (1912). *Essays in radical empiricism*. Longman Green and Co.

Jaspal, R., Carriere, K. R., & Moghaddam, F. M. (2015). Bridging micro, meso, and macro processes in social psychology. In J. Valsiner, G. Marsico, N. Chaudhary, T. Sato, & V. Dazzani (Eds.), *Psychology as the science of human being* (pp. 265–276). Springer International Publishing. https://doi.org/10.1007/978-3-319-21094-0_15

Jenkins, H. (2006). *Convergence culture: Where old and new media collide*. New York University Press.

Jewitt, C., & Oyama, R. (2011). Visual meaning: A social semiotic approach. In T. van Leeuwen & C. Jewitt (Eds.), *The handbook of visual analysis* (pp. 134–156). Sage. https://doi.org/10.4135/9780857020062

Jeziorowska, E. (2021). Conventionality and innovation: *Détournement* in 2011–2012 protest art. *SAUC-Street Art & Urban Creativity Scientific Journal, 7*(1), 70.

Joffe, H. (2008). The power of visual material: Persuasion, emotion and identification. *Diogenes, 55*(1), 84–93.

Khatib, L. (2013). *Image politics in the Middle East: The role of the visual in political struggle*. Tauris.

Kjeldsen, J. E. (2018). Working through immigration with images. *Explorations in Media Ecology, 17*(4), 465–473. https://doi.org/10.1386/eme.17.4.465_1

Klein, N. (1999). *No logo*. Picador.

Klein, O., & Muis, J. (2019). Online discontent: Comparing Western European far-right groups on Facebook. *European Societies, 21*(4), 540–562. https://doi.org/10.1080/14616696.2018.1494293

Kress, G. R., & Leeuwen, T. V. (2021). *Reading images: The grammar of visual design* (3rd ed.). Routledge.

Kristensen, N. R. (2020, *Hvor mange muslimer er der i Danmark?* Tjekdet. www.tjekdet.dk/indsigt/hvor-mange-muslimer-er-der-i-danmark

Kristeva, J. (1980). *Desire in language* (L. S. Roudiez, Trans.). Columbia University Press.

Kuhn, A. (1988). *The power of the image*. Routledge.

Kusenbach, M. (2003). Street phenomenology: The go-along as ethnographic research tool. *Ethnography, 4*(3), 455–485. https://doi.org/10.1177/146613810343007

Landes, J. (1992). Representing the body politic: The paradox of gender in the graphic politics of the French Revolution. In S. E. Melzer & L. W. Rabine (Eds.), *Rebel daughters: Women and the French Revolution* (pp. 15–37). Oxford University Press.

Lauwereyns, J. (2012). *Brain and the gaze: On the active boundaries of vision.* MIT Press. https://doi.org/10.7551/mitpress/9087.001.0001

Le Bon, G. (1896). *The crowd: A study of the popular mind.* Macmillan.

Le Guin, U. K. (2019). *The carrier-bag theory of fiction.* Literary Trust.

Leder, H., Mitrovic, A., & Goller, J. (2016). How beauty determines gaze! Facial attractiveness and gaze duration in images of real world scenes. *I-Perception, 7*(4). https://doi.org/10.1177/2041669516664355

Lee, S., & Feeley, T. H. (2016). The identifiable victim effect: A meta-analytic review. *Social Influence, 11*(3), 199–215. https://doi.org/10.1080/15534510.2016.1216891

Lefebvre, H. (1991). *The production of space* (D. Nicholson-Smith, Trans.). Blackwell.

Lessig, L. (2003). The Creative Commons. *The Florida Law Review, 55*(3).

(2004). *Free culture: How big media uses technology and the law to lock down culture and control creativity.* Penguin.

Levine, M., Prosser, A., Evans, D., & Reicher, S. (2005). Identity and emergency intervention: How social group membership and inclusiveness of group boundaries shape helping behavior. *Personality & Social Psychology Bulletin, 31*(4), 443–453. https://doi.org/10.1177/0146167204271651

LeVine, R. A., & Campbell, D. T. (1972). *Ethnocentrism: Theories of conflict, ethnic attitudes, and group behavior.* John Wiley & Sons.

Lewisohn, C. (2008). *Street art.* Abrams.

Lister, M., & Wells, L. (2011). Seeing beyond belief: Cultural studies as an approach to analysing the visual. In T. van Leeuwen & C. Jewitt (Eds.), *The handbook of visual analysis* (pp. 61–91). Sage. https://doi.org/10.4135/9780857020062

Literat, I. (2017). Refugee selfies and the (self-)representation of disenfranchised social groups. *Media Fields Journal, 12.*

Lonchuk, M., & Rosa, A. (2011). Voices of graphic art images. In M. Märtsin, B. Wagoner, E. Aveling, I. Kadianaki, & L. Whittaker (Eds.), *Dialogicality in focus* (pp. 129–146). Nova Science Publishers.

Lutz, C. A., & Collins, J. L. (1993). *Reading National Geographic.* University of Chicago Press.

MacDougall, D. (2005). *The corporeal image* (Student ed.). Princeton University Press. https://doi.org/10.1515/9781400831562

MacDowall, L. (2014). Graffiti, street art and theories of stigmergy. In J. Lossau & Q. Stevens (Eds.), *The uses of art in public space* (pp. 33–48). Routledge. https://doi.org/10.4324/9781315757018-9

(2019). *Instafame: Graffiti and street art in the Instagram era* (1st ed.). Intellect. https://doi.org/10.1386/9781783209835

Mackenzie, A. (2006). *Cutting code: Software and sociality.* Peter Lang.

Makar, A. (2016, 4 February). *Alan Kurdi: Between reportage and propaganda.* Mada. https://tinyurl.com/2smjzttm
Maner, J. K., Kenrick, D. T., Becker, D. V., Delton, A. W., Hofer, B., Wilbur, C. J., & Neuberg, S. L. (2003). Sexually selective cognition. *Journal of Personality and Social Psychology, 85*(6), 1107–1120. https://doi.org/10.1037/0022-3514.85.6.1107
Manghani, S. (2012). *Image studies: Theory and practice* (1st ed.). Routledge. https://doi.org/10.4324/9780203134917
Marcus, G. E., Neuman, W. R., & MacKuen, M. (2000). *Affective intelligence and political judgment.* University of Chicago Press.
Maricut, A. (2017). Different narratives, one area without internal frontiers: Why EU institutions cannot agree on the refugee crisis. *National Identities, 19*(2), 161–177. https://doi.org/10.1080/14608944.2016.1256982
Marková, I. (2003). *Dialogicality and social representations* (1st publ. ed.). Cambridge University Press.
(2016). *The dialogical mind: Common sense and ethics.* Cambridge University Press. https://doi.org/10.1017/CBO9780511753602
Martikainen, J., & Sakki, I. (2021). Visual (de)humanization: Construction of otherness in newspaper photographs of the refugee crisis. *Ethnic and Racial Studies, 44*(16), 236–266. https://doi.org/10.1080/01419870.2021.1965178
(2024). Visual humanization of refugees: A visual rhetorical analysis of media discourse on the war in Ukraine. *British Journal of Social Psychology, 63*(1), 106–130. https://doi.org/10.1111/bjso.12669
Martin, J. R., & White, P. R. R. (2005). *The language of evaluation* (1st ed.). Palgrave Macmillan.
Mather, G. (2014). *The psychology of visual art: Eye, brain, and art* (1st publ. ed.). Cambridge University Press.
Mead, G. H. (1912). The mechanism of social consciousness. *The Journal of Philosophy, Psychology and Scientific Methods, 9*(15), 401–406.
(1934). *Mind, self and society from the standpoint of a social behaviorist.* University of Chicago Press.
Mendes, A. C. (2023). Visuality and parrēsia: Ai Weiwei's countervisual re-enactment of Alan Kurdi's image. *Visual Studies, 38*(5), 766–777. https://doi.org/10.1080/1472586X.2023.2181210
Mielczarek, N. (2020). The dead Syrian refugee boy goes viral: Funerary Aylan Kurdi memes as tools of mourning and visual reparation in remix culture. *Visual Communication, 19*(4), 506–530. https://doi.org/10.1177/1470357218797366
Miller-Idriss, C. (2018). What makes a symbol far right? Co-opted and missed meanings in far-right iconography. In M. Fielitz & N. Thurston (Eds.), *Post-digital cultures of the far right: Online actions and offline consequences in Europe and the US* (pp. 123–126). transcript Verlag.
Mirzoeff, N. (2011). *The right to look: A counterhistory of visuality.* Duke University Press.

(2016). *How to see the world: An introduction to images, from self-portraits to selfies, maps to movies, and more* (1st ed.). Pelican.

Mitchell, W. J. T. (1986). *Iconology: Image, text, ideology.* University of Chicago Press.

(1994). *Picture theory.* University of Chicago Press.

(2005). *What do pictures want?.* University of Chicago Press.

(2012). Image, space, revolution: The arts of occupation. *Critical Inquiry, 39*(1), 8–32. https://doi.org/10.1086/668048

Mitschke, V., Goller, J., & Leder, H. (2017). Exploring everyday encounters with street art using a multimethod design. *Psychology of Aesthetics, Creativity, and the Arts, 11*(3), 276–283. https://doi.org/10.1037/aca0000131

Moghaddam, F. M. (2024). *The psychology of revolution.* Cambridge University Press. https://doi.org/10.1017/9781009433259

Mortensen, M. (2017). Constructing, confirming, and contesting icons: The Alan Kurdi imagery appropriated by #humanitywashedashore, Ai Weiwei, and Charlie Hebdo. *Media, Culture & Society, 39*(8), 1142–1161. https://doi.org/10.1177/0163443717725572

Moscovici, S. (1976). *Social influence and social change.* Academic Press.

(1984). The phenomenon of social representations. In E. M. Farr & S. Moscovici (Eds.), *Social representations* (pp. 3–69). Cambridge University Press.

Much, N. (1995). Cultural psychology. In J. Smith, R. Harre, & L. v. Langenhove (Eds.), *Rethinking psychology* (pp. 97–121). Sage.

Müller, M. G. (2008). Visual competence: A new paradigm for studying visuals in the social sciences? *Visual Studies, 23*(2), 101–112. https://doi.org/10.1080/14725860802276248

Mulvey, L. (1975). Visual pleasure and narrative cinema. *Screen, 16*(3), 6–18.

Muthukrishna, M., & Henrich, J. (2016). Innovation in the collective brain. *Philosophical Transactions of the Royal Society B: Biological Sciences, 371*(1690), 20150192. https://doi.org/10.1098/rstb.2015.0192

Nagate, O., & Stryker, B. (2013). *Archiving the city in flux: Cairo's shifting landscape since the January 25th revolution.* Cluster.

Naguib, R. (2020). The leader as groom, the nation as bride: Patriarchal nationalism under Nasser and Sisi. *Middle East – Topics & Arguments, 14.* https://doi.org/10.17192/meta.2020.14.8232

Neisser, U., & Becklen, R. (1975). Selective looking: Attending to visually specified events. *Cognitive Psychology, 7*(4), 480–494. https://doi.org/10.1016/0010-0285(75)90019-5

Nissen, A., Awad, S. H., & Christensen, I. L. (2021). Imagining the invasion: Right wing visual narratives. In I. Bresc & F. V. Alphen (Eds.), *Reproducing, rethinking, resisting national narratives: A sociocultural approach to schematic narrative templates in times of nationalism* (pp. 137–160). Information Age.

Noë, A. (2005). *Action in perception.* MIT Press.

Nothias, T. (2020). Access granted: Facebook's free basics in Africa. *Media, Culture & Society, 42*(3), 329–348. https://doi.org/10.1177/0163443719890530

O'Halloran, K. L., Tan, S., Wignell, P., Bateman, J. A., Pham, D., Grossman, M., & Moere, A. V. (2019). Interpreting text and image relations in violent extremist discourse: A mixed methods approach for big data analytics. *Terrorism and Political Violence*, *31*(3), 454–474. https://doi.org/10.1080/09546553.2016.1233871

Olesen, T. (2015). *Global injustice symbols and social movements*. Palgrave Macmillan US. https://doi.org/10.1057/9781137481177

(2018). Memetic protest and the dramatic diffusion of Alan Kurdi. *Media, Culture & Society*, *40*(5), 656–672. https://doi.org/10.1177/0163443717729212

(2020). The role of photography in the production and problematization of online affective debates: Struggles over solidarity and identity during the 2015 refugee crisis in Denmark. *The Sociological Review*, *68*(5), 965–981. https://doi.org/10.1177/0038026119886967

O'Neill, S., & Nicholson-Cole, S. (2009). Fear won't do it: Promoting positive engagement with climate change through visual and iconic representations. *Science Communication*, *30*(3), 355–379. https://doi.org/10.1177/1075547008329201

Orwell, G. (1946). Politics and the English language. *Inside the Whale and Other Essays* (pp. 143–158). Penguin.

Özvatan, Ö., & Forchtner, B. (2019). Towards a 'happy ending'? The far-right in Germany. In A. Waring (Ed.), *The new authoritarianism: A risk analysis of the alt-right phenomenon* (pp. 199–226). ibidem Press.

Panofsky, E. (1970). *Meaning in the visual arts*. Penguin.

Parkin, S. (2022, 17 May). Who owns Einstein? The battle for the world's most famous face. *The Guardian*. www.theguardian.com/media/2022/may/17/who-owns-einstein-the-battle-for-the-worlds-most-famous-face

Patel, R. (2013). First World problems: A fair use analysis of internet memes. *UCLA Entertainment Law Review*, *20*(2). https://doi.org/10.5070/LR8202027169

Pearce, W., Özkula, S. M., Greene, A. K., Teeling, L., Bansard, J. S., Omena, J. J., & Rabello, E. T. (2020). Visual cross-platform analysis: Digital methods to research social media images. *Information, Communication & Society*, *23*(2), 161–180. https://doi.org/10.1080/1369118X.2018.1486871

Peirce, C. S. (1998). *The essential Peirce: Selected philosophical writings*. Indiana University Press.

Pępiak, E. (2019). "Hands off our women!": Ethnicizing sexual difference in recent representations of refugees and immigrants. *Studia Humanistyczne AGH*, *18*(1), 63–79. www.ceeol.com/search/article-detail?id=833718

Perelman, C., & Olbrechts-Tyteca, L. (1971). *The new rhetoric: A treatise on argumentation* (J. Wilkinson, P. Weaver, Trans.). University of Notre Dame Press.

Petty, R. E., Cacioppo, J. T., & Schumann, D. (1983). Central and peripheral routes to advertising effectiveness: The moderating role of involvement. *Journal of Consumer Research*, *10*(2), 135–146.

Pink, S. (2021). *Doing visual ethnography* (4th ed.). Sage.
Pink, S., Horst, H. A., Postill, J., Hjorth, L., Lewis, T., & Tacchi, J. (2015). *Digital ethnography* (1st publ. ed.). Sage.
Postman, N. (1986). *Amusing ourselves to death: Public discourse in the age of show business*. Penguin Books.
Prøitz, L. (2018). Visual social media and affectivity: The impact of the image of Alan Kurdi and young people's response to the refugee crisis in Oslo and Sheffield. *Information, Communication & Society*, 21(4), 548–563. https://doi.org/10.1080/1369118X.2017.1290129
Radley, A. (2010). What people do with pictures. *Visual Studies*, 25(3), 268–279. https://doi.org/10.1080/1472586X.2010.523279
Radley, A., & Kennedy, M. (1997). Picturing need: Images of overseas aid and interpretations of cultural difference. *Culture & Psychology*, 3(4), 435–460. https://doi.org/10.1177/1354067X9734001
Radley, A., & Taylor, D. (2003). Remembering one's stay in hospital: A study in photography, recovery and forgetting. *Health*, 7(2), 129–159. https://doi.org/10.1177/1363459303007002872
Rancière, J. (2013). *The politics of aesthetics: The distribution of the sensible* (G. Rockhill, Trans.). Bloomsbury.
Reavey, P. (2020). *A handbook of visual methods in psychology*. Taylor & Francis. https://doi.org/10.4324/9781351032063
Reavey, P., Brown, S. D., Kanyeredzi, A., McGrath, L., & Tucker, I. (2019). Agents and spectres: Life-space on a medium secure forensic psychiatric unit. *Social Science & Medicine*, 220, 273–282. https://doi.org/10.1016/j.socscimed.2018.11.012
Reicher, S. (2001). The psychology of crowd dynamics. In M. A. Hogg & R. S. Tindale (Eds.), *Blackwell handbook of social psychology: Group processes* (pp. 182–208). Blackwell. https://doi.org/10.1002/9780470998458.ch8
Rettberg, J. W. (2014). *Seeing ourselves through technology: How we use selfies, blogs and wearable devices to see and shape ourselves* (1st ed.). Springer Open. https://doi.org/10.1057/9781137476661
Richardson, J. E., & Wodak, R. (2009). The impact of visual racism: Visual arguments in political leaflets of Austrian and British far-right parties. *Controversia*, 6(2), 45.
Rieder, B., Abdulla, R., Poell, T., Woltering, R., & Zack, L. (2015). Data critique and analytical opportunities for very large Facebook pages: Lessons learned from exploring "We are all Khaled Said". *Big Data & Society*, 2(2). https://doi.org/10.1177/2053951715614980
Rieger, J. H. (2011). Rephotography for documenting social change. In E. M. Margolis & L. Pauwels (Eds.), *The SAGE handbook of visual research methods* (pp. 99–113). Sage.
Riessman, C. K. (2008). *Narrative methods for the human sciences*. Sage.
Robins, K. (1996). *Into the image: Culture and politics in the field of vision* (1st publ. ed.). Routledge. https://doi.org/10.4324/9780203440223

Robinson, N. J., Figgener, C., We, A., Mcdonal, J., Gomez, V., MacCarthy, A. C., Stuart, D., & Koleff, V. (2015). Plastic straw found inside the nostril of an olive ridley sea turtle. *Marine Turtle Newsletter, 147*(1), 3.

Rogers, R. (2024). *Doing digital methods* (2nd ed.). Sage.

Rogers, W. S. (2020). *Perspectives on social psychology* (1st ed.). Routledge. https://doi.org/10.4324/9781315144276

Rogoff, B. (1990). *Apprenticeship in thinking: Cognitive development in social context*. Oxford University Press.

Rogoff, I. (1998). Studying visual culture. In N. Mirzoeff (Ed.), *Visual culture reader* (pp. 24–36). Routledge.

Rose, G. (2010). *Doing family photography: The domestic, the public and the politics of sentiment* (1st ed.). Taylor & Francis. https://doi.org/10.4324/9781315577890 (2016). *Visual methodologies* (4th ed.; this ed. first publ. ed.). Sage.

Roth, J. (2020). Citizenship, migration, and the gendering of modern/colonial inequalities. In H. Winkel & A. Poferl (Eds.), *Multiple gender cultures, sociology, and plural modernities* (pp. 62–81). Routledge. https://doi.org/10.4324/9780429454127-5

Ryan, J. R. (1997). *Picturing empire: Photography and the visualization of the British Empire* (1st ed.). Reaktion Books.

Said, E. W. (1978). *Orientalism: Western concepts of the Orient*. Pantheon.

Sawyer, R. K. (2006). Group creativity: Musical performance and collaboration. *Psychology of Music, 34*(2), 148–165. https://doi.org/10.1177/0305735606061850

Sayan-Cengiz, F., & Tekin, C. (2022). Gender, Islam and nativism in populist radical-right posters: Visualizing 'insiders' and 'outsiders'. *Patterns of Prejudice, 56*(1), 61–93. https://doi.org/10.1080/0031322X.2022.2115029

Schmuck, D., & Matthes, J. (2017). Effects of economic and symbolic threat appeals in right-wing populist advertising on anti-immigrant attitudes: The impact of textual and visual appeals. *Political Communication, 34*(4), 607–626. https://doi.org/10.1080/10584609.2017.1316807

Schober, A. (2020). *Popularisation and populism in the visual arts*. Routledge.

Scott, B. A., Amel, E. L., Koger, S. M., & Manning, C. M. (2021). *Psychology for sustainability*. Taylor & Francis.

Shifman, L. (2012). An anatomy of a YouTube meme. *New Media & Society, 14*(2), 187–203. https://doi.org/10.1177/1461444811412160 (2014). *Memes in digital culture*. MIT Press. https://doi.org/10.7551/mitpress/9429.001.0001

Shweder, R. A. (1991). *Thinking through cultures* (3rd print ed.). Harvard University Press.

Simon, H. A. (1971). Designing organizations for an information-rich world. In M. Greenberger (Ed.), *Computers, communications, and the public interest* (pp. 37–52). The Johns Hopkins Press.

Simons, D. J., & Chabris, C. F. (1999). Gorillas in our midst: Sustained inattentional blindness for dynamic events. *Perception, 28*(9), 1059–1074. https://doi.org/10.1068/p281059

Slovic, P., Västfjäll, D., Erlandsson, A., & Gregory, R. (2017). Iconic photographs and the ebb and flow of empathic response to humanitarian disasters. *Proceedings of the National Academy of Sciences, 114*(4), 640–644. https://doi.org/10.1073/pnas.1613977114

Smith, C. (2015). Art as a diagnostic: Assessing social and political transformation through public art in Cairo, Egypt. *Social & Cultural Geography, 16*(1), 22–42. https://doi.org/10.1080/14649365.2014.936894

Smith, L. G. E., McGarty, C., & Thomas, E. F. (2018). After Aylan Kurdi: How tweeting about death, threat, and harm predict increased expressions of solidarity with refugees over time. *Psychological Science, 29*(4), 623–634. https://doi.org/10.1177/0956797617741107

Sonnevend, J., & Steiert, O. (2022). The power of predictability: How Angela Merkel constructed her authenticity on Instagram. *New Media & Society, 26*(10). https://doi.org/10.1177/14614448221138472

Sontag, S. (1977). *On photography*. Allen Lane.

——— (2003). *Regarding the pain of others* (1st ed.). Farrar, Straus and Giroux.

Steele, C. M., & Aronson, J. (1995). Stereotype threat and the intellectual test performance of African Americans. *Journal of Personality and Social Psychology, 69*(5), 797–811. https://doi.org/10.1037/0022-3514.69.5.797

Stones, M. J., & Bygate, M. (2009). Emotive factors that make photographs memorable. *Photography & Culture, 2*(2), 119–133. https://doi.org/10.2752/175145109X12456654102687

Sturken, M., & Cartwright, L. (2018). *Practices of looking: An introduction to visual culture* (3rd ed.). Oxford University Press.

Suchar, C. (1997). Grounding visual sociology research in shooting scripts. *Qualitative Sociology, 20*(1), 33–55. https://doi.org/10.1023/A:1024712230783

Tagg, J. (1988). *The burden of representation: Essays on photographies and histories*. Macmillan.

Tajfel, H., & Turner, J. (1978). The social identity theory of intergroup behaviour. In H. Tajfel & C. Fraser (Eds.), *Introducing social psychology: An analysis of individual reaction and response* (Repr. ed., pp. 7–24). Penguin.

The Local. (2015, 20 October). Swedish street artist reported to Danish police. www.thelocal.com/20151020/swedish-street-artist-dan-park-reported-to-danish-police

Thelwall, M. (2015). Undermining Aylan: Less than sympathetic international responses. In F. Vis & O. Goriunova (Eds.), *The iconic image on social media: A rapid research response to the death of Aylan Kurdi* (pp. 31–36). Visual Social Media Lab.

Thielman, S. (2020, 29 October). Matt Furie on life after Pepe the Frog: 'You have to lead by example.' *The Guardian*. www.theguardian.com/books/2020/oct/29/matt-furie-on-life-after-pepe-the-frog-lead-by-example-mindviscosity

Thomas, N. (1991). *Entangled objects* (1st ed.). Harvard University Press. https://doi.org/10.4159/9780674044326

Thompson, J. B. (2005). The new visibility. *Theory, Culture & Society*, 22(6), 31–51. https://doi.org/10.1177/0263276405059413

Tinio, P. P. L., & Smith, J. K. (2017). *The Cambridge handbook of the psychology of aesthetics and the arts*. Cambridge University Press.

Topinka, R. J. (2018). Politically incorrect participatory media: Racist nationalism on r/ImGoingToHellForThis. *New Media & Society*, 20(5), 2050–2069. https://doi.org/10.1177/1461444817712516

UN. (1991). *Report to the Secretary-General on humanitarian needs in Kuwait and Iraq in the immediate post-crisis environment by a mission led by Mr Martti Ahtisaari, Under Secretary General for administration and management*.

Valsiner, J. (1987). *Culture and the development of children's action: A cultural-historical theory of developmental psychology*. Wiley.

(2007). *Culture in minds and societies*. Sage. https://doi.org/10.4135/9788132108504

(2008). Ornamented worlds and textures of feeling: The power of abundance. *Outlines. Critical Practice Studies*, 10(1), 67–78. https://doi.org/10.7146/ocps.v10i1.1967

(2014). *An invitation to cultural psychology*. Sage. https://doi.org/10.4135/9781473905986

van Es, K., Wieringa, M., & Schäfer, M. T. (2018, 3 October). *Tool criticism: From digital methods to digital methodology* [paper presentation]. WS.2 2018: Proceedings of the 2nd International Conference on Web Studies, 24–27. https://doi.org/10.1145/3240431.3240436

van Leeuwen, T. (2011). Semiotics and iconography. In T. van Leeuwen & C. Jewitt (Eds.), *The handbook of visual analysis* (pp. 92–118). Sage. https://doi.org/10.4135/9780857020062

Vis, F., & Goriunova, O. (2015). *The iconic image on social media: A rapid research response to the death of Aylan Kurdi*. Visual Social Media Lab.

Vygotsky, L. S. (1978). *Mind in society: The development of higher psychological processes* (M. Cole, V. John-Steiner, S. Scribner, & E. Souberman, Eds.). Harvard University Press.

Wagoner, B. (2017). *The constructive mind: Bartlett's psychology in reconstruction*. Cambridge University Press.

Wagoner, B., Awad, S. H., & de Luna, I. B. (2018). The politics of representing the past: Symbolic spaces of positioning and irony. In A. Rosa & J. Valsiner (Eds.), *The Cambridge handbook of sociocultural psychology* (pp. 443–457). Cambridge University Press. https://doi.org/10.1017/9781316662229.025

Wagoner, B., Brescó, I., & Awad, S. H. (2019). *Remembering as a cultural process* (1st ed.). Springer International Publishing. https://doi.org/10.1007/978-3-030-32641-8

Waldner, L. K., & Dobratz, B. A. (2013). Graffiti as a form of contentious political participation. *Sociology Compass*, 7(5), 377–389. https://doi.org/10.1111/soc4.12036

Warburg, M., Johansen, B. S., & Østergaard, K. (2013). Counting niqabs and burqas in Denmark: Methodological aspects of quantifying rare and elusive religious sub-cultures. *Journal of Contemporary Religion, 28*(1), 33–48. https://doi.org/10.1080/13537903.2013.750834

Wardle, C. (2015). Journalism and death on the social web: The case of Aylan Kurdi. In F. Vis & O. Goriunova (Eds.), *The iconic image on social media: A rapid research response to the death of Aylan Kurdi* (pp. 64–67). Visual Social Media Lab.

Warner, M. (2002). Publics and counterpublics. *Public Culture, 14*(1), 49–90. https://doi.org/10.1215/08992363-14-1-49

Wertsch, J. V. (1985). *Vygotsky and the social formation of mind* (1st print ed.). Harvard University Press.

——— (2004). Specific narratives and schematic narrative templates. In P. Seixas (Ed.), *Theorizing historical consciousness* (pp. 49–62). University of Toronto Press.

——— (2008). The narrative organization of collective memory. *Ethos, 36*(1), 120–135. https://doi.org/10.1111/j.1548-1352.2008.00007.x

Wiggins, B. E. (2019). *The discursive power of memes in digital culture* (1st ed.). Routledge. https://doi.org/10.4324/9780429492303

Williamson, J. (1978). *Decoding advertisements: Ideology and meaning in advertising*. Marion Boyars.

Yilmaz, F. (2016). *How the workers became Muslims: Immigration, culture, and hegemonic transformation in Europe* (1st ed.). University of Michigan Press. https://doi.org/10.3998/mpub.8857103

Young, A., & MacDowall, L. (2017). Visual documentation in hybrid spaces: Ethics, publics and transition. In E. Gómez Cruz, S. Sumartojo, & S. Pink (Eds.), *Refiguring techniques in digital visual research* (pp. 81–91). Palgrave Macmillan. https://doi.org/10.1007/978-3-319-61222-5_7

Yurdakul, G., & Korteweg, A. C. (2021). Boundary regimes and the gendered racialized production of Muslim masculinities: Cases from Canada and Germany. *Journal of Migrant & Refugee Studies, 19*(1), 39–54. https://doi.org/10.1080/15562948.2020.1833271

Zajonc, R. B. (1968). Attitudinal effects of mere exposure. *Journal of Personality and Social Psychology, 9*(2), 1–27. https://doi.org/10.1037/h0025848

Zelizer, B. (2004). The voice of the visual in memory. In K. R. Phillips (Ed.), *Framing public memory* (pp. 157–186). University of Alabama.

——— (2010). *About to die*. Oxford University Press.

Zittoun, T., & Gillespie, A. (2016). *Imagination in human and cultural development* (1st publ. ed.). Routledge.

Zittoun, T., Hawlina, H., & Gillespie, A. T. (2022). Imagination. In V. P. Glăveanu (Ed.), *The Palgrave encyclopedia of the possible* (pp. 753–760). Springer International Publishing. https://doi.org/10.1007/978-3-030-90913-0_68

Index

absence, 105, 111, 182, 201, 206
accessibility, 139, 201–202, 206
advertisement, 130, 218, 221
advertising, 199
affect, 64, 112, 134, 161, 169, 177, 182, 185, 209, 227
   hyper-generalized affect, 112
affordance, 47–48, 53, 126, 131, 138, 149
agency, 19, 21, 35, 89, 137, 217, 230
algorithm, 138, 153, 159, 170–171, 177, 198, 232
answerability, 42
Appadurai, Arjun, 126, 137, 168
appropriation, 139, 143, 167, 173, 177, 185, 203, 205, 208
archiving, 200
art, 231
artefact, 203
artificial intelligence, 87, 205, 232
association, 107, 113, 210
attention, 53, 137, 139, 149, 171, 177, 226, 228
   attention scarcity, 138, 152
   selective attention, 53, 142, 151
audience, 149–150, 156, 217
avant-garde, 175, 231

Bakhtin, Mikhail, 41, 85, 88, 121, 148, 154, 199, 230
Barthes, Roland, 87, 109, 112
Baudrillard, Jean, 216
Benjamin, Walter, 86, 168, 201
Berger, John, 155

capitalism, 216, 219
caricature, 96
censorship, 71, 152, 173, 187, 192, 194
   authority censorship, 72
   community censorship, 72, 187, 196
   self-censorship, 198, 204
circulation, 159, 167–168, 180, 198, 201
citizen journalism, 83

cognitive polyphasia, 110
collective memory, 69, 107, 195, 200, 207, 230
colonialism, 68, 215
commercialization, 175, 200
commodification, 131, 136, 139, 200, 216
commodity, 127
compositional analysis, 104
computational method, 179
connotation, 106
consumerism, 137, 172, 217, 221
content analysis, 160
context, 106, 134
convergence, 125
copyright, 200
counter-image, 156, 198, 226
counter-public, 135, 138–139
countervisuality, 157, 185
creative destruction, 198, 208
creativity, 45, 85, 126, 173, 202, 205
critical discourse analysis, 102
critical psychology, 137
critical visual methodologies, 20
crowd, 137–138
cultural artefact, 31
cultural jamming, 172, 199, 218
culture, 21, 170
   digital culture, 138
   visual culture, 21, 136

death of the author, 87
Debord, Guy, 216
dehumanization, 55, 67, 182
denotation, 104
Derrida, Jacques, 154, 201
desensitization, 188
Dewey, John, 36, 102
dialogue, 38, 41, 63, 110, 129, 131, 134, 143, 149, 154, 173, 179, 187, 192, 206, 218, 222, 231
   dialogical mind, 39
digital ethnography, 179
discourse, 107, 110, 202, 218

documentation, 225
dominant codes, 109
double voicedness, 121

ecology, 19, 124, 126, 167, 172, 228
embodiment, 112, 149, 185
empathy, 229
enactment, 185
engagement, 160
environment, 35, 104, 124, 131, 143, 149
    extended environment, 109, 134
    immediate environment, 106, 108
ethics, 44, 159, 180, 187, 189, 200–201, 205, 221, 224, 230
ethnography, 157
experiment, 158
external image, 17
externalization, 34
eye movement, 151

floating images, 176
Foucault, Michel, 56, 87
framing, 105, 223

gaze, 56, 104, 127, 138, 155, 189
    oppositional gaze, 156, 219
genre, 106, 125
gentrification, 131, 142
gestalt psychology, 102
Gibson, James J., 126
go-along walking interview, 157
graffiti, 123, 130, 142–143, 197, 203, 218
graphic images, 16

habitus, 153
Hall, Stuart, 115, 154, 164
Haynes, Deborah, 42, 88
higher psychological functioning, 32
hooks, bell, 55, 156
humanization, 55, 66, 182

iconicity, 188
iconoclasm, 188, 193, 195
iconographic analysis, 160
iconographical symbolism, 106
iconography, 102, 109
iconological symbolism, 109
identifiable victim effect, 67, 182
identity, 128, 137, 153, 155, 159, 195, 209
    identity politics, 221
imagination, 231
immigration, 160
intentionality, 151–152
internal image, 17
internalization, 34

interpretation, 149, 153
intertextuality, 16, 109–110
invisibility, 26, 111, 152, 171, 185, 192, 196

Juxtaposition, 186

Klein, Naomi, 221
knowledge production, 46
Kristeva, Julia, 110
Kuhn, Annette, 156

language, 57
    linguistic, 16, 58
    textual communication, 16
    verbal communication, 16, 58

Marková, Ivana, 39, 177
Marxism, 219
mass media, 136, 138, 218
materiality, 33, 125–126, 131, 168, 219
mechanical reproduction, 20, 86, 169
mediated communication, 138
medium, 123, 125
meme, 128, 148, 172, 191, 203, 209
memory, 134
    collective memory, 187
mental images, 16
mere exposure effect, 61, 171
mind, 30
Mirzoeff, Nicholas, 151
Mitchell, William J. T., 16, 19, 101
monologue, 44, 218
morality, 45
Moscovici, Serge, 39
mugshot, 127
multimodality, 109
mythologies, 109

narrative, 107, 142, 160
    schematic narrative templates, 110
nationalism, 94, 160
naturalistic modality, 105
news photograph, 181

open system thinking, 59
othering, 55, 67, 121, 154, 159–160, 164, 215
outsideness, 42–43

perception, 149
perceptual images, 16
peripheral routes of persuasion, 62
photo documentation, 141
    longitudinal photo documentation, 131, 142–143
photo-elicitation, 90, 157
photography, 127, 196, 219, 223

Index

photojournalism, 180, 198
photo-taking impairment effect, 69
photo-voice, 91
placement, 131, 133, 146
political campaign, 130
populism, 94
portrait, 128
positioning, 62, 107, 153, 188, 226
poster, 117, 130, 132, 207
postmodernity, 217, 219
power, 46, 56, 111, 130–131, 139, 151,
    153–156, 170–171, 173, 176, 188, 192,
    195, 199, 209, 215, 220, 225
  symbolic power, 48
pragmatism, 36, 215
private images, 18
producer of image, 80, 83
  author of image, 81, 87
propaganda, 136, 151, 186, 220
protest sticker, 130
psychoanalysis, 154, 201
psychogeography, 118, 142, 222
public images, 18
public space, 45
public sphere, 46–47, 135, 138
  private sphere, 135
punctum, 112

qualitative method, 90
  interview, 90, 157
quantitative method, 158
Rancière, Jacques, 47, 55, 135
reality, 127, 137, 215
  hyperreality, 217
recontextualization, 185
re-enactment, 134
referent systems, 109
reflexivity, 25, 230
refugee, 117, 132, 167, 182
relativity, 37, 216, 220
representation, 54, 128, 137
  self-representation, 232
representational meaning, 104
resistance, 84, 130, 137, 156, 211, 217, 221, 232
revolution, 10, 145, 166, 207, 222
rhetorical, 60

Said, Edward, 121, 164
selfie, 127–128
semiotics, 32, 110, 219
  social semiotics, 102, 109
sign, 31, 33, 126, 150, 210, 217
signifier, 104
simulacra, 216
simulation, 216, 221

situationist movement, 175, 222, 231
social actor, 108, 110, 156
social difference, 154
social knowledge, 39, 41
social life of data, 170
social life of discourse, 20
social life of images, 75, 233
social life of things, 20, 126
social media, 176, 217, 232
social position, 81, 148, 153
social practice, 109, 125, 128, 150, 169
social representations, 39, 54, 60, 110, 182, 226
social structure, 111, 219, 221, 225, 229
socialization, 153, 227
Sontag, Susan, 19, 172, 188, 196, 227–228
spectacle, 187, 189, 193, 216
stereotype threat, 64
street art, 130, 142
subject–object dualism, 37
suffering, 224
surveillance, 56, 127, 139, 156, 232
symbol, 33, 65, 114, 137, 162, 195, 209
  affective symbol, 114, 121
  hate symbol, 208
  national symbol, 93, 160
  protest symbol, 65, 169, 174–175, 200, 211, 223
sympathy, 229

technology, 125–126, 136, 140, 156, 168, 170, 232
tool, 31, 126
transformation, 129, 168–169, 172, 181, 203

unconsciousness, 113
unfinalizability, 42–43, 88, 148
urban image, 142
urban space, 131, 134
utterance, 42, 44, 121

verbal images, 17
viewer of the image, 148
  passive viewing, 170
virality, 129, 158, 170–172, 175, 198
visibility, 47, 55, 111, 128, 135, 139, 151–152,
    169, 171, 185, 195, 223, 226
  mediated visibility, 56
visual ethnography, 131, 141
visual perception, 16, 50–51, 126
  vision, 51
  visuality, 22, 51
visual reciprocity, 22
vitality, 19
voyeurism, 187
Vygotsky, Lev, 31

war, 219

For EU product safety concerns, contact us at Calle de José Abascal, 56–1º,
28003 Madrid, Spain or eugpsr@cambridge.org.